JEWISH
VISIONS
FOR AGING

Another Jewish Lights book by Dayle A. Friedman

Jewish Pastoral Care, 2nd Edition
  *A Practical Handbook from Traditional and
  Contemporary Sources*

JEWISH
VISIONS
FOR AGING

A Professional Guide for
Fostering Wholeness

Rabbi Dayle A. Friedman, MSW, MAJCS, BCC

Foreword by Thomas R. Cole, PhD

Preface by Dr. Eugene B. Borowitz

For People of All Faiths, All Backgrounds

JEWISH LIGHTS Publishing

Nashville, Tennessee

Jewish Visions for Aging:
A Professional Guide for Fostering Wholeness

© 2008 by Dayle A. Friedman
Foreword © 2008 by Thomas R. Cole
Preface © 2008 by Eugene B. Borowitz

Library of Congress Cataloging-in-Publication Data

Friedman, Dayle A., 1956–
  Jewish visions for aging : a professional guide for fostering wholeness / Dayle A. Friedman.
    p. cm.
Includes bibliographical references and index.
ISBN-13: 978-1-58023-348-4 (hardcover)
ISBN-10: 1-58023-348-1 (hardcover)
  1. Aging—Religious aspects—Judaism. 2. Older Jews—Care. 3. Older Jews—Religious life. 4. Respect for persons. 5. Dementia—Patients—Care. 6. Aging parents—Care—Religious aspects—Judaism. 7. Jewish ethics. I. Title.
  BM540.A35F75 2008
  296.084'6—dc22

                                        2008019086

10 9 8 7 6 5 4 3 2

Manufactured in the United States of America
♻ Printed on recycled paper.
Cover design: Melanie Robinson

For People of All Faiths, All Backgrounds
Published by Jewish Lights Publishing
An Imprint of Turner Publishing Company
4507 Charlotte Avenue, Suite 100
Nashville, TN 37209
Tel: (615) 255-2665
www.jewishlights.com

To my beloveds, David, Anya, Anat, and Avram,
who fill each new day with possibility
and love, laughter and light.

CONTENTS

PART III
FAMILY CAREGIVING

PART IV
LIVUI RUCHANI: SPIRITUAL ACCOMPANIMENT IN AGING

PART V
AGING AND COMMUNITY

ובטובו מחדש בכל יום תמיד מעשה בראשית

U'vituvo mechadesh b'chol yom tamid maaseh vereishit

In goodness You renew each day the work of creation.
(Siddur, *Shacharit* service)

~

I can scarcely wait till tomorrow
when a new life begins for me,
as it does each day,
as it does each day.

—STANLEY KUNITZ, former poet laureate
of the United States, in the poem
"The Round," published at age 80

ACKNOWLEDGMENTS

Many guides and angels have helped me realize the vision of this volume. First and always, I thank the elders with whom I have had the privilege of working for shining their light on my path. I have shared some of their stories here, always protecting their privacy, but gleaning, I hope, their precious Torah.

I am conscious as well that my students at the Reconstructionist Rabbinical College and my earlier interns at Philadelphia Geriatric Center have immensely enriched my understanding and pushed me always to strive harder to articulate what I am learning. *Mikol melamdei hiskalti*—truly I have learned from all my students. I thank my colleagues who have unstintingly shared their experience and offered insight as the book was taking shape, especially Chaplain Sheila Segal, Rabbi Meryl Crean, Rabbi Richard Address, and Rabbi Leonard Gordon.

I am privileged to work at the Reconstructionist Rabbinical College. The leadership of Rabbi Dan Ehrenkrantz, president, and our Board of Governors has made possible the creation of Hiddur: The Center for Aging and Judaism, a context in which the visions outlined in this book are being nurtured and shared.

I am blessed to have a publisher, Jewish Lights, that embraces my work. I thank Stuart M. Matlins, publisher, and Emily Wichland, vice president of editorial and production, for encouraging and supporting me in each step of this book's creation. I am indebted to Joysa Winter and Sonnie Katz for their invaluable assistance in the technical preparation of this manuscript.

Finally, words cannot express my gratitude to my *haver in leben*, David, and to Anya, Anat, and Avram. Thank you for your encouragement and patience, distraction and its absence, and most of all your love.

FOREWORD

Later life in the Western world is a season in search of its purposes. For the first time in human history, most people can expect to live well into their seventies in reasonably good health. Yet the words of Ecclesiastes—"To every thing there is a season, and a time to every purpose under heaven"—carry little conviction when applied to the second half of life.

Between the sixteenth century and the third quarter of the twentieth century, Western ideas about aging underwent a fundamental transformation, spurred by the development of modern society. Ancient and medieval understandings of aging as a mysterious part of the eternal order of things gradually gave way to the secular, scientific, and individualistic tendencies of modernity. Old age was removed from its place as a way station along life's spiritual journey and redefined as a problem to be solved by science and medicine. Older people were moved to society's margins and defined primarily as patients, pensioners, or consumers.

Because long lives have become the rule rather than the exception, and because collective meaning systems have lost their power to infuse aging with widely shared significance, we have become deeply uncertain about what it means to grow old. Ancient myths and modern stereotypes alike fail to articulate the challenges or capture the uncertainty of generations moving into the still-lengthening later years. The modernization of aging has generated a host of unanswered questions: Does aging have an intrinsic purpose? Is there anything really important to be done after children are raised, jobs are left, and careers are completed? Is old age the culmination of life? Does it contain potential for self-completion? What are the avenues of spiritual growth in later life? What are the roles, rights, and responsibilities of older people? How can frail or demented elders be treated as moral and spiritual beings?

The longevity revolution has created a paradoxical situation: we are younger longer and we are older longer. That is, we are likely to maintain our health and vigor into our late seventies, and we are also likely to live for another decade of frailty and/or dementia. The question is, how should we live those years—both healthy and sick? Questions of meaning and purpose pose themselves with particular urgency for the American Jewish community. Roughly 20 percent of American Jews are sixty-five or over, and half of that group are seventy-five or over.

Traditionally, Jews were born into a covenant from which they could not retire. But in an era when Jewish affiliation is increasingly chosen, that is precisely what many American Jews do—whether they belong to a congregation or not. We do not know how to live covenantally in later life. For some older Jews, the synagogue provides an important source of identity and social support. Congregational leadership often includes influential elders with a lifelong commitment to the covenant. But many older Jews—especially aging baby boomers—are detached from the tradition and do not feel its moral demands, sources of identity, comfort, and hope. And the broader culture socializes older people into the limited roles of patient, consumer, and/or pensioner—effectively undermining a fuller notion of moral agency and responsibility.

It must be said that, like the larger culture, contemporary Judaism lacks a persuasive vision of the good life for our later years. Leisure clubs and life cycle events become the default positions for engagement. The moral and spiritual opportunities and responsibilities of age pale beside the dreams of eternal youth. We have yet to articulate an ideal of spiritually successful frailty. We have only begun to mine Torah, our rabbinic tradition, and our historical experiences for the wisdom, inspiration and guidance to learn about aging and the sacred.

Fashioning authentic Jewish visions, images, and practices of later life is an urgent priority today, though it has been largely neglected in both rabbinical education and congregational life. Three notable American exceptions are Rabbi Richard Address's Sacred Aging project at the Union for Reform Judaism; Rabbi Peter Knobel and Dr. Martha Holstein's initiative on Judaism, aging, and ethics at Temple Beth Emet: The Free Synagogue in Chicago; and Rabbi Dayle A. Friedman's Hiddur: The Center for Aging and Judaism of the Reconstructionist Rabbinical College in Philadelphia. And now, with the publication of this book, we have an exciting new paradigm for Jewish aging. Friedman focuses primarily on working with elders in need of care. Her profound insights apply not only to the caregiving relationship but to the spiritual journey of all in search of meaning, wisdom, and celebration.

American Jews are rightly proud of the exemplary care and service provided to our elders, but it is time, as Friedman demonstrates, to attend to the inner lives of elders and of ourselves. The dominant approach to care for poor, ill, frail, or dependent elders assumes that aging is a problem to be solved rather than a mystery to be lived. In this paradigm, professionals give and do not receive; elders receive and have nothing to give; they have physical and social needs but no spiritual or moral aspirations. By contrast, Friedman calls on us to engage elders as spiritual and moral beings, as teachers and learners, celebrants and worshippers.

Friedman's paradigm is based on a fresh translation of the commandment in Leviticus 19:32, normally translated as, "Rise up before the gray-haired and grant honor (*hiddur*) to the elder." Friedman builds on Danny Siegel's translation of *hiddur*, which reads, "You shall rise before an elder and allow the beauty, glory, and majesty of their faces to emerge."

What does it mean to allow the "beauty, glory, and majesty" of elders to emerge? We cannot fully know in advance, but Friedman, drawing from the nursing home culture-change movement, calls on us to involve elders in visioning and implementing their place in Jewish communal life. Her book is offered as a resource toward that end. The topics include an overview of Jewish texts and tradition, the search for meaning, family caregiving, spiritual accompaniment, elders in community, and intergenerational programming. This volume is practical as well as visionary; it is filled with useful material for rabbis, cantors, educators, chaplains, social workers, family members, psychotherapists, and volunteers. Whether independent or dependent, merely aging or well advanced in years, Friedman's vision speaks to all of us. Like the story of Reb Yitzhak who searched for a far away treasure buried under a bridge in Cracow, Friedman shows us that we have only to come home and dig up the treasures of Jewish wisdom buried under our own front porch.

Thomas R. Cole, PhD

PREFACE
A Beneficiary's View

Most of this richly insightful book is directed to professional and family caregivers—an increasing community these days—of whom, in special ways, I am surely one. But I thought it might be helpful at the outset of this work to remind you of the extraordinary variety of elderly we seek to care for by saying something about my largely fortunate case.

By the time this book is published I will—God willing—be eighty-four, which, we have been told, is the median age of the "continuing care community" in which I have lived since 1999. My wife, Estelle, *alehah hashalom*, and I came to Edgehill for the usual reasons: it was near one of our daughters and seemed like it would be a lovely place in which to live. Besides, I had undergone a quadruple by-pass operation the year before and Estelle was now four-plus years into the pulmonary fibrosis which would end her life in 2004.

We did have some compunctions about coming to Edgehill, which is in Stamford, Connecticut. We remembered the days when the nearby communities of Greenwich, New Canaan, and Darien were not welcoming to Jews and we wondered what sort of slights we might run into. Not only have there been none but the openness and decency of our neighbors here—about two hundred and sixty or so of them—has been a continuing joy. God bless America indeed.

We had considered the possibility of moving into a Jewish community home near one of our daughters but the ones we examined were too big-city, apartment-house-like for us old single-home dwellers with strong memories of our Ohio childhood. At Edgehill, the Jewish population consists of about fifty or sixty of us, the bulk of whom used to live in this area. The rest have come, like us, to be near children. Our cohort here keeps reminding me of the early 1960s, before the days of the Aquarian revolution. That is, it shows few signs of the later turns to the right in practice, spirituality, or learning. Rather, we have a few assimilationists—Jews who do not hide their identity but disassociate by never showing up, for example, at our three "festivals": a second-day Rosh Hashanah reception and shofar blowing; a Chanukah menorah-lighting party; and a second-night Seder. Most Jews here identify but don't go to High Holy Day services perhaps as much because they are no longer *shul* members as because of their old-style agnosticism.

The predominant tone of our lives at Edgehill has been a quite happy one. Mostly, people are delighted to be in this lovely place and part of this friendly, even caring, but non-intrusive community. We well realize that we are the fortunate elderly but like all those in our situation, we are afflicted by two entwined and largely buried anxieties: one stemming from our loss of competence, the other from the potential loss of health and life. But seeing the ninety-year-olds with their reasonably active, interesting lives, changes the horizon of aspiration for everyone younger. And to have recently seen my 101-year-old, handsome, charming neighbor—our eldest resident—come back from the hospital after a bout of pneumonia has given us all a positive sense of life's surprises.

As they say, "Old age is not for sissies," though I far prefer the wisdom encapsulated in the title of the master Protestant theologian Paul Tillich's book, *The Courage to Be*. Fostering that courage, I take it, is one of the great fruits of religious faith that, as this book points out, can have transformative power for us struggling with frailty and searching for perspective.

At Edgehill, I and my fellow residents are helped to find something of that strength by a caring staff. We are not so blessed as to have Dayle Friedman herself available to guide us through the special pleasures and challenges of our unanticipated longevity. But those who care for us, professional and lay, can now have the benefit of her years of dedicated service and wise reflection on what it means "to be there" with us—so simple a phrase but so redolent with meaning in the multiple ways that family and staff and we, the aging, are "there."

And let me add a very personal word: Dayle was my student some decades ago and it was a special pleasure to have in the class what even then seemed like someone with a wise soul. At one session, I called her to task for not following the instructions for her presentation. Later, she called me to task for, as she put it (and you will notice I have not forgotten her words), "creating an emotional situation in which she could not learn anything." She taught me an important lesson that day and, in her professional life since, I and many others have benefited from her pioneering work with the aged.

In these pages she has created an emotional situation in which everyone can learn the contemporary Torah of honoring the old, a teaching which I know will bless many lives.

Dr. Eugene B. Borowitz

INTRODUCTION

Seasons of Splendor—
New Visions for Jewish Aging

Unprecedented Challenges and Opportunities of the Age Wave

The age wave has hit the North American Jewish population with dramatic and undeniable force.[1] This seismic demographic shift will reshape life for individuals, families, and the Jewish community as a whole.

According to the 2000–2001 National Jewish Population Survey, at least 19 percent of U.S. Jews—or nearly 1 million individuals—are sixty-five years of age or older, compared with 12 percent of Americans in general. This growth of the Jewish aging population is seen even more vividly in the fact that 23 percent of American Jews (1.19 million) were already over sixty years of age even before the first baby boomers reached that milestone. Moreover, those seventy-five and older comprise half of Jews over sixty-five, and this is the fastest growing segment of the Jewish population.[2]

We are living ever longer. Many of us can look forward to two, three, or even four decades of being old.[3] The longevity revolution creates the possibility of *both* extended years of healthy living *and* prolonged periods of frailty and dependency at life's end. These interrelated realities create unprecedented opportunities and challenges; they are both part of the new face of Jewish aging.

The Times They Are a-Changin'

Retirement is changing. Many elders may not fully stop working; economics may well drive some to continue working far beyond traditional retirement age.[4] For existential reasons, many people will reinvent themselves in "encore careers."[5] Many of those who do leave paid work behind will choose to invest themselves in serious and demanding community service.

Caregiving is becoming more complex and demanding. Many families have two generations of elderly members—grandparents in their sixties or seventies and great-grandparents in their eighties or nineties. We have new "sandwich generations." In some families, grandchildren in midlife are caring for parents *and* grandparents, as well as for their own children.

The current and upcoming waves of Jewish elders are highly educated and sophisticated. They are overwhelmingly American-born, though one-fifth are immigrants, primarily from the former Soviet Union. Those who are over sixty-five belong to Jewish organizations and give to the community in higher proportions than younger individuals. They belong to synagogues in slightly lower proportions. They participate in volunteering and adult education at similar rates to younger Jews.[6] Baby boomers are not as highly affiliated; even those who once belonged to synagogues or community centers may have let their ties lapse once their children's Jewish education was completed. Other boomers have never been connected to Jewish life, or have not renewed connections they had in childhood through family or Jewish education.[7] These educated, talented individuals are a potentially valuable resource for Jewish communal life.

A Spiritual Hunger

> Behold the days are coming, when I shall send a famine to the land. Not a hunger for bread, nor a thirst for water, but [the longing] to hear the words of God. (Am. 8:11)

Boomers and elders are consumer-oriented; they reach for connection to resources and communities that speak to their current needs and aspirations. As they face the transitions and tasks of later life, they may be open to Jewish connection in new ways. In a 2002 survey that asked older Americans about the components of a meaningful and vital life, 67 percent of those surveyed named spiritual life, 38 percent identified community, and 32 percent pointed to new learning as essential.[8] I believe that these responses reveal a longing for connection and a perhaps inchoate pull toward that which transcends the narrow bounds of the self.

Jewish life can speak to this hunger. I know this from experience—from the many years I served as rabbi for a community of one thousand elders. I have seen that isolation can be pierced, time sanctified, and life imbued with meaning through Jewish observance, study, social action, and spiritual presence. The transformative power of Judaism for elders struggling daily with frailty and loss points to the impact it can have for those whose challenges are perhaps less formidable. Judaism can be every bit as powerful for those who are searching for new meaning and roles, for perspective on life's profound questions, and for solace amid the inevitable loss and change of later life.

A New Paradigm

The Jewish community has a long heritage of honoring elders. For hundreds of years we have developed communal responses that embody the values of *kavod* (honor) and *mora* (awe).[9] Our homes for the aging, family service agencies, community centers, and synagogues have provided for elders' basic needs in an atmosphere of respect and dignity. We can be proud of the exemplary care and service we have provided.

The new realities of aging demand even more from us. Care and service are essential, particularly for those who are poor or ill, frail or dependent. But even for these especially needy individuals, these approaches only ensure that elders *survive*. Our task now is to help aging Jews *thrive*, to bring quality to their lives from the inside out. As Harry R. Moody, author of *Ethics in an Aging Society*, has said, we need to move from aging as problem to be solved to aging as mystery to be lived.[10]

It is time to forge a new paradigm for the Jewish response to aging. The Torah offers us a framework in a commandment included in the Holiness Code, the compendium of core ethical imperatives found in Leviticus chapter 19.

> Rise up before the gray-haired, and grant *hiddur* to the elder. (Lev. 19:32)[11]

The first half of the mitzvah is clear. Literally, it impels us to stand up out of respect when an elder crosses our path. In contemporary Israel, this phrase is emblazoned on placards on every public bus to remind younger passengers to give up their seats to elders. On a deeper level, though, this commandment calls us to rise from our places in the presence of elders, to leave lassitude behind and accord them respect and deference.

The second half of the commandment is less clear, because the word *hiddur* is challenging to translate. Danny Siegel suggests this translation:

> You shall rise before an elder and allow the beauty, glory and majesty of their faces to emerge.[12]

If we are to allow elders' light and beauty to shine forth, we must create a context in which this is possible. The *hiddur* that is hidden within elders has to be brought out and *shared* or *received* by others around them. This interpretation suggests that *hiddur p'nai zaken*, as this mitzvah is known, requires us to *empower* elders, to *engage* them as actors and not just as recipients. We are called upon to enable them to find joy and meaning and to shine their light outward into the world. Engaging elders means reaching out to empower them as:

- Spiritual beings searching for meaning
- Learners and teachers
- Celebrants and worshippers
- Contributors with vast talents, wisdom, and resources to bring to communal life

- People experiencing challenge and joy, trial and heart-
  break, who need to be engaged in a web of caring
  connection

This mitzvah is far more demanding than simply providing care,
service, and shelter. There is much to be done to realize this vision
of engagement. Professionals may need to confront unintentional
ageism in ourselves and in the organizations and communities we
serve. We must consult and involve elders in visioning and implementing our efforts to bring them into the center of our communal
life, and to engage them in forging meaningful and valuable lives.
Existing programs may need enrichment or rethinking. New visions
will need to be articulated, and novel strategies will need to be
tried, evaluated, and revised. *Jewish Visions for Aging* is intended
as a resource in this quest.

Empowering and Engaging Elders with This Book

This book is a tool for those who seek to enable elders' lights to
shine. If you are a rabbi or cantor, educator or chaplain, social
worker or psychotherapist, family member or volunteer, you will
find resources here to support you in involving, empowering, and
engaging elders in your community. If you are a chaplain or clergy
member from another faith, you will encounter another faith community's approach, and perhaps gain sensitivity to Jewish elders
that you encounter. You will find perspectives from text and tradition, as well as practical guidance for the work of *hiddur p'nai
zaken.*

The book has five parts. The first, "Text and Tradition,"
offers a survey of classical Jewish perspectives on growing older.
The second part, "Aging and Meaning," contains perspectives on
the possibility of finding and making meaning in later life, as well
as the value that we can reap from our encounters with elders.
"Family Caregiving," the third part, outlines pastoral, theological,
and ethical responses to the challenges faced by individuals managing the juggling act of caring for relatives and other life responsibilities. The fourth part, "*Livui Ruchani*: Spiritual Accompaniment in

Aging," addresses spiritual care with elders, including tools from tradition and a special look at those in long-term care institutions. Finally, we turn to the fifth part, "Aging and Community," and look at the promise of intergenerational programming, offering a vision and practical guidance for transforming congregations into thriving multigenerational communities.

The material in this book has been developed over the past two decades through my work in accompanying elders as a rabbi and chaplain, and in training rabbis, chaplains, and other professionals through Hiddur: The Center for Aging and Judaism of the Reconstructionist Rabbinical College. The experiences I have had in sharing Jewish life with the "old old" have shaped these writings. The people depicted in the case studies within the book are composites of elders I have met through my students' and my own work. Identities or names have been changed to protect confidentiality.

The themes of accessibility, empowerment, and facilitation pervade all of the chapters. As I review them, I am aware of how urgently we need to apply these concepts to our response to baby boomers and "younger" elders. While I believe that the core principles of *hiddur p'nai zaken* apply to the entire spectrum of experience in the last third of life, I hope that the unique struggles and joys of these younger members of the Jewish community will be specifically understood and addressed in future work. This book is the beginning of a dialogue and, I hope, a spur to creative action.

Most of all, I pray that later life can become a time of wonder and renewal, connection, and contribution. May we fulfill the mitzvah of *hiddur p'nai zaken*, bringing splendor to the face of aging.

PART I

TEXT AND TRADITION

Crown Me with Wrinkles and Gray Hair

Traditional Views and Visions of Aging

When I was a child, I was fascinated by a television commercial for a well-known hand lotion. In the scene, a mother is mistaken for her teenage daughter. The two are then shown together holding their hands up for inspection so that the viewer can see that the mother's hands look as young as her daughter's. The announcer then informs the viewer that this miracle is due to the use of the hand lotion, which can provide the viewer with "younger-looking hands" as well.

What a different scene is presented by one of the classic texts of Jewish tradition! In Genesis Rabbah, the midrash on humanity's beginnings, the Rabbis explain that until Abraham, the elderly had no distinctive physical appearance. The elderly patriarch was distressed that people who saw him and his son Isaac together could not discern who was the elder, and thus failed to offer him the honor and deference due the aged. He pleaded before God to "crown" him with signs of old age. Hence, wrinkles and gray hair entered the world.[1]

These contrasting scenarios encapsulate, to a certain extent, the immense rift between contemporary attitudes toward aging and those conveyed in biblical and rabbinic traditions. In our twenty-first-century North American culture, aging is seen as a plague to be avoided, or at least concealed. In Jewish tradition, attaining and bearing the mark of long years is considered a reward to be coveted. Why this gap in perception? In secular culture, the worth of the individual is measured by what he or she does, by the material contribution he or she makes. Beauty and desirability are equated with youth, and dependency and frailty are dreaded. In Jewish

In our twenty-first-century North American culture, aging is seen as a plague to be avoided, or at least concealed. In Jewish tradition, attaining and bearing the mark of long years is considered a reward to be coveted.

tradition, by contrast, the worth of the individual is intrinsic, since all are created in the Divine image. Our value is not connected to productivity, strength, or physical beauty.

As the Jewish community becomes grayer, it behooves us to search our tradition for perspective and guidance on how to face the period of life that has been called the "third age." Although Jewish tradition is broad and deep, and has developed in varied fashion over the centuries and around the globe, we can discern some prominent themes and values. An examination of traditional Jewish sources on aging reflects an apparent paradox: on the one hand, they realistically depict the impairments and losses of aging, while on the other, they treat old age as a positive and worthy stage of life. Our task is to investigate and analyze the relationship between these two aspects of Jewish tradition's approach to aging. We hope that tradition's positive values and models will help shape our relationships with elders, our own aging process, and our communal responses to aging.

Challenges of Aging

As seen in biblical and rabbinic sources, aging has challenging and sometimes painful consequences. Growing older can be a frightening prospect, as reflected in the renowned lines of Psalm 71:9, "Cast me not off in the time of my old age; when my strength fails, forsake me not." Rabbi Jose ben Kisma laments, "Woe for the one thing that goes and does not return," that is, youth.[2] In the same passage, Rav Dimi similarly describes youth as a crown of roses and old age as a crown of thorns.

Old age is characterized by physical and mental impairments. The Midrash baldly states, "In old age, all powers fail."[3] Isaac becomes blind in his old age (Gen. 27:1), and David is so feeble that his body is constantly cold (1 Kings 1:1). The physical losses of aging are poignantly described by the eighty-year-old Barzillai the Gileadite in 2 Samuel 19:35: "I am this day fourscore years old; can I discern between good and bad? Can thy servant taste what I eat or what I drink? Can I hear anymore the voice of singing men and singing women?" An exhaustive catalog of the sorrows and sensory losses of aging is metaphorically described in Ecclesiastes 12:11–7:

> So appreciate your vigor in the days of your youth, before those days
> of sorrow come and those years arrive of which you will say, I have
> no pleasure in them; before sun and light and moon and stars grow
> dark, and the clouds come back again after the rain:
> When the guards of the house become shaky,
> And the men of valor are bent,
> And the maids that grind, grown few, are idle,
> And the ladies that peer through the windows grow dim,
> And the doors to the street are shut—
> And the noise of the hand mill growing fainter,
> And the song of the bird growing feebler,
> And all the strains of music dying down;
> When one is afraid of heights
> And there is terror on the road ...
> Before the silver cord snaps
> And the golden bowl crashes,
> The jar is shattered at the spring,
> And the jug is smashed at the cistern.
> And the dust returns to the ground
> As it was,
> And the lifebreath returns to God
> Who bestowed it.

The Babylonian Talmud interprets this depressing passage as a catalog of all the physical changes and disabilities brought on by aging.[4] The Rabbis who cite this passage vie with one another to describe the most horrific visions of old age. Several authorities apologetically demur, explaining the terrifying descriptions as applying only to the wicked. By and large, however, the Rabbis see physical debilitation and impairment as a fact of life in old age.

Some Rabbinic sources also view mental deterioration as an inevitable feature of aging. In depicting an individual who today would no doubt be diagnosed with dementia, one text quotes an old man: "I look for that I have not lost."[5] Another old man misinterprets the sound of twittering birds: "Robbers have come to overpower me."[6] Despite the dominant view that the old are wise, some sources dispute this: "There is no reason in old men and no counsel in children."[7] Even Moses, whose physical strength is undiminished at the age of one hundred and twenty, is described in one midrash as having lost his capacity to teach, or even to follow the logic of a presentation given by his disciple, Joshua.[8] This loss of power is so devastating that Moses, who has consistently and passionately pleaded to live, now begs God to let him die.

These texts describe aging as it was experienced hundreds, even thousands, of years ago, but the essential reality they depict remains unchanged in our time. Despite medical and scientific advances that have lengthened the life span from under fifty years at the turn of the twentieth century to over seventy-five today, we have not succeeded in evading frailty and finitude. Our society is loathe to accept and acknowledge the seeming inevitability of physical and mental deterioration for most older people, and this reluctance leads to serious consequences, such as isolation of the elderly, denial of aging, and a loss of self-respect among elders.

Aging inevitably involves losing loved ones, which can be devastating to our sense of meaning. Honi the Circle Maker, a kind of Jewish Rip van Winkle, goes to sleep for seventy years, only to awaken to a world in which no one knows him, and in which everyone he loves has died. In a moment of utter despair he cries out, "Either fellowship or death!"[9] The tradition recognizes that, for some frail older people, there can come a time when living itself is a burden. Yalkut Shimoni, Parashat Ekev portrays an encounter between an old woman and Rabbi Yosi ben Halafta.[10] The woman, who had "aged greatly," says, "Rabbi, I have aged too much and now my life is worthless, for I cannot taste food or drink, and I want to die." The rabbi asks what mitzvah has been part of her daily practice. She answers that she faithfully goes to synagogue each morning. The rabbi advises her to refrain from attending the synagogue for three consecutive days. She follows his counsel and, on the third day, she becomes ill and dies.

The old woman's inability to experience pleasure makes life seem worthless to her. The amazing response of the rabbi is to help her stop doing the very things that seem to be spiritually prolonging her life. This startling text seems to suggest that an individual's evaluation of his or her quality of life is a legitimate element in decisions about life and death, and that prolonging a life that feels burdensome to the individual is not obligatory. For contemporary Jews struggling with wrenching decisions about life-extending medical treatments, this midrash may provide useful guidance. Although it has no halachic authority, it does provide support for basing decisions on an older patient's wishes, as well as for forgoing life-extending treatments when living has become burdensome to the person.

Positive Aspects of Aging

Along with, or perhaps in spite of, these realistic and rather dire depictions of the hardships of aging, our texts hold a fundamentally positive view of aging. Long life is considered a reward for righteous living. While most of the mitzvot (commandments) in the Torah are mandated without assurance of reward, in the few exceptional cases long life is the promised recompense. Length of days is assured for those who honor their parents (Exod. 20:12), for those who do not remove a mother bird's young in her presence (Deut. 22:7), and for those who employ equal measures in commerce (Deut. 25:15). In addition, those who observe "all of the laws and ordinances" (Deut. 6:2) are promised "length of days." According to Proverbs 16:31, one attains old age through *tzedakah*, righteous living.

Many midrashim describe old age as a reward for virtuous living, such as faithful attendance at the house of study, or for a life marked by righteousness and Torah.[11] An entire page of the

*W*hile most of the mitzvot (commandments) in the Torah are mandated without assurance of reward, in the few exceptional cases long life is the promised recompense.

Talmud is filled with various Rabbis' accounts of the particular worthy deeds that explain their longevity.[12] Another example of this reasoning is given by Rav Addah bar Ahaba:

The disciples of Rav Addah bar Ahaba asked him: To what do you attribute your longevity? He replied: I have never displayed any impatience in my house, and I have never walked in front of any man greater than myself, nor have I ever meditated (over the words of the Torah) in any dirty alleys, nor have I ever walked four cubits without (musing over) the Torah or without (wearing) phylacteries, nor have I ever fallen asleep in the House of Study for any length of time or even momentarily, nor have I rejoiced at the disgrace of my friends, nor have I ever called my neighbor by a nickname given to him by myself, or some say, by the nickname given to him by others.[13]

Old age is valued as reward and blessing, and elders are to be treated with deference and respect. In addition to the obligation to honor our parents, the Holiness Code outlines our responsibilities to older adults in general: "You shall rise before the aged (grayhaired) and show deference (*hiddur*) in the presence of the old (*zaken*); you shall fear your God: I am the Eternal" (Lev. 19:32).[14] This mitzvah is understood to dictate deferential treatment toward scholars as well as older adults. *Zaken* (old) is taken to refer to people of wisdom, and not just those who have attained wisdom through life experience.

The Rabbis mandate an attitude of reverence toward all people over a certain age (generally sixty or seventy).[15] "What is the deference (*hiddur*) demanded by the Torah? That you not stand in his [the older person's] place, nor contradict his words, but behave toward him with reverence and fear."[16] Included among those meriting this deferential treatment are elderly non-Jews and Jews who are neither learned nor particularly righteous, since they are assumed to have acquired understanding of God's ways in the world through life experience.[17] Hence, revering the elderly means recognizing the value of their experience. Even if they have forgotten their learning through dementia or other frailty, we still owe them respect: "Take care to honor the old man who has forgotten his learning for reasons beyond his control, as it is said, 'both the [second, unbroken] tablets and the broken tablets [of the Law] were kept in the Ark [of the sanctuary].'"[18] Respect for the elderly is not predicated on their capacity to contribute socially or to benefit those younger than them. They are inherently worthy, even when "broken," and are to be cherished and nurtured, just as Israel treasured the first (broken) set of tablets of the Law.

We must not merely comport ourselves so as to give honor to the older person; we must do this in such a way that the elder will know that the honor is meant specifically for him or her. For example, we must rise in the presence of older people, but we should wait to do so until the older person is within four cubits so that he or she will recognize that this honor is being accorded to him or her.[19] In addition, we must reach out to older persons where they are; thus, if older persons are standing, even if we are sitting and engaged in our work, we must meet them at their level by rising as well. Clearly, tradition obligates Jews to behave with reverence for the dignity of every older person, thereby recognizing the value of that person's experience and perspective.

We might wonder what it is about old age that makes it both desirable and deserving of respect. First and foremost, old age is associated with wisdom in Jewish tradition. The old are viewed as leaders with good counsel to impart. The people of Israel are enjoined, "Ask your father and he will tell you, your elders and they shall instruct you" (Deut. 32:7). Or, in the words of the book of Job, "For wisdom is with the old, and understanding with length of days" (12:12). Among the generation in the wilderness after the Exodus, it is the elders (*zekenim*) who are Israel's leaders. While

We might wonder what it is about old age that makes it both desirable and deserving of respect. First and foremost, old age is associated with wisdom in Jewish tradition.

many sources understand *zaken* as a generic term for leaders of any age, the use of a term that also denotes old age surely reflects the general association of wisdom with age. The guidance of elders is seen as critical to the survival of the people of Israel: "When is Israel able to stand? When it has elders.... For one who takes advice from elders never stumbles."[20]

Rabbinic doctrine urges acceptance of the elders' opinions when there is a dispute between the generations. Even if the elders seem to be arguing for destruction and the youth for construction, the elders should be heeded, for "the tearing down of the old is building, and the building of the young is tearing down."[21] Perhaps elders are uniquely able to critique current conventions with the long view of experience and history. Thus the elders' perspectives are exemplified as particularly valuable for the guidance of the community. So inexorable is the link between old age and wisdom that the sage Bar Kappara exclaims, "If wisdom is not here, can old age be here?"[22]

Later life is not merely a time for savoring lessons gleaned from a lifetime of experience and learning. On the contrary, according to Jewish tradition, old age is a time in which we are called to continue to learn and grow. A person who has been a student of Torah in his or her youth must continue that learning.[23] Not only can we continue in old age to follow paths that have been spiritually fruitful throughout a long life, but we can also transform our life to the very last day. In explaining the verse, "Better is the end of a thing than the beginning thereof" (Eccl. 7:8), Ruth Rabbah states, "A man may act wickedly in his youth, yet in his old age he may perform good deeds" (7:6).

Old age can be a time of broadening our concern, of involvement with others and the world around us in order to create a better life for those who will live in the future. One example of this attitude is reflected in the Talmudic understanding of the central obligation to teach a child Torah. According to the Rabbis, not only is a parent obligated to teach a child, but this responsibility belongs to a grandparent as well.[24] Older people have a unique contribution to make to the lives of the young. One beautiful example of this is the story of Naomi, the old woman whose sons have died childless, and whose daughter-in-law, Ruth, decides to stay with her rather than returning to her people. When Ruth later has a child, he is nursed by Naomi, and he is considered her son as well. The women of the village say, "He shall be to you a restorer of your

Later life is not merely a time for savoring lessons gleaned from a lifetime of experience and learning. On the contrary, according to Jewish tradition, old age is a time in which we are called to continue to learn and grow.

life, and a nourisher of your old age" (Ruth 4:14). Naomi is simultaneously nourished by and a nourisher of the younger generation. She represents a powerful model of generativity in old age.

One other example of concern for the future is seen in two stories about old men who involve themselves in the task of planting a tree, though skeptics around them point out that they will not live to see the fruits of their labors. In Ecclesiastes Rabbah,[25] a one hundred-year-old man is challenged by the emperor Hadrian as to why he wastes his time planting trees. The man answers, "If I am worthy, I shall eat; if not, just as my forefathers toiled for me, so shall I toil for my children." The emperor promises the man a reward should he live to see the trees produce figs. Indeed, the man lives, and is rewarded with riches, for the emperor says, "His Creator has honored him, so shall not I?" In the parallel tale, Honi the Circle Maker gives a similar rationale for planting a tree at age seventy.[26] In both cases, the older adult is depicted as caring about the welfare of those yet to be born. This kind of engagement with the future is beneficial to future generations, and by providing meaning, it also sustains the elder.

Final Words

We have seen that Jewish tradition offers images and understandings of aging that are radically different from those current in contemporary secular culture. Old age is affirmed as a time of meaning and possibility, even as its hardships and challenges are acknowledged. As we face our personal journeys through aging, as well as the momentous impact of the age wave on our community, we may be bolstered by this fundamentally positive view so that we can fulfill the ancient vision of Psalm 92:

> The righteous will flourish like the palm tree:
> They will grow like a cedar in Lebanon.
> Planted in the house of the Eternal,
> They shall flourish in the courts of our God.
> They shall yet yield fruit even in old age;
> Vigorous and fresh they shall be,
> To proclaim that the Eternal is just!
> [God is] my Rock, in whom there is no injustice.

For Further Investigation

Gerald Blidstein. *Honor Thy Father and Mother.* New York: Ktav, 1975.

Rachel Dulin. *A Crown of Glory: A Biblical View of Aging.* New York: Paulist Press, 1988.

Walter Jacob and Moshe Zemer, eds. *Aging and the Aged in Jewish Law.* Pittsburgh, PA: Rodef Shalom Press, 1998.

David Salomon, ed. *Sefer Zikhron Shemuel: Haziknah bimekorot Yisrael, Leket Mekorot v'Iyunim mitoch haTanakh haShas haMidrash haRambam v'Sifrut haSh'elot uteshuvot betzeruf hebet sotziologi u'vibliografiyah.* Israel: Sifre Yahadut ha-Torah, 1989.

Yitzhak Schlesinger. *Ve-hadarta Penai Zaken.* B'nai Brak, Israel: Ha-Mesorah, 1985.

Menachem Mendel Schneerson. *Attaining Sagacity: Reflections on Reaching the Age of Sixty.* Eliyahu Touger, trans. Brooklyn, NY: Sichos in English, 1998.

PART II

AGING AND MEANING

The Mitzvah Model
Meaning and Mission in Late Life

What are you doing with the rest of your life? This is the question for the sixty-three-year-old wondering what he is going to do "when he grows up"—when he leaves the professional position at which he has excelled for thirty years. This is the question for the seventy-five-year-old recently widowed woman who is struggling to redefine her life now that her beloved husband of thirty years is gone. This is the question for a ninety-year-old activist, striving to continue her work in the world from her new home in a retirement community as she contends with painful chronic illness. And this is the question for the eighty-four-year-old engineer, crippled with Parkinson's but intellectually unbroken, struggling to stay stimulated in the nursing home that will be his final home.

This question is also the core of the spiritual challenge of increased longevity. Our twenty-first-century Western society has an instrumental view of people. We are valued for what we do, produce, or create. Aging individuals looking ahead to years or decades without the jobs or roles that previously defined or confined them seek a sense of value and purpose. Elders with energy, economic resources, and good health and those who are severely limited by physical or cognitive impairments wonder: Who are we when we are no longer workers, child-rearers, spouses, professionals? What now is our job? In the absence of clearly defined roles, elders who seek meaning may well find that the social expectations of our culture stymie them. The message of many advertising and media images to those who are retired from remunerative work is that they should spend their time in play, taking up games, travel, or other "self-indulgent mindlessness."[1]

A very different approach comes from a group of eighty- to one-hundred-year-old nursing home residents at the Abramson Center for Jewish Life outside of Philadelphia.

> *They are frail, living with disabilities they never imagined and in a setting they always dreaded. They rely on others to prepare their meals, help them dress and bathe, and move them from place to place. These elders reside in a nursing home, where they also volunteer. Through a program called Hands and Hearts created by their chaplain, Sheila Segal, and her colleagues, these elders reach out to neighbors in need in their long-term care facility. They greet each newcomer, bereaved neighbor, and returnee from the hospital with a card, a handmade gift, and a personal visit. With each act of lovingkindness (g'milut chasadim), they weave this aggregation of strangers into a sacred and caring community. They act to soften suffering, offer friendship, and bring light amid darkness to lonely souls.*

These frail elders have found something to *do* with the rest of their lives. They have decided to make a difference, and in so doing, *they* are transformed as well. No longer do they think of themselves only as sick people, or as recipients of care, but rather they are *gomelei hesed*, human purveyors of divine lovingkindness.

The Hands and Hearts volunteers exemplify mitzvah, a model from Jewish tradition with powerful implications for older people and those who care for them. In Jewish tradition, old age is seen as a time of continued mission in which we are called to a life of meaning. This message is embodied in the concept of mitzvah. Through mitzvah, or religious obligation, the older Jew is offered an existence characterized by a profound sense of self-worth and social value. This traditional framework empowers the physically or mentally incapacitated so that they, too, experience personal significance. This Mitzvah Model, which we will explore in this chapter, provides Jews today with a framework for approaching our relationship to aging, both as individuals and as a community.

From birth the Jew is part of a community that extends through time and space. Membership in this community involves inclusion in the *brit*—the covenant with God established at Sinai that binds each Jewish person to mitzvot.[2] Thus, each Jew is *metzuveh* (commanded), bound to

In Jewish tradition, old age is seen as a time of continued mission in which we are called to a life of meaning. This message is embodied in the concept of mitzvah.

the covenant and the commandments, both ritual and ethical. Our fate beyond this world is traditionally seen as dependent on a lifetime record of observing the mitzvot. The redemption of the Jewish people, and indeed the whole world, rests on the collective fulfillment of this ancient covenant through mitzvot.

In this traditional worldview, each Jew's relationship to the mitzvot has cosmic significance. How and whether we observe mitzvot affects our social as well as religious status. We can gain *kavod* (honor) by exemplary performance of mitzvot—by being faithful, for example, to the mitzvot under difficult or dangerous conditions, or by imbuing observance with particular fervor and intentionality (*kavanah*). Within the social world of the covenantal community, we achieve the highest honor by facilitating others' observance. Thus it is a special honor to lead others in the recitation of the Amidah (standing prayer) or other prayers, and to be counted in the quorum for prayer (*minyan*) or Birkat HaMazon (Grace after Meals). Any Jew can gain importance, success, and honor through the performance of mitzvot.

It is easy to see how valuable this concept and experience can be for elders. Being conscious of obligation, of being *metzuveh*, gives elders what they lack: the opportunity to experience life as meaningful, not empty. In performing mitzvot, older Jews have a chance to participate in valuable activities, to have a meaningful social role in the covenantal community, and to structure their time.

Twentieth-century philosopher and rabbi Abraham Joshua Heschel suggests that it is through this experience of being obligated

Being conscious of obligation, of being metzuveh, *gives elders what they lack: the opportunity to experience life as meaningful, not empty.*

that we truly exist. Older adults who believe that they continue to be obligated understand themselves as engaging in the central human task of *tikkun olam*—repairing and redeeming the world through observance of the mitzvot.[3]

The state of obligation may provide many older people with the "sense of significant being" otherwise sorely lacking. The message that elders are as bound to mitzvot as any other Jew communicates to them that something is expected of them, that their actions matter, that they have the means to transcend the narrow confines of their lives' current context along with some of the damning messages communicated by the culture around them.

Halachah (Jewish law) specifies no special category of obligation for the old. While there is a very clear beginning point of obligation—bar mitzvah—there is no endpoint. There is neither retirement from mitzvot nor a senior citizen discount. There is also no automatic assumption that an older person is any less competent to perform a mitzvah than anyone else.

Yet the experience of aging may present formidable barriers to observing the mitzvot, such as the inability to ambulate without assistance, sensory deficits, cognitive impairment, and memory loss. The question then arises: how does the Mitzvah Model apply to those thus hindered? The tradition understands that observance of the mitzvot should be accessible and attainable for Jews. The Torah itself states:

> Surely, this mitzvah which I enjoin upon you this day is not too baffling for you, nor is it beyond reach. It is not in the heavens, that you should say, "Who among us can go up to the heavens and get it for us and impart it to us, that we may observe it?" Neither is it beyond the sea, that you should say, "Who among us can cross to the other side of the sea and get it for us and

impart it to us, that we may observe it?" No, the thing is very close to you, in your mouth and in your heart, to observe it. (Deut. 30:11–14)

Models for understanding the obligations of impaired elders may be found within the halachic literature regarding the obligations of those who are ill or physically incapacitated. As I read these texts, they offer a model of adaptive obligation, which might be called "sliding scale obligation." According to this model, the mitzvot are assumed in principle to apply to each individual, but the authorities use sensitivity and creativity in defining mitzvot so that impaired individuals can fulfill their obligations by simply doing *as much as they can.*

For example, the obligation of daily prayer is considerably altered for the Jew who is physically or mentally incapable of performing it in its complete form. A person who is old or weak and unable to stand may recite the Amidah (standing) prayers sitting down, or even prone, so long as the person has the capacity to concentrate on the prayers.[4] An individual who cannot speak may discharge the obligation by mentally reciting the prayers or by meditating upon them.[5] A person who does not have the endurance to complete the entire liturgy may abbreviate the Amidah.[6] Even the Shema can be abridged to include just the first line if a person cannot concentrate longer.[7]

What is most significant about this "sliding scale" model of obligation for elders is that, once obligated, we remain so, even in the face of diminished capacity. All of the social and personal benefits of being *metzuveh* continue to accrue, because as long as we perform the mitzvah to the extent of our ability, we are considered to have fully discharged the obligation.

The message of the Mitzvah Model, then, is that old age is a time when much is asked of us and when we have much to give. The Mitzvah Model suggests to aging people that their actions matter, that they have the means to transcend the narrow confines of their lives' current context. The key question for elders is thus, "What is the mitzvah I am called to perform in this moment in my life?" or perhaps, "What can I contribute out of, or even in spite of, my suffering?"

The Mitzvah Model also demands much of those who care for elders, whether in our families or in our professional roles. If we understand aging as a time of obligation, we then need to think about our role in facilitating the contribution or service of those who have physical or cognitive constraints. We need to ask, "What is the gap between the mitzvah this person aspires to fulfill and her capacity? What can we do to help bridge it?" For the elders who volunteer in the Abramson Center's Hands and Hearts program, this kind of assistance is essential; *they* do the mitzvah, but they are able to do it only because of the help from volunteers and staff members who transport them in wheelchairs to gather them together, organize their meetings, and convey information about people who need their help. This work of facilitation—enabling elders to do fully what they are able to do—empowers elders in our lives to make a difference.

The message of the Mitzvah Model, then, is that old age is a time when much is asked of us and when we have much to give.

Final Words

The Mitzvah Model does not speak just to individual elders and their caregivers. It offers a challenge to our society at large. It is not enough to serve elders or to care for them. We are called to invite and facilitate elders' contributions so that they may not only experience meaning but also actually help to repair our broken world.

Being obligated is at the heart of our humanity, according to Heschel:

> What a person lives by is not only a sense of belonging but a sense of indebtedness. The need to be needed corresponds to a fact: something is asked of a man, of every man. Advancing in years must not be taken to mean a process of suspending the

requirements and commitments under which a person lives. To be is to obey. A person must not cease to be.[8]

For Further Investigation

Abraham J. Heschel. "To Grow in Wisdom," in *The Insecurity of Freedom.* Philadelphia: Jewish Publication Society, 1966, pp. 70–84.

Everything I Need to Know I Learned in the Nursing Home

Torah for Confronting Fragility and Mortality

I spent my formative years in the nursing home. Not what the commercials used to call the "Wonder Years, 1–12," but my late adolescence, early adulthood, and early midlife. I arrived quite by accident. Actually, I was dragged. One Saturday morning, a fellow college student begged me to join her group of volunteers to lead Shabbat services in a local personal care home. Initially it was disorienting. What did it mean when Mary invited me back to her house for lunch, when she clearly lived *there* in the institution? What was I supposed to make of Jenny, who called out every couple of minutes during the service, "What page?" Should I wake Max, who was sleeping so peacefully through the whole service and then woke up and told us how "vonderful" it was at the end?

But mostly it was simply amazing. Here we were, college kids and octogenarians, praying, singing, and celebrating together. The gaps between us melted away when our voices joined in the traditional chants. And the change in the older people was nothing short of miraculous. The sleepy, seemingly indifferent and somewhat confused bunch who greeted us when we came in were suddenly animated, funny, proud, and present.

Sacred Wisdom

I was intrigued. These old people seemed to *know* things. By dint of the decades they had lived and the adversity they currently faced, they had gathered Torah, sacred wisdom. They comprised a repository of knowing. Like Torah, their teaching was rich with possibilities for interpretation, explication, and practical application. Like Torah, these elders' sagacity needed to be passed on, from generation to generation. I sensed that theirs was the Torah that I needed to learn.

I continued studying that Torah, mining the text of frail elders' lives for wisdom—in my social work training in senior centers, as a rabbinic student in a large urban home for the aged, and at Philadelphia Geriatric Center, a community of 1,100 Jewish elders I was privileged to serve as a spiritual caregiver while director of chaplaincy services for twelve years.

In the time that I spent in the nursing home, I found that colleagues, family members, and people I met in the community hardly shared my enthusiasm for the riches available in the nursing home. On the contrary, whenever I mentioned where I worked, I was met with expressions of fear and loathing. A neighbor exclaimed, "I've told my family, if I ever need to go to a place like that, they should just shoot me." A rabbinic colleague who asked where my congregation was, and seemed to feel terribly sorry for me once he heard the answer, said, "Was that something you *chose*?" A friend remarked, "You must find that so depressing." Another friend would routinely respond to my tales of inspiring moments with my elders with, "So ... have you seen any good movies lately?" And even a resident of the home said, "You're so young. Why would you want to be *here*?"

Accumulating Wisdom

All of those folks were not wrong. The nursing home is a terrifying and very sad place, a place everyone dreads and almost no one would choose. And yet it is precisely in that place of loss, fragility, indignity, and death that elders are living each day, accumulating wisdom and eager to share it, if only someone will listen. These elders, whose bodies and minds are broken, who are discarded, dismissed, and discounted, still have intact souls, radiant with light that can illumine a path. Like the Burning Bush, you have to stop to notice it; or like Jacob after his dream, you have to be prepared to discover that "God is in this place and I, I did not know it" (Gen. 28:16).

What does all of this have to do with caring professionals—rabbis, chaplains, and social workers? Most do not see themselves working in the field of aging, though as an advocate for the elderly, I'm called to point out that a very significant proportion of us encounter older people and issues of later life in our work every day. I want to suggest that the Torah that frail elders embody is precisely what we need to guide and sustain us as we accompany people through the valley of the shadow, through darkness, despair, brokenness, and to the very end of life.

These elders, whose bodies and minds are broken, who are discarded, dismissed, and discounted, still have intact souls, radiant with light that can illumine a path.

When they came to clean out her room after she died, the daughters of a very tough, very cool ninety-four-year-old nursing home resident named Sue gave me a needlepoint she had made. It bore Bette Davis's immortal words: "Old age is not for sissies." It now hangs in my office next to snapshots of my husband and three children.

I think about Sue's message often. I used to think I understood it, since I saw how crushing the vicissitudes of late life could be. Lately, it has occurred to me that the challenges faced by Sue and the very old are not so different in kind from those we face. We professionals are called to live in the face of death, to find meaning amid suffering, and to fan the smallest spark of light in the darkest place. Our work is not for sissies, and, I believe, we can take fortitude from the Torah embodied by the elderly sages from whom I've been blessed to learn.

In this chapter I will share four pieces of Torah, sacred wisdom, I've learned from frail elders. In Jewish tradition, Torah means literally the first five books of the Hebrew scriptures. It also means the entire oral and written tradition that has grown up around the text as it has been passed from generation to generation over the millennia. Just as the biblical Torah text is adumbrated by rabbinic interpretation, here, too, we look at a piece of teaching from Jewish tradition that sheds light on the Torah of the elder sages. Each teaching can be applied to our own encounters with fragility and mortality.

Learning and Growing

Our first piece of Torah is, "It's never too late to learn and grow." People think of the nursing home as the end of the road because, as one resident put it, "You come in on two feet and you leave in a box." But if you are still alive today, it might be that there is not only something to learn, but something new to become.

This Torah was impressed upon me by a group of twenty nursing home residents, assisted-living tenants, and elders from the community who decided to participate in an adult confirmation program at the home. This program offered an opportunity to affirm a connection to Jewish tradition and study for seventy- to ninety-five-year-olds, most of whom were women who had never been offered a Jewish education.

The confirmation process took seven months. The students participated in a course about Jewish values and contemporary social issues. They had to meet a requirement of "perfect attendance," meaning no unexcused absences. Over the course of the class, members faced both ongoing frailty and major life crises. Rachel broke a hip. Her daughter called me while Rachel was in the hospital: "All Mom wants to know is whether she can still be confirmed. Is there work she can do? Does she need a tutor?"

Despite challenges, the students were remarkably committed to participating in class sessions. In addition to their studies, the elderly students did a

I want to suggest that the Torah that frail elders embody is precisely what we need to guide and sustain us as we accompany people through the valley of the shadow, through darkness, despair, brokenness, and to the very end of life.

mitzvah project helping an after-school program for at-risk Jewish and Arab children in Israel. Though many had almost no access to disposable income, they managed to raise more than six hundred dollars for computers; they corresponded with the Israeli kids, who were amazed and thrilled that this group of elderly Jews on the other side of the world had taken such an interest in them.

On the second day of the festival of Shavuot, twenty confirmands made their processional into the synagogue on walkers, in wheelchairs, and in electric carts. Wearing white robes, they conducted the service, received certificates, and spoke to the two hundred and fifty relatives and friends in the audience. This is what one confirmand said in her speech:

> *I never had a formal Jewish education, though I was raised by wonderful Jewish parents and grew up to be a properly raised Jewish girl.... I wanted to join the confirmation class because I could be enlightened about our Jewish religion and what it means to be a Jew.... I can truly say that in our discussions, I learned that there is a God. I feel wonderful that I was able to complete this course. I'm proud of myself and my fellow confirmands.*

One confirmand literally came from her deathbed to the ceremony. In the end stage of pancreatic cancer, Bertha had continued to attend classes and emphatically wanted to be present for the ceremony. When I arrived for the ceremony, I was devastated to learn that Bertha had been taken to a hospital for an emergency procedure that very morning. Amazingly, thanks to a compassionate nursing home administrator's persistence, Bertha was brought back and wheeled into the sanctuary in a geri-chair in the middle of the service. She was able to chant the Aleinu prayer in Hebrew and to receive her certificate in the presence of her family. Bertha died one week later, having achieved a cherished goal at the very end of her life.

Like Bertha, all of the confirmands felt a profound sense of accomplishment and affirmation; they had reached for something and attained it, despite impairments, serious illness, and loss. They had managed to serve as exemplars of lifelong Torah learning, Jewish commitment, and continual growth and renewal.

These confirmands were fulfilling a holy demand. Maimonides, the great medieval Jewish sage, taught that learning is a lifelong obligation for everyone.[1] Rich or poor, smart or simple, weighed down by family responsibilities or not, all are called to keep studying Torah. Even an elderly person whose strength has waned must continue to learn. Until when does this obligation last? Until the day of your death, teaches Maimonides.

What does this Torah mean for professionals? We need forever to continue discovering. We must never assume we know it all. We must never meet the hundredth person in a given condition or situation and think we know what it is about for him or her. We are called to stay curious, keep open, keep learning—from books, from colleagues, from our own life experiences, and most of all, from those whom we accompany through their suffering.

This Torah also calls us to shift the way we see those whom we accompany. We are invited to recognize in them the striving not just to endure but also to continue to become. The person who is still becoming is always a *subject*, never an object. When we see this individual as reaching, we are barred from becoming condescending. On the contrary, we are inspired to stretch ourselves to become more, better. If we are lucky, we can become like the dream weavers of Second Wind Dreams. This incredible organization's sole mission is to help elders in institutions make their wishes come true, such as enabling a pioneer woman pilot to fly a plane at age ninety-one, taking a wheelchair-bound man on a deep-sea fishing trip, or assisting a retired church organist to put on a concert in the home. We, too, can be dream weavers. We can support aspirations and the thirst to learn and grow.

The Power of Mitzvah

Our second piece of Torah is about the power of mitzvah. As we discussed in chapter 2, a mitzvah is a commanded holy act. In colloquial usage, to do a mitzvah is to do a good deed. My elderly teachers have shown me how much doing a mitzvah can transform them, and us.

Ethel, Esther, and Freda had struck up a friendship in the nursing home. They came from remarkably different backgrounds, but they found that they enjoyed spending time together. Every Friday evening the three of them came into the synagogue, supported by canes and walkers, and found their way to their usual spot, right up front in the second pew, on the right side. (No one sat in the first pew, as is, seemingly, the universal custom in congregations everywhere!)

After a while, Ethel, who had been managing to get around with the help of a walker, could no longer do so. Suddenly Ethel was in a wheelchair, a source of great unhappiness to her. "This is not Ethel," she would say, pointing to the wheelchair and her useless legs. Being in a wheelchair also meant that Ethel could no longer sit in her usual pew in the shul. On the first Shabbat when Ethel arrived in a wheelchair, I noticed that Esther and Freda were also not seated in the second pew. They had quietly moved chairs to the space behind the pews. They were seated on either side of Ethel's wheelchair. Esther and Freda had understood Ethel's sadness. Through this simple mitzvah, they reminded Ethel that she was very much "still Ethel," despite the wheelchair, despite the pain, despite the dependency.

We All Want to Change the World

In my experience, frail elders do not want just to do mitzvot that change the lives of those who cross their paths in the nursing home. Rather, they still want to change the world. For example, a few years ago our nursing home congregation was told by a guest speaker about Yonah, a twenty-six-year-old Ethiopian Jew who had been airlifted to Israel in a remarkable rescue effort, Operation Moses. Yonah's mother and siblings were still in Ethiopia. He was barely subsisting on government stipends and trying to find work in his new land.

The congregation was previously unaware of the existence of the Ethiopian Jewish community and quite surprised to learn that

Judaism had flourished in Africa for many centuries. Nonetheless, once they heard Yonah's story, my congregants immediately wanted to reach out to this fellow Jew. The residents decided to adopt Yonah. They wrote letters, with the help of volunteers, who took dictation from them, since most couldn't see well enough to read or write. They sent photos and expressed sentiments such as, "Don't give up, you'll soon be with your family," and "I remember when I left my family in Russia when I came to America as a young man. You should find the happiness I found in my new home," and "God should watch over you, and by Pesach, you and your family should all be together."

In my experience, frail elders do not want just to do mitzvot that change the lives of those who cross their paths in the nursing home. Rather, they still want to change the world.

Sending encouragement was not enough for these nursing home residents turned activists. They wanted to *do* something. They raised money to help rescue Yonah's family, contributing dimes and quarters from their meager spending money or bingo winnings, and asking family members to donate as well. I told several rabbis of nearby synagogues about my congregants' activism and generosity. "They get a stipend of $10 a month and they have raised $700. What can you and your congregants do?" I asked. My congregants' magnanimity ultimately spurred local synagogues to join in raising more than $6,000 for Yonah's family. Several months later, Yonah wrote back, "When you write, I feel like I have brothers who care about me. Everything you wrote, it has come to be. You wrote that God would bring my family to me. At Pesach, my mother and brother came to Israel."

Through their involvement with Yonah, my congregants came to experience themselves not as patients, residents, or recipients of care, but as redeemers, observers of the mitzvah of *pidyon she-vuyim*, redeeming the captives. Truly, these elders taught me the lifesaving power of a mitzvah, not just for those toward whom it is directed, but for those who perform it as well.

For those who are facing brokenness or mortality, engaging in holy action has a transformative power. You change the world, and you change yourself. Here's the challenge: in order for someone who is frail or impaired to do a mitzvah, someone else may have to help. I suggest that the shaping of the task in a way that is accessible and do-able may well become our responsibility as caring professionals.

How would our work be transformed if we thought about not just how we can comfort and heal, but also how we can help those we are serving to use their will, love, and abilities to comfort, heal, and help? For professionals, part of our task thus becomes empowering those we serve to do and contribute. We need to ask: what part of the task do we need to do or shape so that the people we serve can do *their* parts?

Can the bedridden, homebound elder become a caring phone buddy for a latchkey child of working parents who comes home from school to a house empty of company, nurture, or supervision? Can the person struggling with depression be invited to pray for someone else in the community? Can the dying hospice patient give a lasting legacy to his loved ones by making an ethical will? What do we need to do to make that possible?

This Torah, the Mitzvah Model, can be something of a paradigm shift for us. We are accustomed to thinking about the transformation that occurs when professional caregivers are simply present. We try to quell within ourselves and our students the impulse "to fix" the person we are accompanying. The Torah of mitzvah, though, also calls us to enable those we serve to do and be all that *they* can be. And when we do that, neither we nor the individual we are helping remains the same.

The Courage to Love

The third piece of Torah deals with the courage to love. Residents of the nursing home are veterans of loss. They have withstood legions of tiny as well as monumental bereavements, parting with everything from the furnishings of their longtime homes to their dearest beloveds. There is no one who has survived without losing siblings, friends, parents, and neighbors. Most grieve for spouses or partners, but many have also lost at least one child.

In the home, death is the neighbor next door; crouching at the threshold, it is ever present. You just never know where it will next strike. Will it be your roommate? Your tablemate? Will it be you? You never know from day to day who will be there in the morning when you wake up.

In that land of loss and grief, you would expect that hearts close down. It can be just too painful to open to human connection, only to lose it yet again. Yet I have seen true courage in that barren wasteland, for I have seen that the will to love can conquer the fear of loss.

Dr. Rose was a retired professor of Jewish studies. When his beloved wife died a few short days after they came to live in the nursing home, it seemed Dr. Rose might give up altogether. Suddenly, instead of sharing his home with his wife of more than sixty years, he was rooming with a stranger. Instead of being the teacher, respected by neighbors and students alike, he was "a resident," expected to follow the routines like all the others. His three children lived far away, so in a sense, he was truly alone. Who would have guessed that the stranger in the bed next to him would become a dear and treasured friend? Who could have imagined that Dr. Rose would once again become an honored teacher?

Dr. Rose's new roommate was Mr. Fairstein. Mr. Fairstein prided himself on his intellect, and felt that there was no one in the home whom he could consider a peer. Mr. Fairstein had completed several advanced degrees, run a successful business, and always maintained interest in Jewish life. He reluctantly moved to the home after the death of his second wife, when he could no longer manage alone, as he had lost one leg to diabetes complications and the other was infected.

Somehow, the scholar and the intellectual had a meeting of minds. Mr. Fairstein, always fascinated by Jewish history, asked Dr. Rose to give him a tutorial. Thus began a daily study session, filled with discourse, debate, good humor, and mutual respect. When Mr. Fairstein became confined to his bed for nine months, due to his ever-worsening leg, it was Dr. Rose's lessons that kept him going. Dr. Rose said of Mr. Fairstein, "He is my best pupil." Mr. Fairstein said, "Ours is a true intellectual peership." The two pledged unending friendship and promised each other that they would remain roommates until death separated them, which they did.

~

Lillian and Eric were both seventy-five-year-old residents in independent living. They had each recently lost a spouse after a long illness, and both were volunteers in the nursing home. Eric noticed Lillian's flaming red hair, and one day he got the nerve to invite her to coffee in the cafeteria. One thing led to another, and soon they were inseparable. He called her "carrot-top" and she walked around with an elated grin. One day they made an appointment to see me. They had decided to get married, they said. They wanted the wedding in the home's synagogue and me to officiate.

It is a tad embarrassing to say that, thirty years old and unmarried at the time, I had the chutzpah to suggest premarital counseling. Lillian and Eric and I had some frank and difficult conversations, as they shared the pain of caring for a spouse who became frail, and their fear of how they would feel if it should happen again. I asked if they were prepared once again to face loving and losing. Lillian and Eric were absolutely clear: however long we have, they said, we are going to enjoy each other.

After some delays due to illness, the big day finally came. The wedding was small, simple, and moving. Under the chuppah, the wedding canopy, Lillian and Eric looked with delight into each other's eyes. Her children and grandchildren celebrated with them. Eric was dead a year and a half later. Lillian was bereft but philosophical. "Those were the best months of my life," she said.

Someone observing these loving ties among the oldest old might think that they are cute or sweet. I, however, think that what we see are awesome examples of real grit, from people brave enough to open their hearts and give and get whatever love they can for as long as they can.

We can keep our hearts open to love by learning from the Tanach. Consider Naomi, for example. Bereft of husband and sons, she could not bear to remain connected to her daughters-in-law because she feared being a burden. Or perhaps she could not face the risk of yet another loss should they decide to abandon her. Yet even after Naomi pushed them away, Ruth was persistent, and Naomi let her in. She found the courage to open her heart to the one who wished for connection. And this love bore fruit, for Ruth's child became Naomi's, too. Suddenly, instead of being a bitter old woman, Naomi was connected to present and future, a vital link, a nurturer.

This Torah is also relevant for professional caregivers. Even if we care for well people, our relationships are finite; we become attached to people who will be in our lives for a limited time only. Of course, this is also the human condition. This Torah is particularly rich for those of us who care for people at the ends of their lives. The nature of our work is to love and lose. It is an excruciating condition of our situations. But how are we to cope with this? How do we respond when the person we have come to cherish, whose soul has touched ours, is gone? And when there is another person in her bed, her seat, her place, intensely needing our care while reminding us of the hole left by the one who has died?

Our elders teach us that we can keep our hearts open to love by keeping them open to loss, by crying those tears, stopping to feel the sadness, and remembering just who it is we have lost. Rachel Naomi Remen teaches us that burnout happens to helpers who keep accumulating losses without ever giving themselves a chance to grieve.[2] We simply cannot keep caring when our hearts are broken. We need to acknowledge and mourn those we love and lose in order to keep our hearts soft and open to the next person whom we will be called upon to accompany. We need to mourn relationships lost, not just through death but also through trust betrayed, boundaries transgressed, or illusions shattered. The mourning for a lost relationship might be formal—a prayer or a service—or it might be makeshift—a moment of meditation, a journal entry, or a conversation with a colleague.

We can find the courage to remain open to love through the Torah of the elders, those who have preceded us down this path, for they have shown us that we gain even in loss, and that, as Lillian said, every moment of connection is a blessing, for as long as it lasts.

One Hundred Blessings a Day

Our fourth piece of Torah has to do with blessings. Over the course of the time I worked in the nursing home, all kinds of things happened in my life. I bought a home, I got married. My congregants shared the events in my life with avid interest and great enthusiasm. When my first daughter, Anya, was born, I felt like she had hundreds of *bubbes* and *zaydes*, grandmas and grandpas, many of whom were intensely interested in her every developmental milestone and adorable antic.

And then I got divorced. How could I tell my loving congregants that my heart was broken, my faith shaken, my world turned upside down? I could not figure out a way, so I did not tell them. People would ask how my family was, and I would say, "Fine."

Except for Fanny. Fanny was one hundred years old. We had known each other for nine years, and there was a loving, knowing way about her that just made me feel good in her presence. We had been through so much together: the death of her son-in-law, the conversion of her granddaughter's husband, who found Judaism through attending services with her, and her worries about her daughters' declining health. So when Fanny asked shortly after my husband and I had separated, "How are you, how's your husband, how's the baby?" I just could not lie or evade. So I told her.

Fanny said, "To tell you the truth, I never thought he was your type! But I want to tell you something.... When you were born, God made a *bashert* [destined one] for you. You'll find him in a *vinkl*, a corner." Fanny's blessing cheered me enormously. She had joined me in my suffering and offered me a vision of hope. And, it turned out, she was right. I did find my *bashert*, my beloved husband David, for whom I thank God every day!

Words of Blessing

It wasn't just Fanny who gave me blessings. Early in my work in the nursing home, I noticed that this was a kind of pay that I received daily. In nearly every interaction—casual conversation, hospital visit, exchanged greetings after Shabbat or holiday services—at some point, the person I was with would offer me a blessing.

Some of them were quite simple: "You should be well;" "God should let you live to be my age, but healthy;" "I wish you everything you wish yourself."

Others were amazingly profound: "May God grant you the happiness I've known;" "May we live and be well and be here together next year;" "May God bless you with a future that is unprecedented, and may your congregants appreciate the meaning of your message."

Our elders teach us that we can keep our hearts open to love by keeping them open to loss, by crying those tears, stopping to feel the sadness, and remembering just who it is we have lost.

Some blessings used the language of faith, and others were simply offered as loving, sincere wishes. However they were articulated, these blessings were abundant and powerful. They shifted the nature of my relationship to my congregants. They made our encounter explicitly reciprocal; we were each giving to the other in a holy way. Moreover, these blessings connected us to the Transcendent, the Source of life and love. Privileged to receive these blessings on a daily basis, I felt rich, full, sated.

Avoiding Complacency

Here is a traditional teaching about blessings: in the Talmud, tractate Menachot, we are taught that a person is bound to recite one hundred blessings a day. The justification for the number one hundred is in a reading of "And now, Israel, what does the Eternal your God require of you?" (Deut. 10:12). The word *mah* (what) is read as *meah*, which means one hundred. So what is it that God requires of us? One hundred [blessings].[3]

The blessings to which this text literally refers are liturgical benedictions. In Jewish tradition we offer a benediction to acknowledge the wonders of nature, like seeing the sea or a beautiful tree, or hearing thunder. We say a benediction before doing a commanded act, like lighting Shabbat candles. We recite a benediction when we experience sensory enjoyment or satisfaction, like when we eat or drink, or when we go to the bathroom. We say a blessing when we hear good news, see a wise person, and even when someone dies. It's easy to see how you can get to one hundred in a day!

If we become aware of and share blessings in our relationships with those we accompany, we will deepen our capacity to be present to all of reality.

The wisdom of offering these blessings throughout the day is that it bars us from becoming complacent, from taking for granted what the Siddur calls *nisecha she b'chol yom*, the miracles we experience every day. The Torah of the elders' blessings also sharpens our capacity for gratitude, wonder, and holy connection. It calls us to appreciate and acknowledge the blessings we receive from those we serve. And it invites us to find our own capacity to offer blessings, to elevate an encounter to the holy by invoking the divine, by entering into the dimension of the eternal. As David Spangler teaches in his wonderful book *Blessing: The Art and the Practice*, blessings remind us that "We are made of spirit stuff, soul stuff, love stuff … and therefore kin to life and to each other."[4]

Once we develop the habit of giving blessings and acknowledging the ones that come our way, our whole lives just might be richer and sweeter. Who knows, we might be giving a blessing to our partners as they rush off to work, to our assistant for coming through in a crunch, or even to the person who managed to deliver our newspaper after a blizzard! We might find ourselves *getting* a blessing from the grocery store checkout person, or even from our kids as they cuddle with us before bedtime.

The Torah of blessings is infinitely valuable for caring professionals in confronting fragility and mortality. When we respond to the call to give blessing, we are drawn to notice and celebrate the beauty, nobility, and goodness that exist right in the midst of pain, suffering, and death. If we become aware of and share blessings in our relationships with those we accompany, we will deepen our capacity to be present to *all* of reality. We will be sparked to receive bounty from those we serve, and to give our love back in a transcendent and eternal form.

Final Words

May we who walk with those facing brokenness and the finitude of this life, who ourselves are fragile and mortal, find the strength and inspiration to keep our minds open to learning, our souls open to empowering, our hearts open to loving, and may we find a way, like Abraham, not to just give and receive blessing, but *he'yeh berachah*, to *be* a blessing.

For Further Investigation

Rachel Naomi Remen. *Kitchen Table Wisdom*. New York: Riverhead Trade, 2006.
David Spangler. *Blessing: The Art and the Practice*. New York: Riverhead Books, 2001.

Seeking the *Tzelem*
Making Sense of Dementia

The specter of dementia is terribly frightening for most of us.[1] We dread the humiliating prospect of losing continence, the agitation of no longer knowing where or who we are, the vulnerability of being at the mercy of strangers caring for us. This is terrain no one wants to enter. Undoubtedly, anyone who has encountered dementia in family or work has witnessed scenes of great tenderness and scenes of heartrending pathos. I have been confronting the mysterious world of dementia for more than twenty-five years in my work with elders. What follows is an exploration of the meaning of dementia and an effort to put it in a theological context. My hope is that this reflection will shed light on the spiritual dimensions of life with dementia.

Since the challenge of dementia is not abstract but a lived reality, I begin this exploration by describing a few of the elders whose journeys inform my reflections.[2]

Mr. Shapiro, a retired pharmacist, was always impeccably dressed in a suit and tie when he lived at the nursing home. He often stopped me when he saw me pass by to ask if I ever got headaches, and if I'd like to know how to get rid of them. I replied that I did, on occasion, get headaches and would appreciate learning a technique to cope with them. Mr. Shapiro showed me that by rubbing my forehead with thumb and finger, I could reduce the pain of the headache. Though he did not remember our encounters when next we met, I understood that he was a helper and a healer, and that he was striving to continue to be who he was.

~

I met Shirley as I entered her nursing home floor. Obviously distraught, she was near tears. She asked me to help her. "I must find my way home. I'm very late and my mother is waiting for me. She'll be so worried."

~

Rose was an Eastern European woman with quite advanced dementia. She could no longer speak, but she could sing, and sing she did, all day and all night. She had an amazing ability to take up any melody you started, in any genre—Broadway, folk, liturgical, klezmer. She didn't sing the words, only "la, la" with great gusto. Teenage volunteers in the nursing home adored being with Rose. They lovingly called her "the la la lady" and competed to sit next to her in the synagogue.

~

Sylvia was always brought to Shabbat services on her nursing home floor. She would sit slumped over in her geri-chair all through the entire service; it was not clear if she was asleep or awake. When we sang the Shema, the central affirmation of Jewish faith, though, Sylvia would invariably open her eyes and murmur the words.

Encountering Dementia

Encountering dementia is provocative, at times frightening, often surprising, and sometimes even exalting. Confront it we must, for it is all around us as our community continues to age. In this quest to make sense of dementia, I want to explore what dementia means to the people who have it, to those around them, and, with supreme chutzpah, to God. I will then suggest how these observations can guide our work with individuals with dementia.

The Demographics of Dementia

Dementia currently affects about 4 million Americans. Given the aging of the American population, this number is expected to rise to 14 million by 2050. According to current estimates, about 10 percent of those over sixty-five and 50 percent of those over eighty-five have dementia. Based on the 2000–2001 National Jewish Population Survey's estimate of 956,000 Jewish elders in the United States, there are at least 95,000 Jewish elders today with dementia.[3]

Defining Dementia

The term "dementia" is often equated with Alzheimer's disease. In reality it is broader than Alzheimer's disease. Dementia refers to a number of related disorders that feature "significant, progressive losses in mental ability, usually but not always in the elderly. Symptoms of dementia include impairment in judgment, thinking, memory and learning as well as possible changes in personality, mood and behavior."[4] Dementia can last for years and is sometimes broken down into early, middle, and late stages. The early stage is characterized by loss of short-term memory and mild confusion; the middle stage includes more dramatic confusion and loss of memory and judgment, and also often includes incontinence; the late stage involves nearly total deterioration of physical functioning, including, eventually, the ability to eat, speak, and ambulate.

The Challenge of Dementia:
A Phenomenological Description

What is it like to live with dementia? Is it solely a journey of suffering? Can we even know? Any characterization I offer must be with humility, since I haven't been there, and have only witnessed this experience from without.

Sojourning in the Wilderness: The Experience
of the Individual Living with Dementia

One way to conceive of dementia is as a *midbar*, a wilderness. For the Israelites, the forty years of sojourning in the *midbar* after their liberation from slavery were mysterious and difficult. They wandered with few markers toward an unknown destination. They could not sustain themselves without Divine help. They were vulnerable to unsympathetic people they met along the way and to the harsh realities of nature. They could not return to the place of their memories, Egypt, and they could not truly imagine what lay ahead.

Perhaps people with dementia experience their lives as a kind of *midbar*. Memory loss is the hallmark of their condition. This memory loss is distinct from the ever-duller recall with which those of us in midlife or beyond contend. I am constantly asking where my keys are, and what *was* the name of that colleague I always enjoy running into at professional conferences, and I often search for the word that is on the tip of my tongue. Annoying though it is, this memory loss is normal, and not symptomatic of dementia; it is what gerontologists call "benign forgetfulness."

The person with dementia experiences *progressive* loss of memory, at first short-term, and eventually nearly all memory becomes inaccessible. The awareness of this loss is most acute in the early phase of dementia. The sense that you are losing your memory is terrifying. Depression and agitation often occur simultaneously in early-stage dementia. Losing our memory means losing our connection to pieces of ourselves and, eventually, to significant pieces of connection to those who have shared our lives.

When you cannot remember the past and cannot conceive of the future, what you are left with is the present moment. Being present in and aware of the moment at hand can bring joy if the moment is positive, and despair if it is not—for in that moment of *midbar* nothing else is imaginable. It can be a sweet and tender privilege to simply sit with a person with dementia, just holding hands, just being there, without distraction or agenda.

The *midbar* in which the Israelites wandered held places of beauty and moments of amazing power. This is also true for the *midbar* of dementia. While memory and other faculties may fade, many people experience an unabated capacity for joy and love, at least until the final stages of the disease. Diana Friel McGowin, an author and advocate for people with Alzheimer's disease, wrote a fascinating memoir of her journey through dementia. In it, she passionately asserts her continued engagement with life:

If I am no longer a woman, why do I still feel I'm one? If no longer worth holding, why do I crave it? If no longer sensual, why do I still enjoy the soft texture of satin and silk against my skin? If no longer sensitive, why do moving song lyrics strike a responsive chord in me? My every molecule seems to scream out that I do, indeed, exist, and that existence must be valued by someone![5]

There are remarkable oases of connection to be found amid the *midbar* of dementia. Against the background of so much loss, I have sometimes seen an especially keen appreciation for life's goodness. For example, one daughter described a sublime afternoon spent sitting with her father as they wordlessly watched the autumn leaves falling outside the window of the nursing home. The two of them were completely absorbed in nature's drama. They had no need for words or action.

When short-term memory fails, the world around us can offer many surprises. Psychotherapist Rita Bresnahan was moved by this dimension of her mother's experience amid dementia:

And she [my mother] is constantly surprised—by flowers that have been in her room for days, or by visitors who just step out of the room for a while. "Oh," she exclaims, smiling broadly at their return, delighted to see them as if they have just come. She lives David Steindl-Rast's words: "Any inch of surprise can lead to miles of gratefulness."[6]

In the Yotzer prayer, part of the traditional morning worship service, we praise the Eternal for "renewing in goodness each day the work of creation."[7] The person for whom a familiar, beloved person or object can continually seem a surprise is living the words of the Yotzer prayer. In this experience of surprised delight, each moment seems new. The person with dementia may experience what the rest of us are too busy to notice: each moment is a gift and not to be taken for granted.

Unfortunately, the person living with dementia often suffers through being treated by those around him or her as a nonperson.

In his courageous book *Dementia Reconsidered*, researcher Tom Kitwood decries what he calls the depersonalizing tendencies of malignant social psychology. Among the dehumanizing responses to people with dementia he identifies are:[8]

- Treachery: using deception to distract, manipulate, or force the person into compliance.
- Disempowerment: depriving the individual of control over his or her life.
- Infantilization: treating people with dementia like "wrinkled babies" instead of mature adults with history, dignity, and will.[9]
- Invalidation: failing to acknowledge the subjective reality of a person's experience or feelings.
- Objectification: treating the person as if he or she were "a lump of dead matter to be pushed, lifted, filled, pumped, or drained, without proper reference to the fact that they are sentient beings."

These dehumanizing responses are rampant in settings in which elders with dementia receive care. There are extreme examples, such as a staff member telling an elder who asks to be taken to the bathroom that she wears diapers and should just urinate in them. But there are also more insidious forms of dehumanization, such as using terms of endearment in speaking to an elder; perhaps the retired physician doesn't want to be called "sweetie," nor does the very demure homemaker necessarily want to be told how "cute" she looks. Every time staff members speak about an elder as if he or she is not present, the elder's dignity is assaulted. Each instance an escort pushes a wheelchair without addressing the person in it is a diminution of the elder's personhood.

The experience of wandering in the *midbar* of dementia is made harsher by the social context that surrounds it. Just as the Israelites were at the mercy of sometimes hostile others in the wilderness, so, too, those with dementia are vulnerable to attacks on their dignity through dehumanizing treatment. Conversely, the suffering of the person with dementia can be eased by love, respect, and tenderness.

Loving the Stranger: The Challenge for Those Who Love a Person with Dementia

When our beloved Grammy Anne suddenly became extremely impaired, unable to sensibly converse or relate to anything but frightening delusions, my sister Jill continued to visit almost daily and cared for her with great devotion. Jill sadly remarked, "This is not Grammy. The person we loved is gone." Encountering dementia in someone we love raises painful questions about what it is that makes us ourselves. This questioning is why pastoral educator David Keck teaches that dementia is a theological disease.[10]

As my family discovered, it is demanding to relate to someone you love whose personality has been distorted by dementia. Often the change is negative, as when a distinguished woman disinhibited by dementia suddenly shouts profanities she would never have dreamed of uttering. Sometimes the change can be a salutary one, as I learned when I met the family of Rose, the woman who loved to sing. "You must enjoy her so much. She is such a delight," I said. "We do," her daughter said, "Especially since she was not always like this. She was tough to live with!" Rose's dementia brought her family a new opportunity to know and appreciate her in a way that was never before possible.

Loving a person with dementia means facing a long, slow farewell, losing your dear one a little bit at a time. You experience the loss anew every time you see the person you love and realize, again, the differences in that person. This is an ongoing bereavement, but one without routine social or spiritual acknowledgment or support. Gerontologist Kenneth Doka points out that *disenfranchised grief*, which is not recognized by those around the bereaved person, can be particularly lonely and painful.[11]

The person who loves someone with dementia faces a delicate task of caring for ever-diminishing body and mind with *mora* (reverence) and *kavod* (honor).[12] We may need to adjust to radically changed roles as a loved one copes with dementia. The direction of power and dependency may shift. There may be weighty new responsibilities and knotty dilemmas as we balance respect for the person's wishes with concerns for his or her safety and well-being. Becoming a caregiver for a parent does not mean that you are now your parent's parent, but it is a painful realignment of roles nonetheless.

Psychotherapist Rita Bresnahan suggests that acceptance is a key part of the task in caring for a parent with dementia. It is so painful to surrender to our inability to fix the inexorable fading of the one we love. "More than anything," she writes, "I need to accept Mom where she is—and accept my own limitations as well. I once heard another caregiver explain to a fellow elevator-rider, 'There is nothing I can do for him, and I am doing it.'"[13]

One way of articulating the family caregiver's spiritual challenge is: "You shall love the stranger."[14] The Torah teaches us that we must treat the stranger with care, "for you know the soul of the stranger."[15] The stranger before you is the very person you have known and loved for all these years. In the confrontation with dementia, you are asked: Can you love this so-familiar and yet totally strange person before you? Can you let go of the expectation that the person will behave or appear as he used to, and appreciate him for who he is now? In loving the stranger, can you learn from this person and her journey? Poet Betsy Sholl puts the challenge eloquently:

> This old woman …
> isn't my mother,
> is not what I think.
>
> She's a spiritual master
> trying to teach me
> how to carry my soul lightly
> how to make each step
> an important journey,
> every motion and breath
> anywhere
> as though anywhere
> were the center of the earth.[16]

It is a supreme challenge to love the stranger. Certainly we have a mandate from Torah to do just that, hard and painful though it be. That this challenge of caring for a loved one with dementia can go on for years, or even decades, makes it even more heroic to overcome impatience, grief, and frustration and lovingly do what needs to be done.

Transcending Assumptions: Challenges for Staff Who Care for a Person with Dementia

Taking on the job of caring for a person with dementia as a healthcare or social services worker means facing a terrifying reality. In our society, many of us are hypercognitive, primarily identified with our intellectual sides—we believe we *are* our brains, so we believe witnessing the erosion of cognition is witnessing the decimation of personhood. Tom Kitwood suggests that confronting those with dementia arouses two primal fears: fear of frailty and dependency and fear of dying and death.[17]

Many people distance themselves from people with dementia in order to be spared this frightening prospect. In a study in which researchers observed life in an assisted-living community, Susan McFadden and her colleagues met a local parish clergy person in the elevator. When asked about his visit, he replied, "Well, I have three members here … but two are out of it so I just said hello and left my card."[18]

The stigma that our society attaches to those with cognitive impairments such as dementia can lead caregivers to form powerfully negative assumptions about their limitations. Christine Bryden, an Australian woman diagnosed at age forty-six with dementia, decries what she calls the "toxic lie of dementia," the assumption that "the mind is absent and the body is an empty shell."[19] The impact of caregivers' assumptions can be devastating, as she writes:

> This stigma leads to restrictions on our ability to develop our spirituality. It threatens our spiritual identity. It is assumed

that the limits due to our failing cognition place us beyond reach of normal spiritual practices, of communion with God and with others. But to what extent are these assumptions due to the limits placed upon us due to the stigma attached to our dementia?... The question is, where does this journey begin, and at what stage can you deny me my self-hood and my spirituality?"[20]

Even the most dedicated caregivers face frustration as they seek to respect the person with dementia. It is often so hard to know what the person is feeling, experiencing, longing for. The caregiver is limited in resources to understand the person and his or her wishes. It is therefore invaluable to hear the voices of persons with dementia, which is what makes narratives like Christine Bryden's and Diana Friel McGowin's so valuable. Although each individual's experience is wholly unique, these narratives give caregivers a window into the experience of dementia. This glimpse of their reality may help those of us on the outside to better understand and more respectfully relate to people with dementia.

Seeing the *Tzelem*: How Does Dementia Look to God?

The biblical creation narrative tells us that God created humanity *b'tzelem Elohim*, in God's own image. Religion scholar Stephen Sapp suggests that the task in approaching a person with dementia is "to see as God sees.[21] I would suggest that God sees the *tzelem* in people with dementia, the divine spark within them that is made in God's image. The late Hershel Matt reflected on his experience in providing pastoral care for people with dementia, and wondered where that *tzelem* could be in those diminished by confusion and incapacity. He suggested that what he was witnessing was "the fading image of God."[22]

Others would argue that the image of God can never be diminished in a living human being. For example, the Maggid of Mezeritch, an eighteenth-century Chasidic master, taught that the *tzelem* is an intrinsic element of the human being. The Maggid compared the creation of human beings in God's image to a father who has a son. Even if the son goes far away, the father always holds the son's image in his heart and mind. According to the Maggid of Mezeritch, God had an image of humanity in mind before we were even created, and this image is unchanging in past, present, and future. We always look the same to God.[23]

Based on this teaching and my own encounters with people with dementia, I would suggest that the *tzelem* is not dependent on cognition or capacity. Amid all of the changes of dementia, the *tzelem* remains, for it is our very humanity.

Another way of understanding what God sees in the person with dementia is that God sees the *neshamah*, the soul. We are taught that the soul within us is pure and remains within us until we die.[24] If so, then perhaps the idea that the person with dementia is suffering might be our own projection. How do we know that person with dementia is not on a *higher* spiritual *madrega* (level)?

> *I would suggest that the* tzelem *is not dependent on cognition or capacity. Amid all of the changes of dementia, the* tzelem *remains, for it is our very humanity.*

In some spiritual approaches, the ideal is to be present in the present moment; people with dementia are probably more able to do that than the rest of us. In mystical terms, we speak of the ideal of shedding the *klipot*, the outer shells, of superficial utilitarian identities; dementia accomplishes this purpose, stripping souls down to their essence. This is the experience of one daughter who crosses the country by plane every few weeks to care for her father with advanced dementia. It is not a burden but a privilege to be with him, for, she says, "He's just pure *chesed* [lovingkindness]. That's all that's left."

According to our tradition, God remembers *for* us, even when we can't. In the beautiful words of the Zichronot (remembrance) prayers from the High Holy Day liturgy, "Thus says the Eternal, I remembered for you the kindness of your youth, the love of your wedding day, how you followed Me into the wilderness."[25] Even when we are mired in the moment, bereft of all perspective on our lives, God sees more, in boundless compassion. God holds *all* of who we've been. We may forget, but God does not. God "for eternity remembers all of the forgotten ones … and there is no forgetfulness before Your throne of glory."[26] We are always whole in God's eyes.

Another way of understanding what God sees in the person with dementia is that God sees the neshamah, *the soul. We are taught that the soul within us is pure and remains within us until we die.*

Seeking the *Tzelem*: The Challenge for the Spiritual Caregiver

Our role as spiritual caregivers with people with dementia is to emulate God in seeking the *tzelem*. We need to remind ourselves that even when the *tzelem* is not apparent, it is there. In the person who is disoriented, who is regressed, or even unresponsive, somehow the image of God resides.[27] Christine Bryden reminds us of the power of seeking the *tzelem*: "By rejecting the lie of dementia and focusing on my soul rather than on my mind, I can be free of fear of loss of self, and in so doing can also help you to lose your fear that you are losing me."[28]

Remember *for* Them

Spiritual caregivers can also emulate God by remembering *for* people who cannot remember for themselves. We can connect them to memory. The Talmud contains a poignant narrative about Rav Joseph bar Chiya. Rav Joseph was called "Sinai" because he held all of the laws of the Torah systematically in his head, as if he had heard them directly from God at Mt. Sinai.[29] Rav Joseph apparently became ill and suffered major memory loss. The Talmud recounts a number of cases in which his student, Abaye, gently reminds him of his own teaching. Upon hearing a complex legal discussion, Rav Joseph says, "I have never heard this tradition," and Abaye reminds him, "You yourself have told this tradition to us, and it was in connection with the following that you told us."[30] Abaye connected Rav Joseph not only to his memory but also to his very identity and worth. In reminding his teacher of his own wisdom, Abaye upheld another of Rav Joseph's teachings:

> Rabbi Joseph teaches that the tablets [of the law] and the broken tablets [that Moses shattered upon discovering the Golden Calf] are both kept in the ark. From here we learn that a scholar who has involuntarily forgotten his learning should not be treated disdainfully."[31]

As we recall their personhood, we remember those with dementia in an additional way. According to Stephen Sapp, by recalling the Latin root of *remember*, which comes from the word for limb, we learn that our role is to return the person to the community. "*Remembering* those individuals in the sense of bringing them back into the human community, refusing to let them be cast aside and forgotten, which is in effect to *dis-member* the body. And chaplains are often in an especially critical position to facilitate this process of re-membering ..."[32]

Whenever we respond to an individual as one created in the image of God, we are helping him or her rejoin the community.

Respond to the *Neshamah* (the Soul)

In accompanying individuals with dementia, we are challenged to relate to the soul within them. As Rita Bresnahan writes:

> It is not *Mom* who must remember who *I* am. Rather, it is *I* who must remember who *my mother* is. Who she truly is. Not merely "an Alzheimer's patient." Nor merely "my mother." It is up to me to [continue to be] ... keenly aware of her spirit, honoring her soul-essence. Meeting her with caring and love

and respect in that sacred place of wholeness which nothing can diminish.[33]

We relate to the soul when we let the faces of elders with dementia shine through the power of ritual. We witness the power of symbol, song, and holy times to connect to the part that is whole within the person, as with Sylvia, who found connection through the familiar words, melody, and message of the Shema. When we use ritual to empower individuals to live in sacred time, there is a chance that, at least in the moment, elders will feel that the day is more than an endless expanse of waiting that will never end. We are called to adapt our celebration and worship to make it accessible to individuals with dementia, harnessing our creativity to engage people at the time and in the manner that works for them.

Whenever we respond to an individual as one created in the image of God, we are helping him or her rejoin the community.

The Work of Spiritual Accompaniment

In spiritually accompanying individuals with dementia, we forge a life of connection for them. In our simple presence, in our caring and fervent commitment to striving to understand the individual, we provide a response to the pastor who said, "There's nothing to do with them because they're out of it." Our response is to be with them in the *midbar*. Diana Friel McGowin eloquently states the urgent need for this accompaniment:

> Without someone to walk this labyrinth by my side, without the touch of a fellow traveler who truly understands my need of self-worth, how can I endure the rest of this uncharted journey? I thirst today for understanding, a tender touch and healing laughter.[34]

The work of accompanying elders with dementia requires curiosity. We will do best to follow the advice of pastoral care educator

Melvin Kimble, who suggests we practice "hermeneutical phe-nomenology," inviting the old to be our teachers about aging and meaning.[35] In this learning process, the teaching happens at levels beyond words and surface conversation. We search agitated behavior or speech to unearth the profound concerns the person is trying to communicate. When Shirley tells us she needs to go home to her mother, we may learn worlds about the enduring mother-daughter bond if we inquire into the *derash*, the meaning of this quest.

When we acknowledge and validate the emotions reflected in apparently "unreal" content, we can reach and honor the confused elder. As Rita Bresnahan observes, "I am learning that 'the facts' do not matter. Only the relationship does."[36]

We will learn much if we open ourselves to the person with dementia. I learned from Mr. Shapiro, the pharmacist, not only how to relieve a headache, but also how a person retains his or her essential goodness amid change and brokenness.

This work requires patience. We struggle to be with the person in silence, to be satisfied when nothing seems to be happening. Sometimes we learn that a great deal is happening, as did the daughter who discovered anew the wonder of falling leaves as she sat in silence with her father. In accompanying people with dementia, we ambitious caregivers need to measure accomplishment in a different way. Any progress may register in millimeters, not inches. Yet we must be prepared for "magic moments," when a person who seems generally quite confused may suddenly speak or connect with great clarity and profundity.

> *When we acknowledge and validate the emotions reflected in apparently "unreal" content, we can reach and honor the confused elder.*

Anna was a feisty, fun-loving woman who had formed many close friendships with other elders in the home in the years she lived there. Only when she passed age one hundred and pain-fully fractured a hip did she begin to be confused. One day, as she sat in her geri-chair, Anna was moaning, saying over and over, "Oy, mama, oy, mama." I sat down next to Anna and took her hand. "You're thinking a lot about your mother, aren't you, Anna?" Anna turned to me and said, "It's always Mom in the end."

Anna could not have said what day of the week it was, nor did she necessarily remember the chaplain sitting next to her. Somehow, though, Anna knew what really counted. She realized that she was near the end of life. She was aware that she longed for the comfort of her mother, and she believed she would soon be joining her.

Ultimately dementia is a mystery. If we can find the courage to walk alongside those who journey in this *midbar*, we, too, will be transformed. Debbie Everett, a hospital chaplain, has identified the "surprising paradox" of ministry with dementia: it leads us, the spiritual caregivers, to live more authentically. Everett writes, "As we open ourselves to embracing [persons with dementia] as wholly worthwhile and valuable persons that need motivated and loving care, they expel us from our intellectual theological boxes. In the process, they introduce us to a God who is also dancing and laughing in the bizarre places where chaos reigns."[37]

As we learn from those we accompany that the human being is more than intellect, more than memory, even more than cognition, we learn that we are too. We learn to value ourselves for our very essence.

As we learn from those we accompany that the human being is more than intellect, more than memory, even more than cognition, we learn that we are too. We learn to value ourselves for our very essence.

Practical Tips for Accompanying People with Dementia

The following are some specific suggestions to guide you in spiritually accompanying people living with dementia.

General Approaches

1. Try to remain conscious of the other as a being *b'tzelem elohim*—and know that you can be an important model for staff and family.
2. Work on being with silence, with "nothing happening."
3. Slow down to keep up. Adjust your pace to the person whose life moves slowly, if at all.
4. Be prepared for "magic moments," when a person who seems generally quite confused may suddenly speak or connect with great clarity and profundity.

Reaching a Person with Dementia

1. Use position and touch to establish connection.
2. Always introduce yourself. It can be very embarrassing to a memory-impaired person not to remember who you are.
3. Use "parallel talking"—express what you observe the person is experiencing or expressing nonverbally. Your interpretive comments can "give voice" to the person who cannot express himself or herself.
4. Acknowledge how difficult it is not to be able to communicate better, to understand one another.
5. Use statements, not questions. If you do ask questions, they should be more concrete and closed-ended.

6. When confronting "unreal" content from the person, attend to the reality beneath that content: What is the person feeling? What does this content mean to him or her? Validate the feelings and meanings without validating the content.
7. Use diversion at times (take a walk, change the subject, sing a song) to help refocus a person who is anxious about something unreal.
8. Be sensitive to concrete requests and their meanings; don't discount them.

Caring for Yourself While Caring for People with Dementia

1. Acknowledge that this is hard work.
2. Get support from colleagues.
3. Alternate seeing these most challenging individuals with others who may be more obviously rewarding.
4. Keep a sense of humor and don't be afraid to show it.
5. Measure your accomplishments in millimeters, not inches.
6. Know that some people will be reached through your presence, others through ritual, and others only in *mashiachzeit*, the Messianic age.

Final Words

Confronting dementia puts us in touch with the profound fragility of so much that we cling to in this life—memory, identity, relationship. In this awesome and mysterious journey, may we remain connected to the One whose compassion is boundless, who remembers us, and remembers the covenant that binds us in eternal love. May we bring that compassionate connection to all of our relationships.

For Further Investigation

Virginia Bell and David Troxel. *The Best Friends Approach to Alzheimer's Care.* Baltimore: Health Professionals Press, 1997.

Rita Bresnahan. *Walking One Another Home: Moments of Grace and Possibility in the Midst of Alzheimer's.* Liguori, MO: Liguori/Triumph, 2003.

Christine Bryden and Elizabeth MacKinlay. "Dementia—A Spiritual Journey Towards the Divine: A Personal View of Dementia." *Journal of Religious Gerontology* 13, no. 3/4 (2002): 69–75.

David Keck. *Forgetting Whose We Are: Alzheimer's Disease and the Love of God.* Nashville: Abingdon Press, 1996.

Tom Kitwood. *Dementia Reconsidered: The Person Comes First.* Buckingham, England; Philadelphia: Open University Press, 1997.

Nancy Mace and Peter Rabins. *The 36-Hour Day: A Family Guide to Caring for Persons with Alzheimer's Disease, Related Dementing Illnesses, and Memory Loss in Later Life.* Baltimore: Johns Hopkins University Press, 1981, 1991.

Hershel Matt. "Fading Image of God? Theological Reflections of a Nursing Home Chaplain." *Judaism* 36, no. 1 (Winter 1987): 75–83.

Diana Friel McGowin. *Living in the Labyrinth: A Personal Journey through the Maze of Alzheimer's.* New York: Delacorte Press, 1993.

Jane M. Thibault. "Spiritual Counseling of Persons with Dementia." In *Aging, Spirituality, and Religion: A Handbook,* vol. 2, Melvin A. Kimble and Susan H. McFadden, eds. Minneapolis: Augsbury Fortress Press, 2003, pp. 23–32.

Larry VandeCreek, ed. *Spiritual Care for Persons with Dementia: Fundamentals for Pastoral Practice.* Binghamton, NY: Haworth Press, 1999.

Resources

Forgetmemory.org is a website and blog devoted to reflecting on the possibility for quality of life amid memory loss.

The Foundation for Alzheimer's and Cultural Memory has developed collective reminiscence work that gives voice to elders with dementia (www.memorybridge .org).

Island on a Hill is a CD recording of elders from San Francisco's Jewish Home who became psalmists and singer-songwriters with the help of Rabbi Sheldon Marder and musician Judith-Kate Friedman (www.cdbaby.com/cd /judithkate).

Sacred Seasons celebration kits, produced and distributed by Hiddur: The Center for Aging and Judaism, are designed to enable elders in residential settings, even when a Jewish spiritual caregiver is unavailable. Comprehensive, easy-to-use kits for Shabbat and holidays include everything a staff member or volunteer without Jewish background needs to facilitate a joyous celebration (www.sacredseasons.org).

The TimeSlips Project has collected hundreds of stories, produced plays, and mounted art exhibits based on narratives of individuals with dementia (www.timeslips.org).

Lilmod U'lilamed

Elders as Learners and Teachers of Torah

M any of us who are now working adults will likely have two to three decades of good health and vitality post-retirement, and some protracted period of frailty and dependency as well. Although aging presents other profound challenges and opportunities, the questions of meaning-making and meaning-finding are central.

A lthough aging presents other profound challenges and opportunities, the questions of meaning-making and meaning-finding are central.

With what pursuits will we fill our days? How will we understand who we are when the roles by which we've been identified are no longer ours? What is the purpose of these "bonus years"?

In this chapter, I suggest that engagement with Torah—with Jewish learning and teaching—can bring significance to the experience of aging. The connection with Torah is life-giving, both for older learners and for those they touch, as we learn from Kiddushin 82b:

> R. Nehorai said: I abandon every trade in the world and teach my child only Torah, for every trade in the world gives a person sustenance only in youth, but in old age, one is exposed to hunger. But it is not so with the Torah: it stands by us in our youth and gives us a future and hope in old age.[1]

Lilmod: Elders as Students of Torah

The most rewarding course I have ever taught was the weekly Torah study group in the nursing home I served as chaplain. You

58

might think that an institution for frail elders would be an unlikely place to find a lively community of Torah scholars. Yet that was exactly what I found in teaching—and learning—Torah with twenty-five to thirty-five students aged seventy-five to one hundred over a period of ten years.

We opened each session with the *bracha* for Torah study, acknowledging the commandment "to occupy our-selves with the study of Torah" and framing our work as a sacred pursuit. Each time we met, we explored an issue from *Parashat Hashavua* as we read and discussed a selection reproduced in large type. Most of my students, who gathered in wheelchairs, on walkers, and attached to feeding tubes and other apparatuses, had not previously studied Jewish text. They might well have felt shy about expressing their views about a tradition they knew from childhood observance more than from intellectual exploration. Over time, however, they became adept at *pilpul*, dissecting the text and argu-ing with it and about it.

You might think that an institution for frail elders would be an unlikely place to find a lively community of Torah scholars. Yet that was exactly what I found in teaching—and learning—Torah with twenty-five to thirty-five students aged seventy-five to one hundred.

The students' life experiences were invaluable in our delibera-tions. They could, for example, understand Jacob and Esau's con-flicts from the perspective of parent, child, sibling, and grandparent. They brought a depth of understanding to our investi-gation of the Israelites' doubts and rebellions during their seemingly endless and directionless wandering in the wilderness. My students knew what it was like to lose track of their goals, to question their path, and to feel profoundly insecure.

The students valued the Torah study group and grieved when illness, physician appointments, or treatments kept them from attending. We closed each session by singing Debbie Friedman's arrangement of *Kaddish D'Rabanan*, praying for peace and loving-kindness for "those who study Torah, here and every-where." However improbable, these elders, who might so easily have been dismissed as dependent, frail nursing home residents, counted themselves among the scholars of Torah.

It is not just my nursing home congregants who are powerfully drawn to Jewish learning in later life. Evidence of the appeal of Jewish study is apparent in the remarkable popularity of Elderhostel courses with Jewish themes, and in the burgeoning of Jewish studies courses at community colleges in areas with significant elderly populations. The enthusiasm of elders for serious Jewish study is evident in their prominent participation in community-based adult education efforts such as the Florence Melton Adult Mini-Schools.[2] In addition, a significant proportion of students in many synagogue adult education programs is sixty and older.

These adult learners are clearly a diverse lot. They include at least two generations, ranging from individuals in their sixties to those in their nineties (and beyond!). Some are individuals who are healthy and vital, while others are quite frail. Though highly edu-cated by American standards, many have not been connected to Jewish learning since childhood. They are motivated not only by a desire for connection to a past, but also by a quest for significance, and by a thirst for continued learning and growth.

The benefits of engaging older learners in Jewish study are impressive. Older learners sustain their minds and spirits in the course of Jewish study. Learning together creates community at a time when isolation threatens. Further, adult education may offer a pathway toward new or renewed Jewish connection and affiliation. Conversely, elder learners are a growing and rewarding audience for new and existing adult education efforts.

What does it take to foster late-life Jewish learning? It is not necessary to create age-segregated programs to attract and involve elders in Jewish learning. In fact, I would argue that to do so is to miss opportunities for profoundly rich exchange between genera-tions. It is imperative, however, to design programs that will foster and maximize elders' participation.[3] Attending to the educational approach and to issues of accessibility will help foster dynamic Jewish learning for those in later life.

Educational Approach: Andragogy

We need to employ a respectful and effective educational approach in engaging older adult learners. While research suggests that older learners are indeed able to extend their knowledge and continue to grow intellectually, they do it best when teaching touches and exploits what they already know. The andragogical approach to teaching any adult involves building from the known to the unknown, and allowing the learner to be self-directed in the educational process.[4]

Implications of this approach for Jewish teaching of older students include welcoming (while channeling appropriately) students' sharing of life experience relevant to the topic at hand, and inviting students to articulate and evaluate their own learning objectives.

> *In a Torah study class examining the mitzvot connected to treatment of "the stranger," older students are invited to tell about moments in their lives when they have felt themselves to be strangers. One student, a Holocaust survivor, speaks about feeling excluded in her current community because she has an accent. Another suggests that the residents in their senior housing community are strangers to one another. A lively discussion about alienation and community emerges from the sharing of their personal experiences.*

Sacred study can help aging individuals address the developmental tasks of later life, and bring the wisdom of the Jewish tradition to bear on their experience.[5] Adult educational opportunities that address life challenges of aging individuals, such as discerning a person's mission and facing mortality, will be especially welcome.

Paving the Way: Fostering Accessible Learning Opportunities

Opening educational opportunities to older persons requires sensitivity to issues of accessibility on a number of levels. Older learners may be integrated into general adult education programs if these issues are addressed. First, transportation can be an obstacle for many older people, particularly at night. It may be that younger students would be happy to be matched with elders who are unable to drive themselves. If there is a concentration of older people in one or more apartment complex or neighborhood, perhaps volunteer drivers could bring a group of them to the program or class.

A dult educational opportunities that address life challenges of aging individuals, such as discerning a person's mission and facing mortality, will be especially welcome.

Alternatively, it might be that local para-transit agencies could transport elders to the program, or that classes could be held in the places where they live.

Once they have arrived, older learners will benefit if attention has been given to the physical learning environment. Is there a ramp so that those with difficulty walking or in wheelchairs can enter the space? Are the restrooms handicap accessible? Is the lighting conducive to looking at texts? Will the conversation be audible to those with hearing limitations, or are amplification devices (or microphones) available? Will learners be able to hear one another when they speak? Alternatively, are there seats near the front of the room for those with hearing or vision problems?

Finally, a warm social environment will encourage older learners to participate. Simple steps, such as inviting participants to introduce themselves and share some key life experience connected to the course's focus, will enhance comfort and community among learners. Serving refreshments, or inviting participants to take turns bringing them, also fosters an invaluable sense of connection among learners. Never underestimate the power of food in Jewish education. The rabbinic adage *im eyn kemach, eyn Torah* (if there is no bread, there is no Torah) could not be more vividly borne out than in Jewish education with older learners.

Engaging older learners can be transformative for the older learners, for other learners, and for teachers as well. The motivation, enthusiasm, and wisdom older students contribute to the learning environment can intensify the experience for all involved. The opportunity to examine course content from multiple life-stage perspectives adds depth and nuance to the learning process.

Given all of these benefits, if we only engage elders as learners, we might say *dayenu*, that is more than enough. I would suggest, however, that there is yet more to be gained by engaging elders as *teachers* of Torah.

Older learners will benefit if attention has been given to the physical learning environment. Is there a ramp so that those with difficulty walking or in wheelchairs can enter the space? Are the restrooms handicap accessible?

Lilamed: Elders as Teachers of Torah

One of the great tragedies of our age-segregated society is the deprivation of children, young adults, and even those in midlife of the wisdom and guidance of elders. Many Jewish children grow up at a great distance from their grandparents. Occasional visits do not provide a steady stream of the very special love, nurture, and perspective elders might provide. In many congregations, older adults either fall away from membership entirely or are more involved in senior adult clubs than in "mainstream" congregational activity. In communities to which elders have moved in their retirement, they may have scant interaction with younger families and individuals in congregations and organizations.

I would like to suggest two strategies for using the talent and wisdom of elders in Jewish learning: elders as teachers and elders as mentors.

Elders as Teachers

The teacher shortage in supplemental synagogue religious schools is widely recognized. Frustrated educators fill the classrooms with well-meaning laypeople, Israeli immigrants, and secular school-teachers. These teachers may lack substantive Jewish background or pedagogical foundations. Retired secular schoolteachers could be a fruitful resource for the Jewish school.[6] Such individuals commonly retire at a relatively young age and are in search of meaningful roles for the next stage of their lives. They already have both education and experience in pedagogy, often refined through teaching in very challenging contexts. The Jewish education they lack could be provided through participation in one of the many community-based or university-based Jewish studies programs. Student teaching and mentorship in the classroom, along with seminars on the particular context of the supplemental religious school, could equip these teachers with the skills and knowledge they need to serve as exemplary Jewish educators. A cadre of second-career Jewish educators might well enrich the supplemental religious schools.

A more modest approach might be to recruit elders as adjunct teaching assistants for religious school classrooms. This role might be a volunteer position, or it could carry a stipend. Alternatively, this role might earn volunteers a benefit, such as discounted synagogue membership, tuition for a Judaic studies course, or free admission to a special event. Either approach would require close supervision, clear expectations, and regular feedback.

Elders as Mentors

> When the Temple was standing, the leaders would ask the elders for advice, as it is written, "Ask your father and he will tell you, your elders and they will say to you" (Deut. 32:7), for whoever takes advice from the elders will not fail.[7]

Elders can be invaluable resources for teens and young adults. There is a natural alignment of the older and younger generations. Both feel at times disenfranchised and disrespected, and both eagerly wish to assert their agency and autonomy. Today's Jewish elders have lived through dilemmas about Jewish identity and have made choices about observance, affiliation, and marriage that have shaped their lives.

Who better to join with young people in reflecting on these vital issues of Jewish continuity? Thus, linking adolescents with older partners at key moments, such as bar/bat mitzvah, may be powerful. Connecting old and young at other critical life passages—for example, providing foster grandparents as adjuncts to new parents—may also be valuable.

Programs engaging elders as mentors need not be elaborate, but they should be conscious in preparation of both young and older participants and clear about roles, expectations, and parameters. Older partners might be members of a congregation or residents of a nearby retirement community or assisted-living facility. What is key to this vision is that elders are not *recipients* of an effort of *g'milut chasadim* (acts of lovingkindness), but rather are precious repositories of wisdom who can bring Torah to individuals and communities.

E lders can be invaluable resources for teens and young adults. There is a natural alignment of the older and younger generations. Both feel at times disenfranchised and disrespected, and both eagerly wish to assert their agency and autonomy.

Practical Tips for Engaging Elders as Learners in Jewish Education

1. Create a respectful learning environment.
   - Empower learners to set and evaluate their own learning objectives.
   - Invite older learners to make connections to their knowledge and experience.
2. Foster accessibility in the learning setting.
   - Make sure the space is well-lit and that sound amplification is available.
   - Make handouts available in large type (at least 24-point font size).
   - Set up the space so that students with wheelchairs or walkers can have good seats.

3. Encourage personal reflection, for example journaling or sharing reactions with fellow students.
4. Make the experience warm and welcoming.
   - Give out name tags (at least for a few meetings).
   - Give personal introductions.
   - Set ground rules to establish safety and boundaries on personal sharing (e.g., students won't be called on a second time until everyone has spoken once).
   - Use strategies to maximize participation, such as small groups or *hevruta* (study partner) pairings.

Final Words

The words of the Ahavah Rabbah prayer from our *Shacharit* liturgy offer a beautiful vision for the place of learning and teaching Torah throughout our lives: "Have compassion upon us, and allow our hearts to understand and discern, to hear, learn and teach, that we might observe and uphold and establish all the teachings of Your Torah in love."

I pray that our community will empower and enable the broad range of today's and tomorrow's elders *lilmod u'lilamed*, to be learners and teachers of Torah, so that more wisdom and more love may be present for them, for our people, and for the entire world.

For Further Investigation

Roberta Louis Goodman and Betsy Dolgin Katz. *Adult Jewish Education Handbook*. Springfield, NJ: Behrman House Publishing, 1990.

Malcolm Knowles, Elwood F. Holton III, and Richard A. Swanson. *The Adult Learner: The Definitive Classic in Adult Education and Human Resource Development*. 6th ed. Amsterdam; Boston: Elsevier, 2005.

Jeffrey Schein and Judith Schiller. *Growing Together: Resources, Experiences, and Programs for Jewish Family Education*. Springfield, NJ: Behrman House Publishing, 2001.

Diane Tickton Schuster. *Jewish Lives, Jewish Learning: Adult Jewish Learning in Theory and Practice*. New York: UAHC Press, 2003.

Mel Silberman. *Active Learning: 101 Strategies to Teach Any Subject*. Boston: Allyn and Bacon, 1996.

Henry Simmons. "Religious Education." In *Aging, Spirituality, and Religion: A Handbook*, vol. 1, Melvin A. Kimble, Susan H. McFadden, James W. Ellor, and James J. Seeber, eds. Minneapolis: Augsbury Fortress Press, 1995, pp. 218–232.

Resources

Coalition for the Advancement of Jewish Education (CAJE), 520 Eighth Ave., 2nd Fl., North Tower, New York, NY 10018; (212) 268-4210, www.caje.org.

Lifetime Education and Renewal Network (LEARN), a constituent group of the American Society on Aging, 833 Market St., Ste. 511, San Francisco, CA 94103; (800) 537-9728, www.asaging.org.

PART III

FAMILY CAREGIVING

Help with the Hardest Mitzvah
Spiritually Supporting Family Caregivers

> R. Simeon b. Yohai said, *"The most difficult of all
> mitzvot is 'Honor your father and your mother.'"*[1]

"It's the hardest thing I've ever done." So say sons, daughters, husbands, and wives who have cared for elderly relatives through long, slow declines. They've confronted dear ones with painful realities ("Dad, it's really not safe for you to drive anymore"); made agonizing choices ("Mom will stay in her apartment with a caregiver; Josh will not go to summer camp because we can't afford both"); lost sleep (phone calls throughout the night, every night); and experienced unimaginable stress. They've felt guilty—for what they couldn't do for their frail loved one; for the ways in which their partners and children got shortchanged; for not being able to do it all.

The age wave is creating a parallel *caregiving* wave in the Jewish community. Jewish families are caring for elderly members who are living longer, and with more extended periods of greater dependency, than ever before. Three factors make the demands of the caregiving wave more pronounced in the Jewish community: the higher proportion of elders in our midst; the community's lower birthrate, and consequently ever-shrinking pool of caregivers; and the geographic mobility of the Jewish population.[2] The demands of family caregiving for the elderly will rise dramatically in the near term.

Jewish families are caring for elderly members who are living longer, and with more extended periods of greater dependency, than ever before.

Caring for aging loved ones is one of the greatest challenges facing our Jewish community. The complicated task of family caregiving, while demanding and often sorely trying, is largely invisible and unacknowledged. Caregiving can change your life, whether in the context of supporting a frail parent through a stay in a nursing home, struggling to keep a parent in his or her home, or caring for a spouse or parent in your own home.

The Myth of Abandonment

Many people believe that adult children today fail to care for their parents in the way that previous generations did. The perception that there has been widespread abandonment of the elderly by their families is simply not accurate.

> *Ira, a ninety-seven-year-old assisted-living resident, has just fallen. He is taken to the emergency room and receives twelve stitches for a gash in his head. The resident and attending physician have called his family, but no one has come to be with him. Knowing that Ira has a daughter-in-law, Ricki, who is usually quite involved, the assisted-living facility staff are surprised. They comment that perhaps Ricki isn't as interested in Pop as she once was.*
>
> *When Ricki comes in the next day, she explains that she couldn't come sooner because on the very same day on which Ira was injured, her brother died and her husband was rushed to the hospital with chest pain. Ricki literally didn't know what to do first: should she stay at the hospital with her husband during his cardiac catheterization; make funeral arrangements for her brother; or go to be with Pop, who must be very frightened and upset at being taken to the emergency room alone?*

Like Ricki, many family caregivers of frail elders are performing trying tasks with few supports. Many caregivers are pulled between multiple concurrent responsibilities for dependent elders, not to mention jobs and caring for young children. Often the caregivers' efforts are neither seen nor acknowledged, and their pain is faced alone.

This reality runs counter to the commonly held perception that today's elders have been abandoned by their children and that previous generations were more devoted and more constant in their care. As the gerontologist Elaine Brody eloquently argues, this "myth of abandonment" is rooted in our guilt at the limits of what we can give our aging parents.[3]

Many caregivers are pulled between multiple concurrent responsibilities for dependent elders, not to mention jobs and caring for young children.

The myth also stems from a failure to fully comprehend the unique challenges posed by today's caregiving task. Increased longevity and mobility and decreased birthrates mean that more and more elders are cared for over increasingly long periods of dependency by fewer and fewer caregivers. Despite the tremendously demanding nature of the caregiving task, family members provide the majority of all care for dependent elders, with adult daughters or daughters-in-law most often providing this care.

Challenges Facing Family Caregivers

Family caregivers contend with multiple, complex demands. Caregivers are not in the proverbial sandwich, says one of my friends; they are, rather, living in a *vise*. The emotional and familial consequences are often stress and distress. We will examine three key challenges faced by caregivers.

Guilt

No matter how much they are doing, family caregivers feel that they never do enough. As Elaine Brody points out, in part this is because we can never repay our parents in kind for the care they provided us when we were totally dependent children.[4] In addition, all caregivers have competing claims on their time and resources.

In a profound way, the caregiving task itself is impossible, as frail elders typically do not get better, but instead, become more frail and more dependent over time. In this way, there is actually no such thing as "success" in caregiving. One daughter who has cared for her frail parents for ten years told me, "It's not a task you can succeed at. No matter how creative I am, how much money I throw at it, how dedicated I am, they don't get better, they just get sicker and needier, and, sooner rather than later, they'll die."

Our secular culture values tasks that can be mastered and completed. The caregiving task does not have a neat or happy ending, as it comes to completion only with the death of the loved one. We don't know how to value the gift of presence, the richness and connection we contribute in the moment, in the midst of the inevitable movement toward frailty and mortality.

Conflict among Family Members

Caring for frail older members almost inevitably elicits conflict within families. The daughter who is dutifully caring for Mom is offended when her brother, who lives three thousand miles away, comes to visit and proceeds to tell her what she needs to do about Mom's care. A son who tells his mother he believes she should move from her home to an assisted-living facility receives an angry reply. A wife whose husband has become confused is furious with him when he forgets what she just told him; she blames him for not "holding it together." A daughter who has taken on the role of primary caregiver, managing every aspect of her father's daily care, resents her sister and brother, who visit occasionally and tell her she's "a hero" but don't offer to help. The stresses of caregiving bring long-dormant family conflicts to the fore and may provoke new rifts along those fault lines. Sadly, only rarely do these challenging situations bring previously distant family members together.

Hard Choices

Caring for a dependent elder often presents agonizing dilemmas. Often, the wish of the family caregiver to protect the elder conflicts with the elder's desire for autonomy. Family caregivers wishing to be respectful struggle in deciding how much to do for an older person, and how much to let him or her do, even if doing so might pose some financial, social, or physical risk. When—if ever—does a caregiver need to take over an impaired parent's finances? Should an elder suffering from dementia be allowed to continue to drive? When is it time for a frail elder to move into a nursing home or other long-term care facility? Most distressing is a decision of when it is *et lamut* (time to die). When does medical treatment cease helping to preserve life and instead act to prolong the dying process? Caregivers wrestle mightily with these hard choices and often feel they have nowhere to turn in their search for answers.

Caregivers experience economic, emotional, professional, and physical strain and may feel isolated from their community at precisely the moment they are in most need of support. Caregivers are often too proud, too guilty, too depressed, or too overwhelmed to ask for help from their rabbi, their synagogue, or their community.

What Can Spiritual Caregivers Do?

Spiritual caregivers have an important role to play with family members caring for aging relatives. In the face of the formidable tasks they shoulder, caregivers need spiritual support and succor.

Give Normative Support

Spiritual caregivers can help caregivers by offering normative support. Rather than perpetuating the myth of abandonment, spiritual caregivers can acknowledge family members' heroic efforts and painful challenges. From the *bimah* and at the bedside, the pastoral caregiver can note the efforts of family caregivers. The pastoral caregiver can also support the caregiver in accepting his or her limits in the face of seemingly infinite tasks.

A "Caregivers' Shabbat," in which individuals supporting ill family members are recognized, could not only raise awareness but also lift caregivers' spirits. Sermons that acknowledge caregivers' challenges, courage, and patience and that affirm how no one can "do it all" would be a welcome support. In Germantown Jewish

*R*ather than perpetuating the myth of abandonment, spiritual caregivers can acknowledge family members' heroic efforts and painful challenges. From the bimah and at the bedside, the pastoral caregiver can note the efforts of family caregivers.

Centre, the congregation to which I belong, it has become a treasured Rosh Hashanah custom to make a *mi-sheberakh* (prayer for healing) for family caregivers. As the husbands, wives, children, and grandchildren of the sick and frail stand to be blessed, their invisible burdens are seen, and those around them can note and reach out—on the spot or in months to come.

Offer Guidance

Spiritual caregivers can support family caregivers facing puzzling dilemmas. When asked, they can offer guidance based on the values embedded in Jewish tradition. See Figure 1 for a collection of Jewish values relevant to the dilemmas of caregiving.[5] This guidance must be offered thoughtfully, of course, responding to the needs and concerns of the family caregiver and without imposing a solution or course of action. One insight from tradition that may be particularly helpful is the recognition that obligations to parents have always been understood to be qualified by competing claims, such as obligations to spouses or to children.[6]

Provide Presence

We will learn a great deal if we ask how the caregiving is going (rather than having an awkward or sad conversation) and how we can be supportive.

Harold, a seventy-five-year-old retired housepainter, visited his mother, Becky, who was ninety-seven, nearly every day during the years she was in the nursing home. Although Becky was confused about time and place, she still recognized him. Both Harold and Becky enjoyed the times he pushed her wheelchair

---

Ten Core Jewish Values in Family Caregiving

1. Mitzvah (obligation) and *Lo aleicha* (limits)
2. *Kavod* (honor) and *Mora* (reverence)
3. *B'tzelem* (divine image) and *K'vod habriyot* (honoring beings)
4. *Shalom bayit* (harmony in the family)
5. *L'dor va-dor* (generation to generation)
6. *Pikuach nefesh* (saving life) and *Et lamut* (a time to die)
7. *Dayan ha-emet* (God's justice/acceptance)
8. *Refuah shelemah* (healing spirit and body)
9. *Hesed/rachamim* (love and compassion)
10. *Teshuvah/selichah* (repentance and forgiveness)

Figure 1

out to the garden, and he loved it when she would sing her end-less repertoire of Yiddish songs.

As Becky's Alzheimer's disease progressed, she gradually became less alert, until she could no longer recognize Harold, and then she stopped talking altogether. Harold's visits became more sporadic, and he often looked on the verge of tears as he sat silently holding his mother's hand. The chaplain made a point of catching Harold in the corridor one day when he was visiting at the home. She said, "You look so sad as you sit there with your mom." Harold's tears flowed, and he talked of his love for his mother, his grief at losing her by inches, watching her fade away before his eyes. Harold shared stories about his mother from his youth. The chaplain asked Harold if he would like to say a prayer. He said, "I just pray that Mom knows I love her."

Harold's pain and loneliness were apparent. He had actually lost the mother he'd known, but had had no chance to say goodbye or to grieve that loss. Joining with Harold, enabling him to give voice to his sadness, alleviated his loneliness. Praying allowed him to con-nect to his own spiritual resources. This connection can be enor-mously helpful for burdened, depleted caregivers. Whether those resources are faith, spiritual practices, or communal ties, research has shown that having access to resources can ease the stresses of caregiving and help in coping.[7] Often, caregivers need to be reminded that they are deserving of care, including attending to their own spiritual lives.

Connect Them to Spiritual Resources

*S*piritual caregivers can help caregivers draw upon tools that may or may not be familiar to them.

Judaism is rich in spiritual tools that can "heal the brokenhearted" and enable suffering people to be resilient in the face of the long-term, trying challenges of caregiving. Spiritual caregivers can help caregivers draw upon tools that may or may not be familiar to them. See Figure 2 for a list of ten traditional tools that can sustain family caregivers.[8]

Ten Jewish Tools for Responding to Caregivers' Spiritual Needs

1. Sacred Listening/Shema

   The proclamation of Jewish faith calls us to listen with reverence to the sacred stories of another person's life, and to listen especially for the presence of Oneness.

   • Ask the caregiver, "What is this like for you?" and listen with an open heart to whatever is offered.

   • Create a safe space in which the caregiver can express emotions without fear of being judged.

2. Life Review/Zichronot

   The caregiver may be encouraged to reflect on the life of the one receiving care and on their relationship, with special attention to the connections and blessings that emerge.

   • Ask the caregiver if there are issues to resolve or anything more that needs to be said.

   • Ask the caregiver what she or he can hold onto as this loved one declines. What is the legacy of the loved one's life?

Figure 2

3. Holidays/*Mikra'ei Kodesh*

While holidays can be stressors for caregivers, they also provide the extra motivation for people to come together and affirm their connections. In addition, holidays can offer special insights into the spiritual dimension of the caregiver's situation.

- Talk about an approaching holiday. What does it mean to the caregiver and family? Anticipate practical, emotional, and spiritual challenges.
- Explore the themes of the holiday in light of the family's current situation. How can they bring a spark of light into the darkness (Hanukkah)? What does freedom mean at this time (Passover)?

4. Shabbat/*Menuchah*

Shabbat offers a paradigm and an affirmation of the need for rest and renewal as well as the opportunity for an enhanced sense of divine presence.

- Explore what aspects of Shabbat observance can help create some sacred time and space for the caregiver.
- Help the caregiver accept the imperative of taking a "Shabbat," whatever day of the week it may be.

5. Ritual/Mitzvot

The performance of traditional rituals and mitzvot can connect individuals to each other, to Judaism, and to God. The creation of new rituals can give sacred form to the spiritual dimension of a caregiver's experience.

- Facilitate the performance of rituals that have always been important to the caregiver and/or loved one, and explore what they mean.
- Create new rituals for difficult passages in the journey of caregiving, such as clearing out a parent's home.

6. Prayer/*Tefillah*

Prayer brings the language of holiness and blessing to the caregiver's spiritual distress—whether through the use of traditional texts or through spontaneous, creative prayer.

- Recommend a regular prayer practice, such as bedtime Shema or morning blessings.
- Give voice to the caregiver's pain and yearnings by weaving them into a spontaneous prayer or encouraging the caregiver to create his or her own prayer.

Figure 2 (cont.)

7. Community/*Kehillah*

Community can assuage the loneliness of the caregiver and relieve some of the burdens. Feeling part of a community provides a larger context for the caregiver's struggles.

- Encourage and facilitate the caregiver's participation in the community (attending services, a meeting, or a support group, or helping another).
- Explore ways that the community can support the caregiver (meals, phone calls, rides, respite).

8. Study/Talmud Torah

Many traditional Jewish texts provide affirmation of the caregiver's challenges and yearnings.

- Share a psalm that expresses what you have heard from the caregiver—whether it is feelings of doubt and abandonment or the renewal of faith and gratitude.
- Consider how the weekly Torah portion might resonate with the caregiver's situation (e.g., betrayal by siblings, a journey through the wilderness, a sudden loss, an outburst of song).

9. Meditation/*Neshamah*

Meditation is an opportunity to slow down and listen to the breath of life, to receive each breath as a gift.

- Encourage the caregiver to cultivate some quiet moments of doing nothing other than paying attention to the breath.
- Suggest adding a special word or phrase to accompany the rhythm of breathing.

10. Music/*Niggun*

Music can help us access memories and feelings that words do not reach. Called the purest means of self-expression, music is also the most direct way of connecting to God.

- Encourage the caregiver to listen to melodies that stir the soul, bring back memories, release tears, or create a feeling of peace.
- Encourage sharing of music and song by the caregiver and family.

Figure 2 (cont.)

Forge Connections to Other Community Resources

It is vitally important that the pastoral caregiver be aware of resources in the community that can support family caregivers, such as counseling services, support groups, and respite services, as well as resources available to frail elders, such as adult daycare, in-home services, and long-term care facilities. Professionals who work with caregivers have noted that family members can be resistant to accepting help. Therefore referral in these situations may require extra support and encouragement. Spiritual caregivers in a congregational context may want to specially reach out to congregants who are intensively caring for frail relatives, and inquire about their needs and what can be done to enable the caregiver to continue to participate in the life of the community.

Final Words

Caring for elders in our families demands more resources than any caregiver can muster alone. Just as we have learned that it takes a village to raise a child, so, too, may we come to realize that it takes an entire community to care for frail elders *and* their caregivers.

For Further Investigation

Claire Berman. *Caring for Yourself While Caring for Your Aging Parents: How to Help, How to Survive.* New York: Henry Holt, 2001.

Vivian Greenberg. *Respecting Your Limits When Caring for Aging Parents.* San Francisco: Jossey-Bass, 1989.

Barry Jacobs. *The Emotional Survival Guide for Caregivers: Looking After Yourself and Your Family While Helping an Aging Parent.* New York: Guilford Press, 2006.

Nancy L. Mace and Peter V. Rabin. *The 36-Hour Day: A Family Guide to Caring for Persons with Alzheimer's Disease.* New York: Warner Books, 2001.

Virginia Morris and Robert Butler. *How to Care for Aging Parents.* New York: Workman Publishing Company, 1996.

Philip Roth. *Patrimony: A True Story.* New York: Vintage, 1996.

Resources

Nancy Kriseman. *The Caring Spirit Approach to Eldercare: A Training Guide for Professionals and Families.* Baltimore: Heath Professions Press, 2005.

Stephanie Dickstein. *With Sweetness from the Rock: A Jewish Spiritual Companion for Caregivers.* New York: National Center for Jewish Healing. (212) 399-2320, www.jewishhealing.org.

AARP: www.aarp.org/life/caregiving/.

Association of Jewish Family and Children's Agencies, 620 Cranbury Rd., Ste. 102, East Brunswick, NJ 08816. (800) 634-7346, www.ajfca.org.

Association of Jewish Aging Services. 316 Pennsylvania Ave. S. E., Ste. 402, Washington, DC 20003-1172. (202) 543-7500, www.ajas.org. Publishes *Journal on Jewish Aging.*

Medline on caregiving: www.nlm.nih.gov/medlineplus /caregivers.html.

National Family Caregiver Support Program: www.aoa. gov/prof/aoaprog/caregiver/caregiver.asp.

United Jewish Communities. *The Family Caregiver Access Network Demonstration Project: A Planning and Resource Guide.* (802) 785-5900, www.ujc.org.

Beyond Guilt

Perspectives from Tradition on Obligations to Aging Parents

We are pacing in the family waiting room. Each of us has our eyes on the door to the intensive care unit and an ear affixed to a cell phone. My siblings and I are trying to be in two places at once. We are in the hospital attending to my stepfather, who has just had a serious heart attack. And we are trying, by long-distance phone, to care for our young children, thousands of miles away. We are talking to toddlers, cheering overwhelmed spouses, canceling appointments, juggling work commitments, and feeling generally awful as we wrestle with our decisions about leaving.

My brother decides to go home after two days so that he can be with his son on the first day of kindergarten. I choose to forgo accompanying my two-year-old twins to their first day of daycare. My stepbrother decides to miss yet another day of income from his private practice so that he can be with the folks for Shabbat. We know that whenever we leave it will be too soon for my parents and one local sibling, who are grateful for every moment of presence, encouragement, and advocacy. And however long we stay is too long for our children, who are too young to understand, and for our partners, who are heroically doing the work of two parents.

According to a Yiddish saying, "With one *tuchis* you can't dance at two weddings." With our finite time, energy, and finances, we nonetheless try to find a way, if not to be in two places at once, at least to come close. When we can't do it, we feel guilty and disappointed in ourselves. My siblings and I are confronting the painful dilemmas of multiple and often competing obligations, and the choices we are forced to make are often confusing. Like so many others in our life situation, we desperately need wisdom. We want to know what we owe our aging parents, and how we are to navigate the treacherous terrain of finitude, ours and theirs, and seemingly irreconcilable competing demands.

Our Jewish tradition offers a perspective on relationships between adult children and their parents that can provide us with moral guidance. The tradition urges respectful, attentive care on the one hand and, on the other, recognizes and supports accepting the limits of what adult children can do. This chapter will examine texts that outline our basic obligations to our aging parents. We will also analyze the limits on our obligations and the relevance of these texts for our contemporary quandaries. To prepare for this discussion, we will first examine the demographic and emotional realities that give rise to these questions.

*O*ur Jewish tradition offers a perspective on relationships between adult children and their parents that can provide us with moral guidance.

The Dimensions of the Caregiving Demand

Though the details of each family's situation are unique, the experience of caring for elderly parents is increasingly demanding. The blessings of medical advances and increased longevity have created the challenge of prolonged periods of dependency among older people. Elders may be able to live for decades with considerable frailty and dependency. The decrease in the birthrate and rise in mobility in the Jewish community mean that there are fewer caregivers available to do the formidable task of caring for aging parents. Like me and my siblings, most caregivers feel guilty some, or all, of the time. Not only are caregivers' resources stretched over multiple demands, but also the nature of the caregiving task itself easily induces guilt, as an ancient Jewish folktale teaches:

A mother bird was carrying her three babies across a river. As she carried the first baby in her beak high above the river, she asked it, "When I am old, will you do the same for me?" "Of course, Mother," replied the baby, "It will be my honor." The mother bird dropped the baby into the river, saying simply, "You're a liar!"

As she carried the second baby, the mother again asked, "When I am old, will you do the same for me?" The second baby bird replied as the first, and the mother bird dropped it, too, into the river.

When she carried the third baby across the river, the mother bird asked it, "When I am old, will you carry me across the river as I am carrying you now?" The baby bird answered dolefully, "Oh no, Mother, when you are old, I will have children of my own, and I shall have to carry them across the river. I won't be able to carry you as well." The mother bird replied, "You are my darling child, for you have told the truth." She carried this baby to the other side of the river and gently put him down.[1]

As the tale illustrates, we can never repay our parents for the care they gave to us. Moreover, the nature of caring for a child is different than that of caring for a parent. While a child naturally grows toward greater competency and less dependency, our parents are likely to need *more* care over time. Caregiving for aging parents has no end point besides death. It is difficult to feel we are successful at caring for dependent parents because they usually do not "get better."

Caring for parents is emotionally complex, since it challenges the order of the relationship we've known. We are used to our parents being "in charge" and to their taking care of us. Turning the tables in these regards can be provocative at best. In relationships where there has been conflict, strain, or estrangement, the new situation might create an opening for healing, but it can also dredge up old wounds. Painful past experiences may limit the ways in which an adult child is able or willing to care for a parent.

Caregivers struggle to "do the right thing," to successfully traverse unfamiliar territory without a map. We look to our tradition to provide orienting values, and to replace guilt, which can be paralyzing, with guidance.

Fundamental Obligations of Adult Children toward Aging Parents

The Torah includes two basic commandments regarding children's obligations toward their parents. The first of these is the fifth commandment: "Honor your father and your mother, that your days may be long on the land that the Eternal, your God, is giving you" (Exod. 20:12). In the Holiness Code, the obligation is stated differently: "You shall each revere your mother and your father, and keep My sabbaths: I, the Eternal, am your God" (Lev. 19:3).[2]

It is interesting to note that in both instances, the obligations toward parents are linked directly to our relationship to God. This feature can be interpreted in various ways. Clearly, the connection to God underscores the importance of the mitzvah. Perhaps the texts draw an analogy between our obligations to parents and our obligations toward God. One further characteristic of these texts is worth noting. The fifth commandment is the only one among the Ten Commandments that promises a reward for obeying it. The presence of the promised reward might hint at the difficulty of observing this mitzvah. That the promised reward is long life suggests that caring for parents fits into a system of intertwined relationships. We care for our parents in the hope that we will be blessed to live to a ripe old age, and that we will be cared for by our children when we reach that point.

Although we are commanded by the Torah to love God and to love our neighbors, interestingly neither of these commandments requires that we *love* our parents. In fact, the Torah is silent about how we must feel about them. Perhaps acknowledging the complexity of parent-child relationships, the Torah commands us only to respectfully lend assistance to our parents.

Rabbinic interpretation assumes that even seemingly redundant passages are in the text to teach us something important. Thus the Rabbis suggest that these similar mitzvot teach us about two discrete and fundamental aspects of our obligations to our parents.

We care for our parents in the hope that we will be blessed to live to a ripe old age, and that we will be cared for by our children when we reach that point.

> Our Rabbis taught: What is reverence (*mora*) and what is honor (*kavod*)?
> Reverence means that he (the son) must neither stand nor sit in his [father's] place, nor contradict his words, nor tip the scale against him.
> Honor means that he must give him food and drink, clothe and cover him, and lead him in and out.[3]

Reverence, *mora*, is preserving our parents' dignity. This commandment relates to the attitude of respect that is due our parents. The text identifies and prohibits behaviors that might compromise the parent's dignity. Even if our roles have shifted and we are now caring for our parents, we are called to allow them to keep their place. We must not usurp their position of respect or authority. We must not take advantage of them. And we must not make decisions that fail to respect their wishes.

A daughter is acting with *mora* when she makes a medical decision for her mother who is no longer able to do so, and decides based on her mother's values, goals, and previously stated preferences. The son whose very frail father desperately wants to remain at home can also demonstrate *mora*. Here, *mora* may mean respecting his father's wishes, even if the son is worried that his father will be lonely, and helping his father to hire help so that he can safely remain home. *Mora* may involve respecting what disabilities advocates have called the "dignity of risk," which acknowledges that being allowed to make choices that involve risk to a person is part of the basic human condition. Painful though it can be to refrain from interfering in a decision that seems fraught with risk, adult children may do so for the sake of respecting a parent's desires.[4]

An adult child can show *mora* to a parent in a nursing home by making sure to include him or her in *simchahs* (joyous occasions), such as a grandchild's bar mitzvah, and even *tzures* (sad occasions), such as a funeral for a relative. Rejoicing and crying with their families means that frail elders are still part of life. These and other similar acts of respect grant reverence to parents who have lost much; they allow them to maintain their place.

*R*ejoicing and crying with their families means that frail elders are still part of life. These and other similar acts of respect grant reverence to parents who have lost much; they allow them to maintain their place.

In contrast to *mora*, which is attitudinal, *kavod*, honor, revolves around providing for our parents' material and concrete needs. This mitzvah obligates us to ensure that our parents have adequate shelter, food, clothing, and transportation. It is our responsibility to see that they are well cared for. There is a debate in the sources about the issue of financial responsibility. Some authorities hold that a child must pay for a parent's needs, while others argue that the child is obliged to make sure the needs are met but can use the parent's money to pay for this.[5]

Nearly every adult child caring for an aging parent has had the opportunity to provide him or her with *kavod*, in the sense of responding to concrete needs. Every time a daughter takes her mother to a medical appointment or shopping, she is offering *kavod*. Each act of advocating for the needs of a father who is in a nursing home is an opportunity to provide *kavod*. Every invitation for an aging parent to come to Shabbat dinner can also be an act of *kavod*, as can helping him or her write checks for monthly bills.

The Rabbis emphasize that the *manner* in which we carry out our obligations is as important as the *fact* of doing so.

> Abimi the son of R. Abahu taught: A son may feed his father pheasant, and [yet] be driven from the world [to come]; he may chain him to the millstone, and merit the world to come thereby.[6]

Rashi explains that grudgingly providing material abundance is not enough. Though he might appear to be giving his parent treatment fit for a king, the person who feeds his father pheasant is punished because "he displays a mean spirit as he feeds him." On the other hand, being unable to wrest a parent from scarcity is not a sin. The son who chains his father to the millstone makes his father work in order to help sustain the family. According to Rashi, he is rewarded because "he honors him by speaking good and comforting words, imposing the labor gently by showing him ... that they could not sustain themselves without his labor." Perhaps his dignity is preserved precisely *because* he is allowed to play an essential role in the household. Difficult though it may be, we are called to care for our parents with an attitude of deference, willingness, and compassion.

One additional mitzvah from the Torah guides our relationships with aging parents. This commandment concerns our relationships with all older people, not just our own parents: "You shall rise before the gray-haired person and grant glory (*vehadarta p'nai zaken*) to the face of the elderly" (Lev. 19:32). As we discussed in the introduction, our obligation toward our elders is not just to treat them with respect, but also to enable them to experience joy, meaning, and pride.

Competing Claims: Limits on Our Obligations to Aging Parents

Our tradition understands that adult children may confront the obligation to care for their parents at the same time that they are caring for partners and children, and also as they are working to support their families. Our Rabbis are also realistic about the limits imposed on a child's caregiving capacity by the parent's condition, as well as by problematic relationships. The obligation to aging parents is qualified by these factors.

Marriage and Children

As important as our obligations to our parents are, they are superseded by the preciousness of the marital bond. Honoring our parents and caring for them must not, according to the Rabbis, endanger marital harmony. A married woman, for example, is exempt from the obligation to care for her parents, since her obligation to her husband is given primacy.[7] The care given to a person's parents apparently must not undermine the well-being of that person's spousal relationship. For example, Maimonides rules that a husband may refuse to allow his wife's parents to visit in his home:

> A man who tells his wife, "I do not want your father and mother, brothers and sisters to come to my home" is to be obeyed. She should visit them in their home monthly and on every holiday, and they should come to her only in unusual circumstances, such as illness or birth, for a man is not to be forced to bring others into his domain.[8]

Rambam also extends this right to the wife vis-à-vis the husband's parents.

> Also if the wife says, "I do not want your mother and sister to come to my [home], and I will not live in a shared courtyard with them, because they are mean and cause me grief," she is to be obeyed, for a person is not to be forced to have others live in his domain.[9]

Interestingly, while the husband's right seems to be unqualified, in this case the wife must offer a justification or, according to some authorities, prove her assertion.[10] While the particular gender distinction here may repel us, the value of preserving the spousal bond is evident. Note that a person is still obligated to remain in contact with and care for his or her parents, but to do so in a way that will not compromise *shalom bayit*, domestic peace.

When we are torn between attending to the needs of parents and those of partners and children, this approach suggests we give priority to our partners and children. The needs faced by caregivers often seem limitless, but adult children are mortal, finite beings. Our tradition recognizes these limits. We are encouraged to work to strike a balance. Although our sources are filled with stories exalting exemplary, self-sacrificing care for parents, there is also a sense that we can only do the best we can.[11]

The Adult Child's Well-Being

Caring for a parent is demanding, and can be exhausting as well. But, according to our tradition, it should not be allowed to be destructive to a person's mental or physical health. Maimonides, for example, specifically suggests that there may come a time when an adult child is no longer able to directly provide the care a parent needs.

> If one's father or mother should become mentally disordered, he should try to treat them as their mental state demands, until they are pitied by God [they die]. But if he finds he cannot endure the situation because of their extreme madness, let him leave and go away, deputing others to care for them properly.[12]

It seems likely that Maimonides is referring to a parent who is suffering from dementia. In this situation, he teaches that an adult child may reach a point where he or she can no longer stand to be the hands-on caregiver of his or her parent. Significantly, the criterion for when that point is reached is the adult child's subjective experience. Only the adult child can say when he or she has reached the limit.

As before, the child's responsibility for the parent remains. What has changed is that he or she is empowered to arrange for others to provide that care. Although he does not clearly state it, it would seem that Maimonides would expect the child to continue to provide *mora*, respect for the parent's dignity, even while the obligation for *kavod* is being carried out indirectly.

Maimonides' teaching was relevant in the situation faced by a fifty-five-year-old woman named Shirley.

> *Shirley cared for her mother, Rose, for three years after she was diagnosed with Alzheimer's disease. At first Rose was only mildly forgetful, and Shirley helped her by calling to remind her of doctor's appointments or of activities in her assisted-living facility. Over time, however, Rose became more disoriented and began to call Shirley up to twenty times a day, asking over and over, "Where is Daddy? He's late home from work and he hasn't called," searching for her husband, Al, who had died seven years before. The only way she would calm down was if Shirley would come over and comfort her. Rose began to miss meals and could no longer remember to get dressed when she left her apartment.*
>
> *Shirley was becoming frazzled, and the manager of the assisted-living facility told her that Rose was no longer safe living there. Shirley, who worked full-time and lived in a one-bedroom apartment, felt she could not have her mother live with her. She ultimately decided to place Rose in the Jewish Home for the Aged. She visited every few days and spoke to her mother at least once a day until her mother died two years later.*

Maimonides teaches us that, like Shirley, we are allowed to respect limits of our endurance engendered by our parents' condition. We also learn from the Rabbis that we may need to withdraw from direct care in the case of abusive or highly conflicted relationships.

> It is best that a father and a son separate if they quarrel with each other, for much pain is caused; and I do not mean only the pain of the father or teacher, but even the pain of the son.[13]

In this instance, the medieval moral text *Sefer Hasidim* teaches that caring for a parent should be done at a distance if coming into contact produces arguments that are painful and destructive for the adult child. We can assume that the text is not addressing the kind of periodic disagreements or conflicts that are part of the fabric of normal relationships, but rather conflicts and behavior that are truly pathological. We are obligated to preserve our own wholeness, as Hillel so aptly taught: "If I am not for myself, who will be for me?"[14]

Although we tend to think of caregiving in terms of the child's obligations toward the parents, our tradition teaches that the parent has obligations, as well. The parent is forbidden to make things harder upon the child, or to be overly demanding.

> Although we are commanded (regarding honoring parents), a person is forbidden to add to the burden upon his child, and to be particular regarding his honor, lest he bring them to a stumbling block,[15] rather, he should be forgiving, and ignore [behavior which is not strictly in keeping with the mitzvah], for when a parent is forgiving regarding his or her honor, his or her honor is preserved (a parent has the right to forgo the honor due him). One who strikes an adult child is to be ostracized, for he has transgressed the commandment, "Do not place a stumbling block before the blind."[16]

Maimonides wisely counsels the parent who is the recipient of care to be forbearing. He realized that approaching your children with an attitude of generosity and forgiveness is more likely to yield the desired result of respectful treatment than critically judging their every action. A parent must not look for what a child has failed to do; the parent who acknowledges and appreciates the child's care will be the richer for it.

Although we tend to think of caregiving in terms of the child's obligations toward the parents, our tradition teaches that the parent has obligations, as well.

Our tradition recognizes that a person's obligations to provide care are brought into question in cases where there has been abuse or mistreatment by the parent. While some sources suggest that the child's obligation is in force even if a parent has wronged him or her, others suggest that the child is obligated only when the parent has repented, when there has been acknowledgment of the wrong, and restitution. The teaching of Joseph Caro, the author of the *Shulchan Arukh*, the Code of Jewish Law, seems to be contradicted by that of Moses Isserles, the author of the gloss on that text.

> Code: A bastard is obliged to honor and fear his father; even if his father is an evil-doer and a violator of the law, he must honor him and stand in awe of him.

> Gloss: And some say that one is not obliged to honor one's wicked father unless he repents.[17]

One way of harmonizing these views is to suggest that a child of an abusive parent is called to at least avoid doing anything active to hurt or dishonor a parent, but may not be obligated to provide direct care or take active measures to honor him or her. Thus a child who survived sexual abuse by her father could feel she had done the right thing by avoiding contact with him, while a son whose father was in recovery from alcoholism and asked for his forgiveness might feel called to attend to his care needs.

Final Words

Adult children of aging parents face a daunting task. Not only are the needs of aging parents extensive, but our responsibilities toward them are also enormous. Jewish tradition helps us to find our way between our obligations to our aging parents and the very real tensions between those and our responsibilities to our spouses, our children, and ourselves.

The texts and values we have explored affirm both our powerful obligations and our very real limits and humanity. Our caregiving can be guided by the teaching of Rabbi Tarfon: "It is not your obligation to complete the task, but neither are you free to desist from it."[18] Our tradition thus urges us to stretch mightily in bringing our physical presence and our spiritual and material resources to the work of caring for our aging parents, but to forgive ourselves for not being able to do it perfectly. This, ultimately, can help us move beyond guilt and into empowered responsibility.

For Further Investigation

Richard F. Address and Hara Person, eds. *That You May Live Long: Caring for Our Aging Parents, Caring for Ourselves.* New York: UAHC Press, 2003.
Gerald Blidstein. *Honor Thy Father and Mother.* New York: Ktav, 1975.

8

Balancing Parents' and Children's Quality of Life

Ethical Dilemmas in Family Caregiving

In the face of elders' increasingly complex and protracted caregiving needs, their children must discern what they are obligated to do and how to balance their obligations to parents with compelling competing responsibilities, including work, children, and partners. Whose quality of life takes precedence in this harrowing juggling act, the parent's or the adult child's? Seeking guidance, we look to precedent from our tradition. Our texts are filled with accounts of exemplary, self-sacrificing deeds of filial piety. For example, in a single passage in the Babylonian Talmud tractate Kiddushin, we find the following:

- Dama ben Netinah, a gentile, gave up a profitable business transaction rather than disturb his sleeping father to get to his merchandise.
- The same Dama ben Netinah allowed his aged mother to strike him on the head, rip off his golden cloak, and spit in his face. Having suffered all of this, he nonetheless did not rebuke her.
- Rabbi Tarfon allowed his mother to use him as a footstool, climbing on his back as he bent over, so that she could get into bed comfortably.[1]

These accounts clearly emphasize the parent's quality of life over the adult child's. Reading them, we might deduce that the adult child's quality of life counts not at all. These texts portray children sacrificing financially, physically, and emotionally, attending assiduously to their parents' quality of life and ignoring or surrendering their own. As we shall see in our investigation, both the realities today's caregivers face and the values of our tradition are far more complex.

As we explore the challenge of balancing quality of life in filial caregiving, it is useful to make some phenomenological observations. First, caregiving for aged parents as described in Jewish tradition is equally obligatory for men and women; interestingly, the examples we find in the text above are sons caring for parents. We can only guess whether these examples are cited because they represent the rare exception to the norm. Perhaps these cases of male caregiving attracted the male Rabbis' attention, while they were hardly conscious of women's routine caregiving for elders, so expected and so of a piece with their caring for children and spouses.

We do know that the reality in our contemporary North American culture is stark: caregiving at both ends of the life cycle is nearly universally a woman's role. Men typically become primary caregivers only when women are unavailable. The burden of parent care falls disproportionately upon women. This inequity sharpens the dilemmas we are examining. Further, the plight of caregivers is made even harsher by the nearly universal tendency for one child in the family to become the primary caregiver, even when others are present and potentially available to share. At this end of the life cycle, as at the other end, women render care in exquisite isolation.[2]

There are therefore important gender dimensions to these questions. Some feminist ethicists have suggested that an ethic of care replace or supplement an ethic of justice. In the ethic of care, moral reasoning emerges out of the context of the particular relationship at hand.[3] Practical experience, not abstract principles or external authority, provides the basis for correct choices.[4] Using an ethic of care, we would examine the dilemmas of caregiving in terms of the "activity of care,"[5] not just abstract notions of obligations.

We would also consider the situation in light of the interdependence and reciprocity of the parent-child pair.[6] A Jewish ethic of care would address the needs and well-being of caregivers and care receivers alike, both in individual families and in society at large. It might well lead us to attend as a community to the expectations and demands placed on "women in the middle" of work, child-rearing, and caring for parents, and might even prompt the allocation of communal resources to the support of these women.[7] A Jewish feminist ethic of care could be a fruitful resource for the caregiving wave.[8] While not yet fully articulated, we will use this approach's focus on relationships and mutuality below as we grapple with a specific case example of family caregiving dilemmas.

Now, to the issue at hand: how can our tradition guide us in navigating among the treacherous shoals of caregiving? In our exploration we seek values that emerge from halachah, from aggadah (Oral Torah in its broadest sense, including midrash, folk culture, and literature), and from the lived experience of the Jewish people. This broad approach to the sources is preferable to a narrow focus on halachic discourse, which runs the risk of becoming halachic formalism, which identifies precedents from rabbinic texts in order to extrapolate norms to yield authentic Jewish prescriptions on specific issues.[9] We are searching out values that an individual or community would need to weigh in evaluating choices in the situation.[10] Not surprisingly, our tradition is much more nuanced and rich than the aggadot cited earlier would suggest.[11]

Fundamental Aspects of Filial Piety

Clearly, filial piety is a weighty responsibility. As we saw in chapter 7, there are two fundamental dimensions to our obligations toward parents, *mora* and *kavod*, as outlined in Torah and rabbinic explication.

Reverence, *mora*, is preserving our parents' dignity. This commandment relates to the attitude of respect that is due our parents. The text identifies and prohibits behaviors that might compromise the parent's dignity. Even if our roles have shifted and we are now caring for our parents, we are called to allow them to retain their place. We must not usurp their role or authority. Moreover, we are not to make decisions that fail to respect their wishes.

In contrast to *mora*, which is attitudinal, *kavod*, honor, revolves around providing for our parents' material and concrete needs. This mitzvah obligates us to ensure that our parents have adequate shelter, food, clothing, and transportation. It is our responsibility to see that they receive exemplary care. In the face of these overwhelming obligations of *mora* and *kavod*, how are we to balance competing claims? How is the caregiver's quality of life to be factored into the equation?

Countervailing Values

Our sources suggest that in addition to the compelling need to provide for quality of life for an elderly parent, the quality of life of the caregiver is also worthy of attention. We can find examples of adult children making choices to fulfill their own dreams and aspirations as early as Abraham.

Midrash Rabbah tells us that Abram, as he was then known, left his father, Terah, to follow the divine call. The midrash takes pains to explain why Terah's death is reported in the verse before God calls to Abram, "And Terah died in Haran" (Gen. 11:32). This is puzzling, since according to the biblical text, his death occurred sixty-five years later. The midrash reports that Abram was reluctant to leave when called by God, as he feared people would criticize him, saying, "He abandoned his father in his old age." God reassures Abram, stating "I exempt you (*lecha*) from the duty of honoring parents, though I exempt no one else from this obligation. Moreover, I will record his death before your departure."[12]

Our sources suggest that in addition to the compelling need to provide for quality of life for an elderly parent, the quality of life of the caregiver is also worthy of attention.

This text is provocative. Reading it, we may wonder if this is a parallel to the *Akedah*, the binding of Isaac, in which God's demands of Abram supersede his obligations to his human family. If so, is it truly only a one-time exemption, or might a contemporary son or daughter have a calling that could be considered adequate justification for putting a parent's needs second? It is worth noting that the midrash's solution to the dilemma actually only removes the *appearance* of a choice to put calling before parent care, as Terah did not die until years after Abram's departure.[13]

As we have discussed in chapter 7, Maimonides suggests that an adult child might need to delegate caregiving tasks in certain circumstances. Significantly, the criterion for when that point is reached is the adult child's *subjective* experience. Only the adult child can say when he or she has reached the limit. Contrary to the first-blush impression we received on looking at the Talmudic texts cited earlier, caregivers are entitled, or perhaps even *must* attend to their own needs and limits. Traditional sources reflect a recognition that caregivers are often balancing multiple competing caregiving responsibilities.

We have seen that the values embedded in our tradition impel us to provide for our aging parents' physical care and to maintain their dignity while also attending to our own personal and familial well-being. We have also seen that parents are obligated to avoid placing their children in impossible binds.

Values embedded in our tradition impel us to provide for our aging parents' physical care and to maintain their dignity while also attending to our own personal and familial well-being.

The ethic of care described above urges us to conduct moral reasoning in the context of a particular set of relationships, and to take *interdependence* and *mutuality* into account. This approach brings the endeavor of ethics to our concrete realities in a way abstract discussion cannot. We can thus best explore how our tradition's values outlined above illuminate contemporary caregiving dilemmas through the analysis of one caregiver-parent crisis.[14]

Myra and her husband Sam raised their family in Queens, New York. When they retired in 1983, they moved to Florida where they bought a small condominium. They made new friends and reconnected with friends from earlier parts of their lives. Their daughter, Roberta, lives in Boston with her husband, Michael; their elder daughter, Sherry, died several years ago.

After Sam's stroke five years ago, he was able to walk with a walker, but he could no longer drive. Suddenly, life in the condominium was no longer feasible. Roberta offered to help Myra and Sam move closer to her home, but Myra and Sam chose to remain in Florida, where their friends were. Roberta helped Myra and Sam move into an independent living facility.

Roberta and Michael again offered to help Myra move north after Sam's death six months later, but she felt strongly that she wanted to stay in Florida. She made new friends and enjoyed the activities in her building. Roberta, Michael, and their two daughters visited two or three times a year.

Four years ago Roberta noticed that her mother was beginning to be forgetful; in the following year, a neurologist diagnosed Myra with Alzheimer's disease. Roberta, who had recently opened a psychotherapy practice after years of working part-time, began to travel to Florida every two months; on these trips, she took Myra to the doctor, arranged a companion a few hours a day, and watched her mother decline. Whenever they discussed the possibility of moving near Roberta, Myra refused. Although many of her friends had died or moved to other facilities, she felt at home in Florida and didn't want to move to a place where she would know no one.

Although the frequent trips were financially and emotionally draining, Roberta was committed to respecting her mother's wishes. She worried about her mother constantly and called her every morning and evening. Her mother's confusion was increasing. Finally, Roberta got a call from the manager in her mother's building. Myra had wandered away from the complex and, in her disorientation, could not find her way home. Roberta would have to move her mother to a nursing home or assisted-living facility.

Roberta is torn between her mother's stated wishes and her own well-being. Should Roberta move her now eighty-six-year-old mother to a facility in Boston or find one in Florida, as her mother wishes? We have seen that there are obligations on *both* sides of the elderly parent-adult child relationship. The parent has the right to make her own decisions, but not to "intensify the child's burden." In an effort to apply our values to this case, let us first examine each party's quality-of-life concerns. In her newly frail state, Myra needs *kavod*, care, more than ever. She cannot arrange for her care, or assure that it is competently or humanely provided. Beyond *kavod*, Myra needs to have her dignity preserved (*mora*). She needs to have her preferences and her values respected. Staying in her familiar surroundings reduces strain on her, especially as her confusion grows.

Roberta, on the other hand, needs to be able to care for her mother. She is obligated, and truly wishes, to attend to Myra's well-being. At a distance, she is not able to do this to her satisfaction. Even if she were to increase the frequency of her travel, she would not be content with the level of involvement and advocacy she could contribute toward her mother's care. She cannot follow up on medications, appointments, home care, and medical care from one thousand miles away. In addition to her need to care well for her mother, Roberta needs to fulfill her responsibilities to her husband and her clients. Finally, Roberta needs to stay well, physically and emotionally.

Myra's and Roberta's quality-of-life needs are in painful tension with each other. While Myra was cognitively intact, she could choose to "waive her honor," absolving Roberta of her obligations of *kavod*, or at least tempering her expectations of her daughter with understanding of the limits her choice to be far away imposed. It is doubtful that Roberta would *feel* absolved, but she would certainly not be accountable for the gap between the kind of care she would ideally like to provide and what would be possible from a distance.

Now Myra is confused and not capable of affirmatively waiving the honor due her, and Roberta is unable to retreat from her obligations. Sadly, due to her decision to stay in Florida, Myra has caused Roberta to stumble. Roberta is faced with either stumbling literally by pushing herself to exhaustion in her effort to care well for her long-distance mother or stumbling in her obligations of *mora* by contravening Myra's stated wishes and moving her close by.

Roberta is now bearing not only the burden of her own multiple obligations but also the burden of the choices her mother has made. I would suggest that this unreasonable burden tips the scales in the quality-of-life equation, and justifies Roberta's decision to move her mother to an assisted-living facility near her home in Boston. In taking this action to ensure that she can provide *kavod* for her mother, Roberta should endeavor to foster her mother's dignity throughout the process. She should, if possible, involve her mother in the choice of the facility and in furnishing her room, as well as in the process of discarding belongings and packing up her Florida apartment. Roberta might create a ritual of leave-taking so that her mother can bid farewell to the friends, surroundings, and memories in that home she has loved so much. Involving Myra in the transition, heeding her wishes within the confines of necessity, and honoring the pain she is feeling will allow Roberta to relate to Myra as a *subject* in her own life, and not an *object* of care. Doing this will enable Roberta to continue to fulfill her obligation of *mora*.

> Rav Assi had an aged mother. "I want jewels," she said, and he got her jewels. "I want a man," she said, and he said, "I will look for one for you." [When she said], "I want a man who is handsome like you," he left and went to Eretz Yisrael [from Babylon, where they lived].[15]

While Rav Assi was an exemplar of extreme filial piety, he, too, had limits. At a certain point he had to give precedence to his own quality of life and well-being and literally distance himself from his mother. Dedicated son that he was, we would imagine that he arranged for others to provide the care he was no longer able to render personally.[16] In the case of Roberta, another exemplary caregiver, giving precedence to her own quality of life requires bringing her mother closer to her, but the principle is the same in both cases.

Final Words

Nothing can take away the complexity, intensity, and weight of caring for those who brought us into the world. At the same time, there is nothing in our tradition that says that we must be consumed by caregiving, wrung dry, and left with nothing for ourselves and our own families. May we support caregivers in discerning both obligations and their limits, helping them to stay whole as they foster well-being in their dear ones.

For Further Investigation

Rabbis Daniel S. Brenner, Tsvi Blanchard, Brad Hirschfield, and Joseph J. Fins. *Embracing Life and Facing Death: A Jewish Guide to Palliative Care.* New York: CLAL, 2002.

Center for Jewish Ethics. *Behoref Ha-Yamim: A Values-Based Guide to Decision Making at the End of Life.* Wyncote, PA: Reconstructionist Rabbinical College Press, 2002.

Tanya Fusco Johnson. *Handbook on Ethical Issues in Aging.* Westport, CT: Greenwood Press, 1999.

Harry R. Moody. *Ethics in an Aging Society.* Baltimore, MD: Johns Hopkins University Press. 1996.

Resource

The Soul of Bioethics. Electronic newsletter published by International Longevity Center and Office of Academic Affairs, AARP, edited by Harry R. Moody (www.aarp.org/research/academic/aarp_office_of_academic_affairs_enewsletters. html).

PART IV

LIVUI RUCHANI

Spiritual Accompaniment in Aging

Enabling Their Faces to Shine
Spiritual Accompaniment with Aging Individuals

Issues of aging touch every Jewish pastoral caregiver in one way or another. Acute-care chaplains report that the majority of those whom they serve are elderly. Significant proportions of synagogue members are older, and issues of aging may well dominate congregational clergy members' pastoral counseling work. Even if the caregiver does not work directly with older persons, he or she may encounter aging issues in the struggles of family caregivers, including those who are simultaneously caring for aging parents and young children.[1]

This chapter offers guidance for the pastoral caregiver working with elders. In the discussion that follows, I begin by addressing the special spiritual challenges posed by the aging process. Next, I derive from the Mitzvah Model three core aspects of the pastoral caregiver's role with aging persons: fostering a life of meaning, facilitating a life of celebration, and enabling a life of connection. Finally, I identify some of the unique rewards of working as pastoral caregivers with aging persons.

Spiritual Challenges of Aging

Aging is a time of opportunity and also of great spiritual challenge. Despite the heterogeneous nature of the elderly, it is possible to outline three basic challenges that the aging person is likely to encounter on his or her journey from midlife to life's end: finding meaning; confronting empty, burdensome time; and counteracting disconnection and disjunction.

Finding Meaning

Anna is the only one left. She has outlived her husband, her siblings, her close friends, and even some of her nieces and nephews. Once a dynamic professional, she is now frail and is cared for in her home by a home health aide. She can no longer go to the meetings of the many boards on which she is a director, or work on political campaigns. Still, Anna remains vitally engaged in the events of the day, reads voraciously, and, when asked how she is, she replies, "For an old lady in a troubled world, I am doing okay."

The aging process challenges a person's sense of who she is, who she has been, and who she will yet be. The accumulation of losses, of the "little deaths" of the aging process, moves us to redefine ourselves. As people grow older, they are almost inevitably stripped of roles and capacities. What are our lives about if the people with whom we share a history are no longer alive? Who are we, outside of our roles as workers, as children to our parents, as partners to our spouses? Can we find new meaning, or are we to merely live with our losses? It is easy to lose a sense of self-worth amid so much change and loss.

Aging is a time of opportunity and also of great spiritual challenge.

The frailty that often accompanies the later phases of aging is particularly provocative, as it forces us to confront dependency.[2] How can we understand our place in the world when we are no longer creating or giving but rather needing the support of others? In a society that trivializes older people, it is a challenge for elders to find a way to continue to make a contribution, to reach beyond themselves, to share the wisdom accumulated over many years.

As people age, they are drawn to look back on their lives, to take stock of their accomplishments and failures.[3] This process of life review can be affirming if the picture we see is of a full, satisfying life. On the other hand, life review can also make us aware of our failings, of relationships that have broken down, of dreams unfulfilled. Like *cheshbon hanefesh*, the self-examination and appraisal that precedes the High Holy Days, this life review process can potentially spark repentance. Growing older can provide us with an opportunity to turn our lives around, to mend damaged relationships, to take on new life missions, and to make peace with our limits.

Growing older can provide us with an opportunity to turn our lives around, to mend damaged relationships, to take on new life missions, and to make peace with our limits.

For many older people, this promise is sadly unfulfilled because they are paralyzed by fear, grief, or resentment, wishing somehow that things could just be the way they used to be.

Shirley is an eighty-four-year-old widow. She has been a leader in Jewish communal organizations and is active in her country club. When her sight declines and she can no longer see well enough to play bridge, drive, or read materials distributed at meetings of the many nonprofit boards on which she sits, she becomes depressed. "This is no kind of life," she bitterly complains to anyone who will listen.

Structuring Time

When older people leave behind their well-established routines, time can weigh heavily. A man who has worked since the age of twenty-one may find he does not know how to fill his days once he retires. A woman who has invested her energy in caring for her children and her spouse may be daunted by the empty time ahead when her spouse has died and her children have established homes and families a great distance away. Cut off from her moorings, she may "kill time" through habitual television watching or compulsive shopping. Without external or long-established structures, old age can feel like a desert in time.[4]

In addition, older people may find themselves cut off from past and future. If dear ones who shared precious past memories are gone, the past itself may feel out of reach. If his or her present home or activities are not linked to previous roles or physical settings, an older person may feel bereft. Similarly, hopelessness may alienate the older person from the future. Even well elders know that they are temporarily able-bodied; the path ahead will likely include disability and will certainly lead eventually to death. Older people may be unable to look forward to the future if no one around them is willing to acknowledge this reality or explore the profound feelings with them.

Disconnection and Disjunction

Old age can bring on isolation or disconnection. Well elders who have moved or retired may be stripped of relationships that have sustained them. Losing friends, siblings, and partners to frailty or death is an inevitable part of growing older. Resilient individuals find ways to forge new relationships; many others find their web of social connection gradually thinned by these successive losses. This experience of isolation may be heightened by physical incapacity. For example, macular degeneration may not only deprive an older man of his ability to drive; it may also mean that he can no longer attend synagogue because he has no transportation. The age segregation in our society may also rob elders of opportunities to relate to younger people. This disconnection further contributes to elders' anomie.

Applying the Mitzvah Model to Spiritual Accompaniment with Elders

As we have discussed in chapter 2, Jewish tradition offers aging persons a unique perspective on their lives, one that addresses the spiritual challenges of meaning, time, and connection. This perspective, the Mitzvah Model, provides spiritual resources that can empower the Jewish person to meet the key challenges of aging. The Mitzvah Model does not eliminate the painful aspects of aging, but it can foster resiliency in response to them. The mitzvot enable an older person to participate in a life of meaning, a life of celebration, and a life of connection. The central role of the pastoral caregiver is thus to enable aging people to participate in these three aspects of a life of "significant being."

Fostering a Life of Meaning

The pastoral caregiver can make a tremendous difference in the lives of elders by facilitating opportunities for them to take part in a life of meaning. Fundamentally the caregiver's task is to create opportunities for older people to perform adaptive mitzvot, doing sacred acts *to the fullest extent of their capacities.* This approach is relevant to pastoral relationships with individual older adults and to work with communities and groups that include elders.

> *Estelle is a ninety-two-year-old woman who has been a treasured member of her synagogue for decades. She served the congregation as a religious school teacher, women's club member, and faithful volunteer haftarah reader. Everyone admires her beautiful singing voice. After a hip fracture, Estelle can no longer live independently. She continues to come to Shabbat services in her synagogue whenever she is offered a ride from her assisted-living facility. The entire congregation prizes the occasions on which she chants the haftarah, and she beams with pride as she hears their accolades at the Kiddush.*

Estelle is able to read haftarah for the congregation because she gets a ride to synagogue, and because she can stand with her walker at a reading table that requires climbing no steps. Estelle's gifts and religious leadership inspire congregants of all ages; they also enable her to find affirmation at a challenging time in her life.

ACCESS

In facilitating full participation in the life of mitzvot, the pastoral caregiver needs to address issues of access on many fronts. Making

Jewish life accessible can be costly in terms of money and human resources, thus it is essential that the pastoral caregiver be a leader in this effort. Transportation is critical, both for elders living in the community and for those in long-term care facilities who are not independently able to get to programs and services. If getting the person to the activity is not possible, it might be possible to "bring" it to him or her using the telephone, the Internet, a radio, or a television broadcast.[5]

The pastoral caregiver can make a tremendous difference in the lives of elders by facilitating opportunities for them to take part in a life of meaning.

The physical accessibility of the space in which activities are held is also vitally important. Not only must people in wheelchairs or walkers be able to get in the door, they need also to be able to sit in a space that is part of any group and, of course, to have accessible bathrooms as well.

The perceptual challenges of older persons require another aspect of access. Prayer books or printed materials need to be in large type and lightweight to be usable by those with impaired vision.[6] A microphone should be used in speaking with groups that include older people; it is also essential that the sound system have as little distortion as possible.[7]

In enabling full participation of older persons, timing is of the essence. Daytime events may be preferable for those who do not drive or go out at night. Many frail elders are strongest and most lucid in the earlier part of the day. If an evening event is planned, even more attention needs to be given to transportation. Program length is another aspect of accessibility because some older adults will find it difficult to participate in events that are very long.

HELPING AGING PERSONS TO CONTINUE TO LEARN AND TO GROW

Everyone is required to study Torah. Whether rich or poor, of sound body or suffering from infirmities, young or very old and weak.[8]

Aging can present wonderful opportunities to study Torah and to grow in knowledge. The wisdom gained from experience makes the encounter with sacred text a rich dialogue. The pastoral caregiver can help bring this wealth to aging persons by teaching in a way that begins with what is familiar and extends toward the unknown, as we discussed in chapter 5. This approach, called andragogy, is deeply respectful of the older person.[9] It does not require either that we focus on topics or texts directly connected to the aging experience or that we offer older adults study opportunities only in age-segregated settings. Rather, teaching andragogically is the best way to teach any adult.

For some elders, later-life learning is simply a natural extension of lifelong study. For most, this part of the life cycle may present a new chance to engage seriously in Talmud Torah, mining our tradition and history for meaning. The pastoral caregiver can nurture the thirst for knowledge and wisdom and provide sustenance both through direct teaching and through helping people to learn by themselves.

In addition to learning more about Judaism, old age can be a time to grow spiritually. The very old often lose much of their body fat, literally being reduced to a life closer to the bone, the *etzem*, the essence of life. There is a way in which life is taken down to its essence in old age. As roles and relationships fall away, as a person's equilibrium is challenged by the ever-present specter of death, grappling with existential questions becomes more urgent. The pastoral caregiver can help nurture spiritual growth, fostering connection to meditative and reflective spiritual practices, as well as engaging older people in dialogue about their spiritual lives.

"What are you thinking about?" This was the question the rabbinic intern asked Miriam, a ninety-two-year-old nursing home resident. "Oh, I am just remembering last night. It was one of

my thinking times. I often can't sleep, so I use those times to think back on my life, or to think about my family." The rabbinic intern was touched by this organic spiritual practice and told Miriam she would like to share it with other elders with whom she worked.

EMPOWER ELDERS TO MAKE A CONTRIBUTION

The Mitzvah Model suggests that aging individuals have much to contribute to their community and their world. Fostering a life of meaning empowers older people to make that contribution. Giving help to others helps transform difficulty and suffering. The Jungian psychoanalyst Polly Young-Eisendrath teaches that compassion is an antidote to suffering and counteracts alienation: "In learning the freedom and wisdom of suffering-with ... [sufferers] discover a new, bigger context in which their lives make sense."[10] Becoming aware of the suffering of others and reaching out to help them can actually salve the wounds of one who suffers. One natural forum for this contribution is sharing the wisdom of elders with young people through intergenerational ties.

*B*ecoming aware of the suffering of others and reaching out to help them can actually salve the wounds of one who suffers. One natural forum for this contribution is sharing the wisdom of elders with young people through intergenerational ties.

At seventy years of age, Frances, a retired executive secretary, was one of the youngest residents of the nursing home. Some of the others, in fact, were old enough to be her mother! But Frances had a progressive neurological disease that confined her to a wheelchair and had destroyed the use of her hands. Frances was the first person Adam met when he came to visit the nursing home with his synagogue youth group. Adam was fourteen and more than a little bit shy. He sat down at Shabbat dinner with Frances and worried that they would have nothing to talk about.

Before he knew it, Frances had drawn him out about his two great passions: baseball and guitar. The two discovered they were both Yankees fans, and Frances had played piano, so they had music in common as well. As they shared Shabbat dinner once a month, Frances asked Adam many questions about Jewish observance because she had come from a socialist family and had only become interested in the religious aspect of her tradition recently. Adam, who attended Jewish day school, patiently answered all of her questions. He felt proud that he could actually teach Frances something. Adam continued to visit Frances throughout his high school years, and even wrote her occasional cards when he went to college.

Frances and Adam's connection illustrates some key features of successful intergenerational connections. Older persons have much to give. Children who live far away from grandparents revel in the loving attention of caring elders. Elders' long view on life can help put the dilemmas of adolescence in perspective. Adam was not there to serve Frances; their sharing was mutual. Reciprocal relationships between elders and adolescents can build self-esteem for both sides.

Programs that bring children simply to perform for elders or for one-shot visits often fail to tap this precious resource. Children need to be well prepared for encountering older people, to learn how to communicate with people whose vision or hearing is impaired, or who are confused. They need an opportunity to express fears about the upcoming encounter and to be equipped with strategies for coping.

Reciprocal relationships between elders and adolescents can build self-esteem for both sides.

They also need opportunities to "debrief" their experiences, articulating strengths they found in themselves, sharing struggles, and remembering lessons learned from the elders. See chapter 13 for more guidance on facilitating intergenerational programs.

In addition to intergenerational relationships, older people can be helped to make a contribution through volunteering. Using skills gained from long years of work, family life, and community service, older people can help fill the vacuum in Jewish life left by two-career families and the over-busy schedules of today's families. Supporting older people to give of themselves requires assessing their particular gifts and interests and matching them with programs, organizations, and individuals who can benefit. Here, too, adapting opportunities in order to facilitate maximal opportunity is key. A homebound older woman might be just the person to edit a congregational bulletin. A frail older man might not be able to come to services, but he might indeed be able to call ill members of the congregation to offer support. Even residents of a long-term care facility can make a difference.

> *Rabbi Meryl Crean promised herself that she would only preach about current events if she was asking her congregants to get involved. In a conventional pulpit, this might not be surprising, bur at the life-care community where she serves as rabbi, the results have been especially powerful. On a recent High Holy Day, Rabbi Crean preached about the humanitarian crisis in Darfur. She asked her congregants to take part in a campaign to generate one thousand signatures in favor of action by the American government to ease the suffering of the oppressed minorities in Darfur. She handed out large-type petitions with the community's address filled in, so her congregants could become advocates by simply signing their name and apartment number. Some thirty or forty chose to take action in this way, including at least one individual who took petitions to get signatures from residents who were not present as well as from family members. The congregants were proud that they had done something to help suffering people thousands of miles away.*

With the help of the pastoral caregiver, older persons can find their own way to change the world. These efforts do not just offer the elderly a life of meaning; the elders genuinely help repair our broken world.

Maggie Kuhn, founder of the Gray Panthers, reflects in her memoir:

> What can we do, those of us who have survived to this advanced age? We can think and speak. We can remember. We can give advice and make judgments. We can dial the phone, write letters and read. We may not be able to butter our bread, but we can still change the world.[11]

When inviting elders to give of themselves, devise structures to facilitate their participation. Think of what *you* need to do to make it possible for them to give what they can.

Facilitating a Life of Celebration

The pastoral caregiver can facilitate a life of celebration for elders by enabling them to live "in Jewish time." As Abraham Joshua Heschel has eloquently pointed out, time is the sanctuary in which we meet God.[12] In contrast to the empty time that can stretch out endlessly before an aging person, in Jewish life, time is filled with moments of celebration. We live in cycles of significant moments: the cycles of the week, the month, and the year. We are always living in relationship to holy moments. Today is not just Wednesday, which looks just like Tuesday; it is the fifth of Iyar, Yom HaAtzma-ut (Israel's Independence Day), the twentieth day of the Omer, the period between Passover and Shavuot, and three days before Shabbat.

This moment, and every moment, has a "location" in time. There is always something to look forward to, always something to savor. Significant moments are actually stretched, through this anticipation and savoring, in what sociologist Fred Davis calls "the accordion effect."[13] Participating in Jewish time offers older people what Heschel calls "the marvel ... discovered in celebration."[14]

Jewish time also connects an older person to past and future. When Reba, an assisted-living resident who is eighty-one years old, is invited to bless the Shabbat candles, she remarks, "I remember my mother doing this." In this act, Reba experiences a thread of connection to her previous life, to beloved experiences and people.

The loneliness and frustration of her current life are, for a moment, softened.

The past is not lost, and change and discontinuity are muted through the emphasis on what the groundbreaking anthropologist Barbara Myerhoff called the "enduring elements of life that do not pass away"; time is experienced as "flowing duration."[15] Most importantly, the elder experiences *herself* as the same through time. Linked by these ritual moments, her life is as a continuum, a "single phenomenological reality."[16] In other words, participation in religious life provides a thread of continuity that connects the older person's life now to the whole of her past.

> *Max is quite depressed. He recently lost his wife, Sophie, and his visual impairment and advanced heart disease make him unable to live alone. He's come to the nursing home at age seventy-six. Often he confides in his rabbi, "I know I shouldn't say this, but to tell you the truth, every night I pray that God should take me." This night, however, Max has something different to say. He is just leaving the synagogue of the nursing home at the end of the Shabbat. As he greets his rabbi, Max says, "We should live and be well and do the same thing next year."*

Max is still bereaved and frail after the Shabbat service, but participating in that moment of holiness and community has made him hope for a future of more such moments. Jewish time connects older people to the future in another way. Aging individuals living in Jewish time know that these cycles of holy moments went on long before them and will continue long after them. This awareness offers a foothold in a future they will not personally witness. Something precious to them will endure beyond their lives; their values, customs, beliefs, and community of faith will be around even when they are not. This point is particularly powerful when ritual is shared intergenerationally.

> *The nursing home congregation has just observed Tishah B'Av. Helen comments as she leaves the service, "That was great!"*

What was great? We have sung songs of lament, read from the Book of Lamentations, and recounted moments of loss and destruction in our Jewish past! What was great for Helen was that the community's worship touched the brokenness and sadness in her own life. As she sat and cried in the service, Helen's feelings were acknowledged, validated, and even sanctified.

The life of celebration available through Jewish time contains more than moments of lightness and joy. The holy days that punctuate the Jewish year reflect the entire spectrum of human emotion. From the outrageous levity of Purim to the solemnity of Yom Kippur, the pure joy of Sukkot to the abject sorrow of Tishah B'Av, every feeling a human being experiences finds reflection in Jewish religious life. This spectrum of emotional opportunity is a powerful resource for older people. Living in Jewish time, elders can touch and affirm, frame and share in sacred community their own joy and sorrow, grief and rejoicing.

The pastoral caregiver's role is to link elders with this life of celebration. First, we are called to make sure that older persons in our care have opportunities to participate in the holy moments of Shabbat and the holidays. For example, consider Shabbat. What are the ways in which individuals with different levels of capacity can participate in Oneg Shabbat (Shabbat joy)? For older people living in their own homes, transportation to services might be what is needed; for those living in the community who are too frail to attend services, a volunteer might deliver challah or the congregation might arrange a telephone connection so that they can listen to services. Rabbis, cantors, or teams of volunteers could hold services for elders in nursing homes and other long-term care facilities. For many older adults, living the life of celebration requires such enabling action on the part of the pastoral caregiver.[17]

The life of celebration need not be limited to rituals and ceremonies that are familiar from an older person's past experience. For instance, Rosh Chodesh can be a beautiful occasion on which to mark time for older people, either on their own or with younger people. Stopping to note and to hallow the beginning of each month can add a dimension of holiness to life. Offering prayers for the coming month for that person, his or her family, the community, and the world connects that person to hope and to his or her power as a source of blessing. (See Figure 3.)

A Rosh Chodesh Ceremony

- Introduction to the Hebrew month ahead: holidays or significant dates in history.
- Words of gratitude: participants individually say, "I am grateful for … " and then sing a setting of *Halleluyah* (Psalm 150).
- *D'var Torah*: brief teaching related to the month ahead.
- Hopes for the month ahead: the group together recites this prayer: May it be Your will, our God and God of our mothers and fathers, that we be renewed in the month of ___. May it be a month of [participants add a word about what they are hoping and praying for in the coming month] … and a month of … and a month of…. and let us say, *v'nomar*: Amen.
- Kiddush for Rosh Chodesh and refreshments (fruit, cake, or cookies that are round or crescent-shaped).

Figure 3

Lastly, the pastoral caregiver can facilitate a life of celebration by helping elders mark the transitions of later life with ritual. We know the power of ritual to aid in transitions early in life. Wedding ceremonies contain the tremendous anxieties and fears about entering marriage and give expression to the elation felt by the bride, groom, family, and community. Funerals and all of the traditional mourning rites help to hold us together in times of loss.

The many transitions of aging also call for such acknowledgment and celebration. Retirement is an enormously challenging passage from past engagement and accomplishment toward an often-uncharted future territory; leaving a home of long standing can be a loss of great significance; becoming a grandparent may represent a precious new beginning; giving up driving can signal an end to independence; entering a nursing home or care facility may be frightening and sad. All of these moments, joyous and sad, can and should be marked ritually.[18] The pastoral caregiver can both respond to requests for such rituals and actively encourage their creation.

Enabling a Life of Connection

The third pillar of the pastoral caregiver's work with aging persons is to facilitate a life of connection. The connection we enable is multidimensional. We have already explored a kind of vertical connection, the link through time to past and future. Another vital aspect of connection is the horizontal link, the connection to community. As mentioned earlier, building intergenerational ties is one way of linking elders to community. Making it possible for elders to participate in the religious life of a congregation is another.

Caring relationships, such as those created through *bikur cholim*, are still another way of touching older people and of ensuring that they are not cut off or left behind. This last dimension of connection cannot be characterized by a physical direction, for it is the connection to God, to the soul. The way in which we forge this connection is through accompanying aging persons on their journeys.

Accompanying Aging People on Their Journeys: *Livui Ruchani*

Rabbi Margaret Holub, who has served as a rabbi with homeless people on skid row as well as in the congregational context, suggests that the essence of the rabbinic task is accompaniment.[19] More than fixing or changing people, our job, she says, is to walk along with people through the sorrows, joys, and everyday moments of their lives. This description is apt for pastoral care in aging. The pastoral caregiver is a witness, companion, and tangible manifestation of God's caring. Here, *livui ruchani*, spiritual accompaniment, is often the most powerful thing we can offer.[20]

To accompany older adults on their journeys through change, loss, frailty, and limits, we may have to notice and seize opportunities to reach out to them. They will probably not ask for our care and support because they are not aware of their needs, they are embarrassed to call attention to themselves, or they hesitate to burden us. We need to be present to them, sometimes grasping opportunities for pastoral intervention at unlikely moments, whether it is in conversation at the synagogue Oneg Shabbat or while making rounds at tables in the nursing home dining room. I call this approach "guerilla counseling." We make ourselves available in settings and situations that are normative and not stigmatized. We listen deeply and faithfully to a person's expressions of need, pain, or joy, and we carefully decide how and when to respond. With information gleaned in a casual encounter, we might decide to follow up in greater depth in a more private setting. Our response always begins with making ourselves available.

The pastoral caregiver is a witness, companion, and tangible manifestation of God's caring.

Two qualities essential in *livui ruchani* with older adults are humility and respect. Working with people who have seen the world for seven or eight decades, or even a century, we have to assume that they know better than we do about what they need and what is right for them. We should also assume that we have much to learn from elders with whom we work.

> Humility and respect are key to accompanying elders. Never infantilize or patronize.

Furthermore, we must approach elders with awe and respect, careful in every interaction to accord them the dignity mandated by our tradition: "Rise before the gray-haired, and grant glory to the face of the elder" (Lev. 19:32). We need to watch our tone of voice, choice of salutation, and physical situation, for example, lest we inadvertently embody the fear expressed in the Talmudic folk saying, "Now that we're old, we're treated like infants."[21] We need always to take them and their struggles seriously. We can serve as faithful companions on older persons' journeys only to the extent that we do so with love and honor.

Telling Their Stories: Life Review

When we are present and available, one important role we can perform is to support elders as they engage in life review. Through telling their stories, older people have an opportunity to savor successes and pleasures and to acknowledge their strengths. Viktor Frankl, twentieth-century founder of logotherapy, points to memory as a powerful source of meaning. Older people can draw upon "the full granaries of the past into which they have brought the harvest of their lives: the deeds done, the loves loved and lost, but not least, the sufferings they've gone through with courage and dignity."

Although elders may not have further opportunities for creating meaning in their future, they can draw upon the assets of their past accomplishments, "the potentialities they have actualized, the meanings they have fulfilled, the values they have realized—and nothing and nobody can ever remove these assets from the past."[22]

Our pastoral task is to listen attentively and to reflect the triumphs, losses, and conflicts that are of primary concern for the person at this stage of his or her journey. Life review also enables older people to work through unfinished business. Long-ago hurts compounded by years of resentment may come into stark relief in looking back on our lives. Coming on these experiences anew can impel an elder to work toward forgiveness, toward letting go of anger and healing old wounds.

Harry is ninety-one years old. Over the past few years he has become completely blind. He has a loving daughter and grandchildren and has made a positive adjustment to living in the nursing home despite his difficulties in getting around. In a conversation with the chaplain, Harry says, "I know why I became blind. God struck me blind because I didn't go to my sister's funeral."

After exploring Harry's feelings of guilt and remorse, the chaplain suggests that Harry ask for forgiveness from his sister.

*She encourages him to write a letter to his late sister, sharing
his shame and regret and requesting forgiveness. She invites
Harry to perform an act of* tzedakah *as part of his* teshuvah
*(repentance), and he makes a gift to a local charity. Lastly, the
chaplain and Harry pray together, "Forgive us, God, for we
have sinned; have mercy upon us, for we have transgressed."*

Rabbi Zalman Schachter-Shalomi, the father of the Jewish
Renewal movement, was moved to investigate aging as he retired
for the first time. He created an approach called Spiritual
Eldering. His methodology for consciously preparing for and welcoming old age includes some very useful techniques to support
older people's work of forgiveness and spiritual healing.[23]
Conveying the message that *teshuvah* and transformation are possible until the very moment of death, the pastoral caregiver can
foster courage and hope.

In the course of telling their stories, older people may also
identify losses for which they have never truly grieved, providing an
opening for pastoral care intervention.

*Hannah lost a two-week-old baby forty years ago. With the
birth of her first grandchild, a daughter, she finds herself
recalling long-forgotten details of that experience, which was
never mentioned in her family. Hannah is very emotional,
crying frequently and constantly anxious about the health
and safety of her granddaughter. Hannah speaks to her rabbi
about this. He suggests that she visit the cemetery where her
infant daughter is buried. Hannah reports that she went to
the cemetery with her son (which she had never done before),
and together they said* Kaddish *for the child whom they never
got to know.*

The pastoral caregiver accompanies older people reliving unfinished grief. Through presence, compassionate listening and rituals,
he or she can aid the individual in marking and containing the
feelings of loss.

Sharing the Spiritual Search

"God forgot about me." "God is with me every moment." Older people often search for God with greater intensity than younger people. They may profoundly feel God's presence amid their joys and suffering. On the other hand, in coping with frailty, loss, and mortality, a person's faith can be shaken fundamentally.

Accompanying aging people involves sharing their search for God. The pastoral caregiver will find that many elders welcome the opportunity to talk about faith, religious experience, doubt, and evil. These questions are not filed away in some remote recess of the mind, but are right at the surface, gnawing, challenging, and urging the older person toward exploration and growth. Sharing the questions is, of course, far more important than attempting to provide answers, although sometimes careful attention to the person's experiences and relationship to God will foster clarity or comfort.

Praying with elders can be a concrete way of sharing the spiritual search. Using traditional psalms and blessings may be sustaining. In addition, empowering the older person to articulate and to utter his or her own prayer or blessing, including his or her very personal hopes, fears, doubts, and dreams, may touch the person profoundly. Sometimes we as pastoral caregivers have to get over our own shyness, embarrassment, or fear of rejection in order to allow the elders whom we serve the gift of prayer.

The chaplain had a warm and moving visit with Elizabeth, an eighty-eight-year-old retired teacher coping with end-stage congestive heart failure. Elizabeth faced ever more frequent hospitalizations, and "good days" were more and more infrequent. Elizabeth said, "I know I don't have long to live." The chaplain asked Elizabeth if they could pray together. When she agreed, the chaplain asked, "What are you hoping for, Elizabeth?" Elizabeth answered, "I'm only hoping I can live to see my granddaughter's wedding in the fall." The chaplain offered this prayer: "Mi-sheberakh imoteinu Sarah, Rivka, Leah, v'Rachel, hu yivarekh et Aliza bat Soreh ... May the One who blessed our mothers, Sarah, Rebecca, Rachel, and Leah, be with Elizabeth as she faces this final stage of her journey. Give her courage, help her to find comfort, and sustain her to celebrate with her family." Elizabeth's eyes filled with tears, and she and the chaplain both said, "Amen."

Looking to Death and Beyond

For all aging persons, death looms large. However long this third stage of the life cycle may be, what will inevitably follow it is death. Death is an omnipresent specter. Perhaps its next appearance will be for the older person herself or himself, or perhaps for a dear friend or family member.

Edith, an eighty-year-old woman, is sharp and always has a humorous word to say. She stops the cantor visiting the assisted-living facility and says, "Where do you think we go when we die? What happens to us? Do we just rot, or do we go some-place? My husband, he's been gone twenty years. Not a letter, not a phone call! Whatever that place is, nobody's come back to tell us about it!"

The pastoral caregiver can accompany the older person as she or he prepares for the journey away from this life. Although Edith's remarks were humorous on the surface, in reality she was deeply curious and troubled by her lack of knowledge about what lay ahead for her. She welcomed an opportunity to talk about her beliefs, and also to hear about Jewish teachings about the afterlife.[24]

Most of us do not take a major trip without rather careful preparation. We pack the things we'll need, we put in order the home we are leaving behind, and we may read and learn about the place we're going. There is no greater journey than the one to the unknown after this life. It behooves us as pastoral caregivers to support older people with whom we work in preparing for death. It may be that, like Edith, a person will wish to speculate on life after death. However, someone else may be moved to put his or her affairs in order, attending to passing on material goods in an orderly fashion. That same individual may also choose to create a spiritual legacy by writing an ethical will, a document spelling out the values she wishes to pass on to loved ones who will survive her, and her hopes and dreams for them.[25]

Bioethical Dilemmas

Elders may need practical help to prepare for dying. In this context, pastoral caregivers can be particularly helpful. We can assist older adults to execute advance directives, living wills, and healthcare proxies to ensure that their wishes regarding their medical treatment will be carried out should they be unable to express them at the time. We can encourage them to speak openly and frankly with their families about their feelings and preferences. As part of this process, we can help people clarify their own values and goals. We can also teach about the Jewish tradition's perspectives on care at the end of life, balancing reverence for the sanctity of life with a realistic acceptance that there is "a time to die."[26]

In the painful dilemmas that can emerge in end-of-life medical care, the pastoral caregiver is a resource for older people and their families. With every more powerful and sophisticated medical technology, it is possible to extend life far beyond what many elders could have imagined or wished. Medical technology has outstripped our capacity to discern its appropriateness.

Moreover, many deaths have become "deaths by decision." Aside from withdrawing life-sustaining treatment, many other issues of forgoing treatments may present themselves to patients or family members. For example, the family might have to decide whether to use antibiotics for pneumonia for a woman who is ninety-nine years old and has recently been rendered unconscious by a stroke; whether to consent to the amputation of a foot for a diabetic man who is eighty-five years old and in the end stages of congestive heart failure; or whether to agree to insert a feeding tube for a woman who is seventy-nine years old and in the final stages of Alzheimer's disease and hasn't spoken for years.

The pastoral caregiver can be a resource in analyzing the choices facing a patient or family. He or she can help them look at the bigger picture, including the individuals' most fundamental values and goals, hopes and fears. The pastoral caregiver may assist decision makers to weigh the potential benefits and burdens of a proposed treatment. The pastoral caregiver can provide a forum for patients and family members to hear one another out, which is often difficult in the heat of emotional disputes. He or she can share teachings from Jewish tradition that illuminate and clarify the choices at hand. And he or she can accompany those who must ultimately make choices in the face of uncertainty, offering them support and compassion.

Final Words

Those who do not work with the elderly often believe that their pastoral care is a dreary, draining affair. On the contrary, serving older adults is work that can be truly transformative. If we endeavor to link elders we accompany to celebration, meaning, and connection, we may just see their faces shine, the beautiful light within them ignited. And we will no doubt be warmed and inspired by the light they shed.

For Further Investigation

Richard F. Address and Hara E. Person, eds. *That You May Live Long: Caring for Our Aging Parents, Caring for Ourselves.* New York: UAHC Press, 2003.

Richard F. Address and Andrew L. Rosenkrantz. *To Honor and Respect: A Program and Resource Guide for Congregations on Sacred Aging.* New York: URJ Press, 2005.

Susan Berrin, ed. *A Heart of Wisdom: Making the Jewish Journey from Midlife through the Elder Years.* Woodstock, VT: Jewish Lights Publishing, 1997.

Lynn M. Huber. "Aging as Pilgrimage: Spiritual Potentials of Late Life." In *Aging, Spirituality, and Religion: A Handbook*, vol. II, Melvin A. Kimble and Susan H. McFadden, eds. Minneapolis: Augsbury Fortress Press, 2003, pp. 7–22.

Journal of Religious Gerontology. The Haworth Press, 10 Alice St., Binghamton, NY 13904-1580; e-mail: getinfo@haworthpressinc.com, www.haworthpressinc.com.

Melvin Kimble et al., eds. *Aging, Spirituality, and Religion: A Handbook.* Minneapolis: Augsbury Fortress Press, vol. I, 1995; vol. II, 2001.

Lois Knutson, *Understanding the Senior Adult: A Tool for Holistic Ministry.* Washington, DC: Alban Institute, 2000.

Harold G. Koenig and Andrew J. Weaver. *Counseling Troubled Older Adults: A Handbook for Pastors and Religious Caregivers.* Nashville: Abingdon Press, 1997.

Amy L. Sales and Shira Kandel. *Synagogue Hope: Help, Opportunities and Programs for Jewish Elders.* Waltham, MA: Brandeis University, 1998.

Zalman Schachter-Shalomi and Ronald S. Miller. *From Age-ing to Sage-ing.* New York: Warner Books, 1995.

Henry C. Simmons. "Spirituality and Community in the Last Stage of Life." In *Dignity and Old Age.* Robert Disch, Rose Dobrof, and Harry R. Moody, eds. Binghamton, NY: Haworth Press, 1998.

Resources

Forum on Religion, Spirituality, and Aging, American Society on Aging, 83 Market St., Ste. 516, San Francisco, CA 94103-1824. (415) 974-9600, www.asaging.org. Holds annual conference and publishes *Aging and Spirituality*, a quarterly newsletter.

Hiddur: The Center for Aging and Judaism of the Reconstructionist Rabbinical College, 1299 Church Rd., Wyncote, PA 19095. (215) 576-0800, www.hiddur.org. Works to transform aging through professional education, scholarship, and innovative spiritual resources.

Religion, Aging, and Spirituality: An Online Annotated Bibliography: http://tech.union-psce.edu/aging/.

Sacred Aging Project, Department of Family Concerns, Union for Reform Judaism, 633 Third Ave., New York, NY 10017. (212) 650-4294, e-mail: jfc@urj.org, http://urj.org/jfc.

PaRDeS

Compassionate Spiritual Presence with Elders

Those of us who work with older adults know that often the most precious gift we can offer is our presence. But truly being present, reaching to enter and understand another's reality, can be a daunting task, especially when the other's world is vastly different from ours. One tool I've found helpful is PaRDeS, a model from Jewish tradition that can help us conceptualize our helping encounters with older adults. The word *pardes* in Hebrew means "orchard" or "paradise." The model is based on founder of Clinical Pastoral Education Anton Boison's insight that pastoral interactions are encounters with "the human document." The pastoral theologian Charles Gerkin suggests that:

> To understand the inner world of another is ... a task of interpretation—interpretation of a world of experience that is in itself an interpretation of the myriad events and relationships that make up a life. Said another way, the task of understanding another in the depth of that other's inner world is a hermeneutical task.[1]

In other words, we can bring what we know about reading texts to the task of understanding the living person we are encountering. As Rabbi Rachel Mikva has noted, the Jewish idiom for the human document is the *human text*.[2] If our effort to fathom the depths of another's soul is a kind of textual encounter, then what we know about interpreting sacred texts may provide us with tools for understanding the *human text*. PaRDeS is one particular set of

Jewish hermeneutics that can teach us about unlocking the mysteries in our connections with aging persons.

PaRDeS is a four-tiered system of textual analysis articulated by Moses deLeon, a thirteenth-century rabbi and the author of the Zohar, the greatest work of Jewish mysticism. DeLeon, like many rabbis and Christian exegetes who came before him, realized that the biblical text is infinitely rich in meaning, and that not all of that meaning is apparent on the surface. He suggested that texts can be read on four distinct levels.

If our effort to fathom the depths of another's soul is a kind of textual encounter, then what we know about interpreting sacred texts may provide us with tools for understanding the human text.

In deLeon's system, *peshat* is literal interpretation, *remez* is searching out allegorical meanings and philosophical truths, *derash* is hermeneutical, homiletical, or ethical interpretation, and *sod* is the mystical understanding that ties words and events of the text to events in the world of the *sefirot* (emanations) of the divine presence. Together, the four levels constitute the PaRDeS. We know from Rabbinic sources that the PaRDeS can be both an exalted and forbidding place to visit. We'll return to this important note later in this chapter.

PaRDeS Applied to Our Encounters with Older Persons

This system of multiple levels of interpretation and understanding can be applied to our helping encounters with elders. Just as a text bears multiple meanings, so, too, there are many levels on which we experience and connect to the older person we serve. By examining our work in light of this interpretive scheme, we have an opportunity to meet those with whom we work in the PaRDeS and maybe, just maybe, to have a glimpse of the Divine.

Peshat: Fact

The first level of listening in the PaRDeS model is *peshat*, the level of *fact*. When we are encountering another on the *peshat* level, we're relating on the surface. We inquire about the basics, the "who, what, where, when." We spend most of our lives on the level of *peshat*. We ask our children at the end of the day, "What did you do in school today?" or our partners, "What were you up to? Did you pick up the dry cleaning, pay the bills, feed the cats?"

When we are encountering another on the peshat *level, we're relating on the surface.*

In our helping encounters with elders, we often start at *peshat*, and sometimes end there too. My chaplaincy students often bring verbatim reports packed with factual inquiries. They can sit down with a nursing home resident, inquire about the person's background, and spend an hour learning facts about jobs, family, synagogue, and home. When all is said and done, they say, "I don't feel I really heard what was on the person's mind."

> *Marsha tells her rabbi that her husband has been diagnosed with advanced prostate cancer and may be dying. The rabbi asks many questions: "Where is Bill now? Is he in the hospital? When did all of this begin? Have you gotten a second opinion? When will the treatment begin?" Marsha quickly ends the conversation, saying, "I have so many things to take care of, I'd really better be going." As Marsha gets up to leave, the rabbi adds, "I'll be thinking of you. Please keep me posted."*
>
> *While she is no doubt genuinely pressed for time, perhaps Marsha has found this conversation with her rabbi unsatisfying because the rabbi did not connect beneath the surface of her crisis to touch her* neshamah, *her soul.*

Of course, the *peshat* can help us to get at essential information. It may well be relevant to know that this eighty-eight-year-old woman before us worked as a teacher, was born in Europe, or had a stroke a year ago. But often, when we are encountering another on the level of *peshat*, we are not quite meeting them. We have a sense that we are not truly connecting. Staying only on the level of *peshat* can distance us from the elder and his or her needs and agenda. I would suggest that we remember that *peshat* can actually emerge not just from directly focusing on it but also in the course of interacting on the deeper levels of PaRDeS.

Remez: Emotion

The second level of PaRDeS is *remez*. In the human text of our helping encounters, *remez* is the level of emotion. We are connecting on the level of *remez* when we are listening and responding to *feelings*. We can learn about *remez* not only through verbal exploration but also through careful attention to what pastoral counselor Charles Taylor calls body messages.[3] We discern emotion in the person we're helping by carefully observing facial expression, posture, focus, movements, and physical reactions (breathing, blushing, crying, sighing). Taylor points out that nonverbal data help us understand a person because they "are usually more spontaneous and less contrived than verbal responses."

> *We are connecting on the level of remez when we are listening and responding to feelings.*

We can powerfully connect by reflecting feelings that are apparent from nonverbal communication alone, as when we sit down next to the elderly woman in the nursing home who is exuding sadness from every pore of her being and say simply, "You're looking really down today." Naturally, nonverbal cues are especially helpful when we're confronted with a person whose verbal communication is compromised.

> Ruth, a woman in her seventies, had been through a devastating stroke and could utter only a few stereotyped phrases. Often I would find Ruth using her good hand to hit the table in front of her and saying, "the bastards, the bastards, the bastards!" I

didn't know, and often couldn't learn the *peshat*, for Ruth was unable to give me the *facts*. But I could reflect and acknowledge her emotions.

When I got beyond my own sense of inadequacy and frustration, I might say something as obvious as, "Ruth, I wish I could know all the words you are thinking but can't say. But I do sense that you are feeling really angry!" On those occasions, sometimes, Ruth's whole presence would change—her body would relax and she would grasp my hand and look me straight in the eye. It was paltry communication on the verbal level, but in those moments, it felt like Ruth and I had truly met.

We are often able to connect to *remez*, the level of emotion, through what Taylor labels the "spoken messages" in the pastoral encounter. We ask: what are the emotions the person is expressing explicitly or implicitly? Taylor submits a list of six basic groups of feelings, formed by three pairs of opposites:

- Guilt-Acceptance
- Anxiety-Hope
- Anger-Love

It can be useful to acknowledge the emotions of the elder with "feeling words" in reflective listening. When Sarah, agitatedly wringing her hands, says, "I don't know what to do with myself now that my husband is gone," a spiritual caregiver might respond, "Sarah, it seems like you are feeling confused, is that right?" or perhaps, "Maybe you are feeling a little afraid as you face a new life without Michael." Sarah might just well then allow herself to cry and say, "It's just so hard."

Often the access to *remez* information is intuitive. It's not that the older person before us articulates his or her feelings and labels them for us, but rather that we engage in *gut listening*. We open our hearts and souls to listen to emotions that emerge within us in hearing the other. It may be that the emotion evoked in us is the very one the other is feeling, or maybe *not*. We need to check out what

we're feeling, even if only to distinguish between our countertrans-
ference and the experience of the person we're serving. Clearly, in
order to hear the person on the level of feelings, we have to be
ready to experience our own feelings.

To elicit the *remez*, it can be helpful to try out a hypothesis.
Instead of asking, "how does that make you feel," which is not only
trite but off-putting, we inquire, "it seems like you may be feeling …"
We offer such a reflection with humility and respect, and we invite
the other to confirm or correct our impression. In risking reflecting
an emotion, we signal to others that we are listening hard and want
to *know* them on the level of *remez*.

Silence can be a helpful tool in connection to emotions.
Somehow, when we sit in stillness with the other, manifesting
through our calm attention that we are truly present and available,
elders often sense and share their feelings.

It can be particularly challenging to connect on the level of
remez with elders, since many of them are unaccustomed to speaking about feelings, and they may even be conditioned to believe that
it is inappropriate or a sign of weakness to do so. We need to
respect an elder's boundaries, but also give permission and open the
door to emotional sharing if that
would be welcome.

Remez is a very real connection,
and not always easy. Quite early on in
my work, I encountered a woman
whose mother suffered from severe
dementia. The mother couldn't speak
or respond in any tangible way, and
she was experiencing one devastating
medical crisis after another. The
daughter, whom I'll call Sheila, visited
her mother for hours every day. She
had never married, had lived with her
mother before her admission to the
home, and did not work. I earnestly stopped by on some kind of
regular basis, especially when Sheila was faced with a decision

> *Somehow, when we
> sit in stillness with
> the other, manifesting
> through our calm
> attention that we are
> truly present and
> available, elders often
> sense and share their
> feelings.*

regarding amputating her mother's leg. I never quite knew what to say to this apparently hostile and forbidding woman who had alienated nearly all of the staff. I was especially stymied when she turned to me one day and practically spat out, "You know, there's nothing very spiritual about this, Rabbi!" I don't even want to recall what kind of response I made as I tried to regain my composure, but I am sure that I didn't think to simply acknowledge her anger, fear, and pain. (I probably thought it was my job to defend God or Judaism, or both!) I misunderstood Sheila, as I was intimidated by her raw feelings, and failed to see that her fury was the very place she needed to be touched.

When we get there, *remez* offers a deeper and richer entry into the world of the human text than *peshat*.

Derash: Meaning

The third level of PaRDeS is *derash*, the level of meaning. The word *derash* comes from a Hebrew root that means to dig or to seek out. Just as midrash (rabbinic exegesis) endeavors to dig out the meanings buried in a text, here *derash* means listening to the elder's narrative. As we analyze the material a person shares with us, Charles Gerkin suggests that we ask, "What does it *mean*?" [4] He urges us to place the person's narrative in the larger theological/ethical context, a context of ultimate meaning, as we listen for "the story of the self" to which we are relating. To connect to *derash*, we need to investigate what meaning elders are making of their experiences. This requires us to be especially open and curious, for each elder's *derash* is completely individual and idiosyncratic.

I will never forget a visit I had with a ninety-five-year-old rabbi whom I had watched steadily decline over several years. One morning when I visited this lovely man, I found him hooked up to both oxygen and a feeding tube. I said, "Rabbi, I wonder what you're thinking about as you lie there this morning." I felt rather sure that I knew the answer he'd give, something along the lines of ad matai *(how long, God?) or, why doesn't God just take me? What he actually said was, "I'm thinking how wonder-*

ful it is to be alive!" I could not have been more stunned, and humbled as well; I could never have imagined the meaning the rabbi was making of a life that looked from the outside to be filled with burdensome suffering. I nearly missed the opportunity to acknowledge it and learn from it.

It is on the level of *derash* that we can both understand the meaning the person is making of her experience and, perhaps, support her in finding additional meaning. The late Viktor Frankl powerfully taught us about the salvific potential of meaning to transform suffering. Frankl defined despair as "suffering without meaning," and suggested that "even a life which has been wasted, meaningless, can be flooded with infinite meaning by admission of the lack of meaning."[5]

Sol was a ninety-year-old nursing home resident who had recently had his second leg amputated. Sol had a deep spiritual and intellectual life, and even in the nursing home had taken on great challenges, such as studying the weekly Torah portion on his own. Sol had been forced to come to the home after the amputation of his first leg. He struggled during the years he was there with mind-altering phantom pain and had gone to great lengths to avoid a second amputation, including spending nine months in bed in order to allow his leg to heal.

As I visited with Sol, it was easy to get at the peshat. *Sol was anxious to tell me the details of his surgery and hospitalization. It was not too difficult to get to the* remez. *Though incredibly proud and generally reserved, Sol was voluble in sharing his sadness and resignation. But it seemed to me that the crux of Sol's experience was on the* derash *level. Clearly the amputation was a trauma, but I wondered what else—would he see it as a loss, a defeat, or yet another hurdle to be overcome?*

The most important part of our dialogue occurred in exploring the meaning he found in the amputation. "I'm not fooling myself," he said. "I know I don't have much longer. I'm just trying to get through each day. It's been pretty rough; I'm ready for whatever God has in store for me. I'm not afraid."

Sol saw his story as coming to its conclusion, and the amputation was the signal to begin wrapping up. He was not stopping living or loving or learning, but now he was also getting ready for the moment when *Malach haMavet* (the Angel of Death) would come. He needed to be met at that place in his journey.

Derash can be an especially rewarding level on which to connect to elders, since they are uniquely available for questions of meaning. It seemed to me in my years as a nursing home chaplain that existential quests and questions were the bread and butter of life. Scratch the surface, ask any one of the people in the home what they are thinking about, and you are likely to learn that they are pondering questions like: "What has my life meant, after all?" or "Why has God forgotten about me?" or "What will become of me after I die?" Those whose days are filled with these profound preoccupations cry out to be met *ba'asher hem sham*, in the place where they are.[6]

Sod: Soul

The fourth and final level of PaRDeS is *sod*, which is the mysterious point of connection to *soul*. When we are present on the most profound plane, we feel linked to the other's soul. Martin Buber described the listening person as "one who grasps the buried latent unity of the suffering soul."[7]

When we are present on the most profound plane, we feel linked to the other's soul.

It is difficult to articulate what it is in our responses that makes possible a *sod*-level connection. We cannot catalog particular words or interventions that will necessarily get us there, for, in a very real way, a *sod* connection is a loving gift from the Eternal. Perhaps what we can say of this connection is that you will know *sod* when you *feel* it. Nonetheless we can prod ourselves to investigate whether our connection has approached this level by asking:

- Do I *get* this person on an intuitive level?
- Do I honor the mystery of this soul and his/her journey?
- Do I see the image of the Divine in this person?
- Is this an I-Thou encounter?

Joe, an eighty-nine-year-old engineer, was a lifelong member of Temple Shalom. He was treasured for his knowledge of the synagogue's building and his ability to figure out its quirks. Since his recent stroke, he no longer attends services as he did every week. He is cared for at home by his wife, Betty. Joe's rabbi has known him for fifteen years. The rabbi visits Joe for the first time since the stroke. Joe can't talk much, and at first he is agitated, trying to speak but only able to utter a kind of angry growl. The rabbi sits and holds Joe's hand, saying, "We don't have to talk. We can just be together." Joe's body relaxes and he grows quiet. The rabbi sees a tear on Joe's cheek and says, "I think I understand. You are oysgemitchet, *worn out." Joe emphatically nods and the rabbi makes a prayer for peace and comfort for Joe.*

Elders may uniquely welcome and facilitate a *sod* connection, for the aging process, in all of its blessings and challenges, opens doors onto spiritual awareness and connection that may have previously been closed.

Another way of understanding *sod* is as God's presence. When we are listening for God's "still, small voice" (1 Kings 19:22) we are open to *sod*. That voice may come in the electrical charge of a profound soul connection or in our intuitive sense that we are being guided in the interaction by the Merciful One. While we can't will *sod*, we can practice spiritual reflection and strengthen our facilities of discernment and openness to the divine.

Perils of the PaRDeS

Opening ourselves to relating to elders we serve on the deeper levels, entering the PaRDeS, is a perilous mission. As pastoral theoretician

J. L. Cedarleaf reminds us, "Ministry of presence ... means vulnerability to and participation in the lifeworld of those served."[8]
Classical rabbinic sages understood the dangers of the encounter
with the Ultimate. We recall the account of the four who entered
the PaRDeS. They didn't fare so well, on the whole:

> Ben 'Azzai cast a look and died. [Of him Scripture says:
> Precious in the sight of the Eternal is the death of God's saints.]
> Ben Zoma looked and [became demented]. [Of him Scripture
> says: Have you found honey? Eat as much as is sufficient for
> you, lest you be filled with it, and vomit it.] Aher [Elisha ben
> Abuyah] mutilated the shoots. R. Akiba departed unhurt.[9]

Rashi explains that entry into the PaRDeS was really a visit to the
heavens, a sojourn in the immediate presence of the Divine. Most of
us, he warns, are not prepared to meet the Ultimate. So, it behooves
us to examine some hazards along the way of entering the pastoral
PaRDeS.

Assuming or Jumping to Conclusions

In the Talmud's account of the four who entered the PaRDeS,
Rabbi Akiba warned his colleagues before they set out, "When you
arrive at the stones of pure marble, say not, water, water!"[10]
Perhaps he meant: Watch out that you don't jump to conclusions
about what you're seeing before you really have evidence. Akiba's
warning applies to the pastoral PaRDeS as well. It is so easy for us
to assume we know what we're dealing with when we approach an
elder.

> *The chaplaincy intern was working with a woman with severe
> dementia. The woman was obviously unhappy and kept repeat-
> ing, "You can't give me what I need." The intern earnestly
> attempted to help her. "Do you need a glass of water?" "Can I
> get you a blanket?" Still, the woman repeated, "You can't give
> me what I need." The intern assumed that the woman, whose
> sense of reality was so tenuous, was simply in another world,*

when the woman said, "You can't give me what I need, because what I need is love." The intern knew that the resident's husband, who visited much of every day, was away from her side for an hour, and understood that this woman, broken in mind as she was, knew exactly what she needed and made a world of sense!

An additional example of assuming and jumping to conclusions comes from the Talmudic account of Rabbi Yochanan's bedside visit to Rabbi Elazar, who is ill (Babylonian Talmud, Berachot 5a).[11]

Rabbi Yochanan enters the room and finds Rabbi Elazar sitting in the dark. Thinking this is the problem, he quickly uses his unique abilities to provide a *tachlis* (practical) solution; he rolls up his sleeve and light radiates from his arm to illumine the room. Then he notices that this hasn't been terribly efficacious, for Rabbi Elazar is crying. "Why are you crying?" he asks, in good pastoral form, and then goes on to answer his own question: "Is it because of Torah that you didn't succeed in learning? Don't worry, in the eyes of God it's not important how much you learned, but that your learning was *l'shem shamayim* (for the sake of Heaven). Or perhaps you are crying because of your meager means? Not everybody is rich! Or perhaps you're crying because you don't have children? Here's the bone of my tenth son!" (You think you have problems!) Finally, Rabbi Elazar interrupts his esteemed colleague: "[It's not because of any of these things that I'm crying], but because of this beauty of yours which will rot in the earth." In other words, "I'm crying because we're all going to die!" Now, Rabbi Yochanan responds, "This is certainly worth crying about!" and the two of them cry together. Then Rabbi Yochanan is able to offer healing to Rabbi Elazar and restore him to wholeness.

This is a marvelous and powerful story because even the great Rabbi Yochanan falls into the many traps of assuming, jumping to conclusions, and failing to really listen on the levels of *remez, derash,* and *sod.* But when he is able to experience his own vulnerability, he is able to truly see and hear Rabbi Elazar, and only then, to help and heal him.

Suffering and Pain Become Overwhelming

Assuming is a hazard that keeps us from offering our most useful presence to elders. The other risks of the PaRDeS are more about our own well-being. Just as entering the PaRDeS drove Ben Zoma mad and Elisha ben Abuya to despair, so, too, the pastoral PaRDeS can take its toll. Encountering intense suffering and pain can easily become overwhelming. In every group of chaplaincy interns I've supervised there are always a couple who come in at some point early in the year with rings under their eyes. They tell me that they can't stop thinking about the people they work with. They dream of them, worry about them, psychically take them home with them. Of course, pastoral caregivers must constantly work on creating boundaries, and most of us get better at it, but at times of high load or special personal stress, it can get hard to cope. Sometimes the sheer horror of situations we face challenges our own faith. In the face of tragedy and trauma, we can feel like we have no affirming vision to lean on. It is a frightening and devastating thing to confront horror on the deepest levels, and it shakes us.

Intensity of Real Connection Is Overwhelming

The final risk of the pastoral PaRDeS is not far from the PaRDeS entered by the Rabbis. Rashi understood the power and danger of the "four who entered," that they entered into the divine presence.

When we experience real connection in a pastoral encounter, the intensity of the experience can also be overwhelming. It is akin to seeing God's face, and we're not always prepared for it.

When we experience real connection in a pastoral encounter, the intensity of the experience can also be overwhelming. It is akin to seeing God's face, and we're not always prepared for it. On the one hand, there is a sense that, as my colleague Rabbi Margaret Holub has said, "nothing is more real than this."[12]

There is a kind of sensation of electrical charge that can be exhilarating. On the other hand, this can also make it hard to return to the mundane. How do we buy groceries, help with homework, or watch mindless TV when our souls are still caught up with the most powerful spiritual encounters with elders? We don't always know how to come back to earth, and the transition can be jarring, both for us and for those close to us.

Survival/Thriving Skills: What Do We Need to Enter the *Pardes* and Emerge Whole?

Given these risks, we need to think about what will help us not only to survive the PaRDeS but also, like Rabbi Akiba, to be able to emerge whole at the end of the day or an entire career.

Self-Awareness

Since being present on the deeper levels of PaRDeS connects to our guts and our *neshamas*, we need to develop and constantly deepen our self-awareness. We can be present to the spectrum of emotions in the other only to the degree that we have access to our own. We need to hear our "counterstory" and at the same time be able to get it out of the way to really make room for the other.

Emotional Support

The second thing we need to enter the PaRDeS is emotional support. We all need a place to feel and discharge the pain of the other, as well as our own pain and brokenness. This place could be clinical supervision, therapy, spiritual direction, or a close friend or partner. It doesn't matter what it is, as long as it is fairly constant and totally safe.

Spiritual Nurture

Finally, and perhaps most importantly, in order to toil in the pastoral PaRDeS, we need spiritual nurture. We who are engaged in facilitating religious life for others need to be sure that we have a religious life that is engaged, growing, and nourishing. We need spiritual practice that comforts us, study that challenges us. We need opportunities to find affirmation, and means of expressing our despair. And we need, in whatever way works for us, to be in ongoing conversation with God.

Final Words

By mobilizing our skills and sensitivity, by caring for ourselves and attending to our own well-being, we can meet elders we serve on the deepest level of their being. We can truly be present with them *ba-asher hem sham*, in the place where they are. And we can, *b'ezrat haShem* (with God's help), make that place, barren though it might be, a PaRDeS, a place of meeting the Divine.

For Further Investigation

Charles V. Gerkin. *The Living Human Document: Re-Visioning Pastoral Counseling in a Hermeneutical Mode.* Nashville: Abingdon Press, 1984.

Rachel Mikva. "Text and the Human Document: Toward a Model for Rabbinical Counseling." *Journal of Reform Judaism*, Summer 1990, pp. 23–33.

Charles W. Taylor. *The Skilled Pastor: Counseling as the Practice of Theology.* Minneapolis: Fortress Press, 1991.

Spiritual Challenges and Possibilities for Jews in Long-Term Care Facilities

Elders living in a long-term care setting are sojourners on a painful journey through loss, change, and disjunction.[1] The spiritual challenges they face are shaped by the dual factors of frailty and institutionalization. Older people enter long-term care institutions as a result of failing physical and/or cognitive health. Residents typically suffer from multiple, chronic illnesses that together make them unable to independently perform the tasks of daily living. More than 45 percent of nursing home residents have a dementing disorder, such as Alzheimer's disease.[2] These health problems result in the loss of independence and capacity, which prompts the decision to seek placement in the long-term care institution.

Admission to an institution entails giving up your home and personal environment and living amid the routines and structures set up by a large organization. Alienation and anomie are frequent parts of life in a total institution, as sociologist Erving Goffman eloquently pointed out.[3] We have explored spiritual challenges faced by elders in chapters 2 and 9. Here we investigate the particular realities of life in a long-term care institution, including empty and burdensome time, meaninglessness, and disconnection. We then offer practical guidelines for bringing religious life into the long-term care setting, as well as models for Jewish communities that seek to specifically address the needs of elders in non-Jewish institutions.

Time

In chapter 9 we discussed some general aspects of the way time can be challenging for elders. In the long-term care setting, time can feel especially burdensome.

The Tyranny of Routinized Time

Institutionalized older adults live in an environment characterized by rigid time routines. For the staff of the long-term care facility, time is organized into distinct blocks, composed of shifts, work-days, and weeks with workdays and weekends. Days are structured by tasks that must be done "to" the residents, such as meals, med-ications, bed-making, bathing, and toileting. For staff trying to accomplish these demanding tasks in a limited time frame, it seems there is never enough time. Staff "tied to the clock" may approach care tasks in a regimented way.[4]

Like the staff, residents' lives are organized by the institutional routines. Their time is structured by staff schedules and sometimes staff whim, not by their own needs, desires, or rhythms. When they rise, eat, go to the bathroom, and go to sleep may have little to do with their own personal rhythm or previous habits. Part of the day may be marked off by meals, as a nursing home resident remarked in Jabier Gubrium's sociological study of a nursing home called Murray Manor: "You go from one meal to the next. That's about it."[5]

Other markers in the day are television programs and recre-ational programs. Unfortunately, the latter often come without warning or anticipation; suddenly, someone swoops down and takes the elder to bingo, a concert, or some other activity. The elder, however, has not had an opportunity to prepare for this moment, so time seems irrelevant. As another resident in Gubrium's study remarked, "Time doesn't matter here because I don't go out any place unless here for bingo and they always take me up there."[6]

The Burden of Empty Time

In her memoir, playwright Florida Scott-Maxwell called old age "a desert of time."[7] Paradoxically, despite the degree to which it is structured, to the resident time seems empty and burdensome. As sociologist Kathy Calkins has observed, time in the long-term care institution can seem much like a treadmill—it moves but nothing happens.[8] The routines of institutional life create a kind of sameness in which days run together; there is little to distinguish Monday from Tuesday or Saturday. One of Gubrium's subjects said, "You eat, you sleep and sit around."[9]

Much of the institutionalized older person's time is spent *waiting*. Given that residents are dependent on staff to meet many needs, and given that they have little sense of tasks that are theirs to perform, they *wait*—for medications, meals, toileting, bedtime, and the recreational activities that break up the routine. "We wait all the time," said one resident of Murray Manor.[10]

Time seems limitless when a person is waiting. The resident who waited ten minutes for assistance to return to her room after an activity reports, "I waited forever." A woman with dementia paces anxiously and approaches staff members asking, "What am I supposed to do now?" Upon being told that she can take a nap, watch television, or wait for dinner, she exclaims in utter exasperation, "This day is *never* going to end!" Time clearly weighs heavily without meaningful markers and momentum toward them. As anthropologist Renee Rose Shield notes, time is thus "unfillable and fraught with peril."[11]

Now Is All There Is

In a curious way, the present is the only time there is for the resident of the nursing home. The past is absent. There is no one around who shares his or her personal history, and there is nothing that evokes it. The resident may cry out to staff in despair, "You don't know who I am," for the staff truly does not know about Mrs. Jones's special reputation as the best cook in the neighborhood, or Mr. Green's status as the pharmacist on whom everyone could rely for help in a pinch. Staff members relate to the impaired older person before them, and the older person experiences a loss of his or her past.

The future for the nursing home resident is, in a way, crystal clear. Nearly all who enter a nursing home know that this will be

The present is the only time there is for the resident of the nursing home.

their last home. So the future awaiting the residents is of incapacity and death. Everyone knows the future, yet there is no recognition of it; deaths, when they occur, are often handled in silence and secrecy. Seldom are other residents informed or given an opportunity to respond to deaths in the environment. Thus, in addition to the qualities of routinization and emptiness, time has a disconnected sense about it, as if the present moment were somehow suspended in time.[12]

The Loss of Meaning

Elders in long-term care institutions internalize powerfully negative messages from society and suffer from low self-esteem. An older person who is no longer working can feel useless and rejected, for he or she is perceived as a "functionless person, an onus on the majority."[13] These negative feelings are intensified for the nursing home resident, who is not only unproductive but is also now in a dependent role. Because American society idealizes independence and abhors dependency, those who find themselves "counting on kindness," as Wendy Lustbader puts it, feel that they have failed, that they are somehow deficient.[14]

> *Esther, a pious Eastern European-born eighty-three-year-old nursing home resident, remarks, "All my life, I always did for others. I helped my husband, my nieces, and nephews. I used to put money in the* pushke *[tzedakah box] every Friday night. I always gave money to the synagogue and to religious schools. Now I'm here, and I can't do anything for anyone. What good am I anymore?"*

Perhaps the saddest aspect of the self-perception of institutionalized older persons is their feeling of personal insignificance and impotency.[15] As individuals who have ceased to play a role in the community, they lack means of attaining social status or self-respect. Nothing is expected of them, and there is a distinct sense that they are not taken seriously.[16]

Theologian Abraham Joshua Heschel, in addressing the 1961 White House Conference on Aging, decried the diminution of worth embodied in the cultural messages to elders reflected in an emphasis on recreation, as opposed to engagement in learning, growing, and other meaningful activity:

> The popular approach is "Keep alive a zest for living in the elderly, by encouraging them to continue old hobbies or new ones." Now preoccupation with hobbies, the overemphasis on recreation, while certainly conducive to eliminating boredom temporarily, hardly contribute to inner strength. The effect is, rather, a pickled existence, preserved in brine with spices.[17]

The sense that a person cannot make an impact on his or her environment, "the perception of uncontrollability, leads not uncommonly to 'learned helplessness,'" which in turn yields passivity, anxiety, and antisocial behavior.[18]

Given the social stigma regarding aging and dependency, and the lack of meaningful roles, it is not surprising that institutionalized elders have a more negative sense of self-esteem than their noninstitutionalized peers.[19] Feelings of inferiority and low self-esteem contribute to the prevalence of depression among institutionalized older adults.[20]

Disjunction and Disconnection

Even more than elders in general, the long-term care resident experiences disconnection. He or she has lost the moorings of home and community, familiar surroundings, and past life roles. Often, residents have lost most of the significant people in their lives, through death, disability, or distance. Although institutionalization thrusts the older person into a social setting, isolation persists within it. The sense of community you might expect simply does not develop

for the older people cast together within the institution, as Renee
Rose Shield notes in her observations of one long-term care facility:

> Instead of *communitas* [a spirit of community], residents stay
> by themselves and try to be "good" patients. Rather than find
> similarities among themselves to bind them together, residents
> emphasize and maintain their differences. Instead of creating
> the exuberance found in *communitas*, residents often distrust
> one another, compete with one another and denigrate one
> another ... there seems little reason for the residents to bond
> together, little reason to help one another and to reciprocate.[21]

Jews in Non-Jewish Long-Term Care Facilities

The experience of isolation and discontinuity brings further spiritual challenges to elderly long-term care residents, particularly
those in non-Jewish settings. It is likely that more than half of
Jewish elders in long-term care institutions are in facilities that are
not under Jewish auspices.[22] They come to these settings for a host
of reasons: proximity to family members, cost, availability of space
at the time they need placement, and lack of capacity in facilities
under Jewish auspices. Some communities have closed their Jewish
long-term care facilities, other smaller communities have never had
them, and even communities with excellent long-term care facilities
do not have adequate space for all Jewish elders requiring that level
of care.

Most of these elders have little means of connection to Jewish
life.[23] Even those who still maintain synagogue membership generally cannot participate, as transportation and accommodations are
not readily available. Synagogue volunteers and rabbis may engage
in some outreach to members in long-term care, but the very disper-
sion of these individuals makes these efforts challenging. These
elders are also unlikely to be connected to other Jewish communal
organizations. Consider this experience of a Jewish resident of a
Protestant-sponsored life-care community:

> *When I entered [a Protestant-sponsored] life-care community, I was a little concerned that I'd have to give up going to synagogue. It was difficult for me to walk there. But I had belonged to a synagogue for forty-two years, and I felt terrible about not being able to go—about not having any connection with my yiddishkeit.*

The need for connection is obviously profound.

The Impact of Religious Life in the Long-Term Care Facility

Religious life can offer elders living in nursing homes a radically different experience of time, personal meaning, and connectedness. While religious life can in no way remove the losses and hardships of institutionalization and frailty, it can provide valuable solace. There is persuasive evidence that connection to religion, tradition, and community are particularly meaningful in a person's later life and in the institutional context. Research suggests that religious involvement enhances physical health and psychological coping and also decreases depression.[24] In the case of the Jewish elder, the tie is both ethnic/communal and religious/spiritual. I suggest that this multidimensional nature of Jewish identity only makes the connection more powerful and its absence more harmful.

Religious life can offer elders living in nursing homes a radically different experience of time, personal meaning, and connectedness.

My experience as a chaplain suggests that religious life offers:

- A sense of significant time and a thread of connection to past and future
- A sense of significant being
- An experience of connection to community
- A connection to transcendence

Models of Building Connection to Jewish Elders in Long-Term Care

How can we bring these dimensions to the long-term care context? There are many possible models for communities to reach and serve Jewish elders in long-term care settings. Some communities have identified this outreach as a central priority. Programs to serve this population are commonly under the auspices of Jewish family service agencies, though some reside in separate Jewish healing centers or aging networks. The following is not a comprehensive catalog, but rather an outline of the diverse range of programs currently in existence.[25]

Community Chaplains

Many communities employ community chaplains to serve elders dispersed in multiple non-Jewish long-term care facilities. Typically these trained pastoral care professionals make visits at regular intervals to elders in various facilities and also offer Shabbat and holiday celebrations and/or study sessions. Pastoral care training enables these professionals to offer meaningful connection to individual elders and family members. However, because the very nature of such a position involves travel and visits to multiple settings, an individual professional in this role may have a limited impact. Most community chaplains extend their reach by involving volunteers recruited and trained by their agency or by congregations. In some communities, facilities pay for the services of a chaplain for their Jewish residents.

Trained Volunteers

Such communities as Denver and Philadelphia train and deploy volunteers to provide pastoral care to nursing homes and assisted-living facilities. Called "parachaplains," these individuals typically participate in substantial training (twelve weeks or longer) that focuses on spiritual and emotional aspects of aging, skill-building in pastoral presence, and conducting prayer and celebration. Parachaplains may serve one or more facilities and generally receive some level of ongoing supervision, usually in the form of periodic group meetings.[26] Parachaplaincy programs can bring talented and dedicated volunteers into connection with elders in long-term care. To be maximally effective, these efforts require professional leadership and ongoing supervision.

There is persuasive evidence that connection to religion, tradition, and community are particularly meaningful in a person's later life and in the institutional context.

Another model is training and placing volunteers for nursing home visits without the pastoral care dimension implied by the parachaplaincy title. In this model, organizations such as Chicago's Jewish Healing Network recruit, screen, and train volunteers. A chaplain provides training and equips volunteers to lead services. Jewish Eldercare of Rhode Island's project CHAVER (Caring Helpers and Visitors Empower Residents) offers an eight-week training program for volunteers who wish to become "spiritually friendly visitors" to elders in nursing homes or at home.

Mobilizing Volunteers through Synagogues and Other Community Groups

Many communal groups reach out to synagogues as a source of volunteers, either as individuals or as part of synagogue groups, such as existing *bikur cholim* committees. Others recruit new volunteers for their purposes. Volunteers may be screened, trained, and placed in nursing homes. In Los Angeles, volunteers recruited by the Jewish Family Service are paired with individual elders in long-term care facilities. Social workers placed in synagogues through UJA-Federation of New York help train and recruit volunteers from the congregations to work with nursing home residents. Agencies also mount initiatives to engage volunteers for particular occasions. For example, Jewish Family Service Metrowest of Framingham, Massachusetts, has recruited synagogue members to send Rosh

Hashanah cards to every Jewish elder in a facility in their area. They also conduct regular interactive intergenerational workshops with elders and youth.

Social Workers/Jewish Communal Service Professionals

In some communities, the responsibility for serving elders in non-Jewish facilities is undertaken by a social worker or Jewish communal service professional. This individual may coordinate volunteers, lead services and conduct programs, and enlist volunteerism and involvement from local synagogues. One model is the Jewish Healing Connection of Boston's Jewish Family and Children's Service, which employs a Jewish communal service professional to offer spiritual outreach to nursing home residents.

Creating Tools to Promote Jewish Life

In addition to providing human resources in the form of professionals or volunteers, efforts are underway to develop and disseminate educational and ritual materials to bring Jewish life to elders in long-term care. One model resource is Sacred Seasons celebration kits, a tool created by Hiddur: The Center for Aging and Judaism of the Reconstructionist Rabbinical College to empower staff or volunteers without a Jewish background to help residents celebrate Shabbat and holidays within long-term care facilities. Each easy-to-use kit includes the resources needed to lead a celebration; a leader's guide with background information on the observance and step-by-step instructions; master copies of large-type participant handouts with the words of songs and blessings in Hebrew, English, and transliteration; and a CD recording of all of the songs and blessings. Sacred Seasons kits are disseminated free of charge through a website.[27]

Here is an example of how the Sacred Seasons kit has been used to enrich the lives of Jewish residents of long-term care facilities. The Jewish resident of the Protestant-sponsored life-care community (quoted earlier), who was grieving her connection to Jewish life at the time of her admission to a non-Jewish life-care community, was overjoyed last Hanukkah. Using the Sacred Seasons kit, the Christian chaplain and recreation staff in her facility helped her and other residents light the (electric) menorah. Each night, they sang, ate latkes, and delighted in the opportunity to share in the Festival of Lights. Basking in the light, she commented, "I'm rejoicing at what they're doing for us."

Other efforts are being developed to provide Jewish resources for long-term care facilities serving Jewish elders. The Joan Grossman Center for Chaplaincy and Healing of the Philadelphia Jewish Family and Children's Service, for example, regularly mails resource packets on major Jewish holidays to recreation therapists at facilities with Jewish residents. The Ohr Tikvah Jewish Healing Center of New Jersey has created and distributed a CD recording of a healing service to long-term care facilities in its area.

Jewish Cultural Competency Training

There is a great need to educate staff members who serve Jewish elders in long-term care facilities about Jewish beliefs, customs, and traditions. Cultural competency training can help staff better understand and support Jewish elders. One noteworthy example is a video series, *The Art of Jewish Caregiving*, created by Jewish Home and Aging Services in Detroit to train health care workers about Jewish customs and traditions. Jewish Eldercare of Rhode Island offers in-service training for nursing home staff on Jewish observances, traditions, and dietary customs. Clearly, as increasing numbers of Jews receive care in non-Jewish settings, the need for such programs will increase.

There is a great need to educate staff members who serve Jewish elders in long-term care facilities about Jewish beliefs, customs, and traditions. Cultural competency training can help staff better understand and support Jewish elders.

Practical Guidelines for Bringing Religious Life to the Long-Term Care Context

The guidelines presented here both describe ideas for religious programming and offer tips for working within the long-term care milieu.

Timing

In order to facilitate religious life within a long-term care facility, it is essential to work within institutional rhythms and time frames. Timing programs means taking into account mealtimes and other established time commitments, as well as staff schedules. Among the challenges facing those who take on this work is balancing the need to schedule when important resources are available, such as staff, with the desire to be authentic, and to hold observances as close as possible to the "real" time. Because a large proportion of nursing home residents suffer from dementia, and many people with dementia exhibit sun-downing behaviors (disorientation increases as night draws near), daytime services and activities may be preferable. Finally, in this setting where attention spans may be quite short, brevity is truly next to godliness. Abridging a service or celebration to half an hour may result in significant prayers being omitted, but it will also ensure more active participation of worshipers for the time period of the service.

Facilitate Accessibility

Accessibility is a vital concern in creating religious life in the nursing home. Residents' multiple impairments must be taken into account as programs and services are developed. Consider these aspects when creating an accessible experience:

- The space needs to be amenable to wheelchairs, walkers, and geri-chairs.
- Elders may need assistance in "transportation" from their rooms to the service.
- Elders may require repeated reminders, verbally and/or in writing, about the event.

- Sound amplification should enable hearing-impaired individuals to participate.
- Liturgical materials should be large-type and light-weight; even so, residents may require assistance in turning pages. Alternatively, images of key prayers might be projected onto a screen using a computer and PowerPoint projector.

Maximize Participation

Attending a religious service or program can be a boost to an elder's sense of spiritual well-being. Active participation provides a further sense of personal significance. For this reason, wherever possible, residents should be encouraged to participate in leading or setting up a service. Calling upon a participant to read or recite or to help others to participate is extremely helpful. In addition, elders can be validated further by the leader's acknowledgment of their experience, knowledge, and perspective.

Involve Families

Visiting loved ones in a nursing home can be a trying experience. When their daily reality has become so removed from the web of family and community life, it can be hard to think of topics for conversation. When cognitive or physical impairments make communication difficult, simply remaining present can be agonizing. When precious relatives have lost significant parts of their functioning, spending time with them can be a painful reminder of the gap between who they were and who they are.

Attending a religious service or program can be a boost to an elder's sense of spiritual well-being.

Participating in religious life can be an affirming experience for elders and family members to share. In the context of religious observance, the older person is most connected to what is whole within her. Often the elder is more expressive and actively participatory in worship than in any other activity in the nursing home. Worshipping, celebrating, or studying provides the visiting family member and the elder with something concrete to do, something in which both can participate and that both enjoy. Finally, family members can be encouraged to participate in religious life within the institution through ritually marking important events in *their* lives, such as marriages, births, and confirmations, within the context of religious observances in the nursing home.

Partner with Staff

Staff chaplains, community clergy, or volunteers who take upon themselves the responsibility for facilitating religious life within the nursing home will be effective to the degree that they collaborate with the interdisciplinary team that makes up the nursing home staff. It is essential to work in close coordination and communication with recreational therapists, social workers, and nurses. Sometimes those involved in fostering religious life will act as advocates regarding elders' spiritual needs; and, often, staff will provide information that will be essential in understanding and serving the elders. Chaplains or community volunteers can come to be seen as a resource for the institution and the staff in caring for the whole person.

Since many nursing homes are multicultural environments, staff may well be from a different religious background than elders. Therefore, education of staff is important to help them understand elders' religious orientations and needs. One way of fostering positive collaboration with staff is to acknowledge their religious and spiritual inclinations and to create appropriate opportunities for them to participate in religious life. Elders and staff can find common ground through celebration of more universal holidays, such as Thanksgiving and Martin Luther King Day. Staff's contribution to elders' lives can be acknowledged through ceremonies for times of recognition, such as National Nursing Home Week, Nursing Week, and Social Work Month. Finally, staff can be given important support through opportunities to mourn individuals who have died in regular or episodic memorial services.

Unmet Needs

Despite the extensive and creative efforts in place in communities around North America, the unmet Jewish needs of this population are considerable. Most communities lack any kind of systematic coordination of outreach to long-term care residents. In many communities, several Jewish communal agencies and many synagogues are helping elders in such facilities without any coordination of their programs. Most professional and lay leaders would agree that more and better organized efforts are needed.

Although there are many dedicated and passionate volunteers and professionals working to bring Jewish life to elders in long-term care facilities, most communities lack consistent and diverse Jewish programming that can connect elders to more than sporadic experiences, as good as they may be. More resources of all kinds—funding, professional and volunteer personnel, and tools—are needed to make a connection to the rich fabric of Jewish life. In general, there is a need for more educational programming to connect elders to Jewish learning and more efforts to enlist elders in long-term care facilities in sharing their wisdom or talents.

The spiritual challenges of life for frail elders in long-term care facilities are profound and represent perhaps the greatest unmet need. As they face loss, debilitation, and the prospect of death, frail elders are grappling with the meaning of life, with sin and regret, and with forgiveness, fear, and hope. Jewish chaplains are the professionals trained and committed to accompanying people through this awe-filled "valley of the shadow."

Today chaplaincy resources for Jewish elders in non-Jewish long-term care settings are scant. If chaplains are involved in a facility at all, their presence is seldom or even on a weekly basis, and it is more often biweekly or monthly. In some communities, a chaplain is called in only for elders in hospice care. Clearly, additional funding is needed to create positions for professional Jewish chaplains, who, in turn, could broaden their reach by training and supervising volunteer parachaplains. It should be noted that relatively few rabbis are trained in working with aging individuals and issues. More training is needed, both in rabbinical seminaries and for rabbis and chaplains in the field, to equip pastoral caregivers to meet the special needs of this population.[28]

Final Words

On Yom Kippur we ardently pray that our worst fear will not be realized. *Al tashlicheynu l'et zikna*, we cry, forsake us not in our old age, when our strength fails, abandon us not. Fostering connection to Judaism and Jewish community allows us to ensure that this fervent prayer is answered for elders in long-term care institutions. In bringing Jewish life to those who might otherwise be forgotten, we allow them to experience meaning, connection, and celebration.

For Further Investigation

Leah Abramowitz. "Prayer as Therapy among the Frail Jewish Elderly." *Journal of Gerontological Social Work* 19, no. 3/4 (1993), pp. 69–74.

Kathy Calkins. "Time Perspective, Marking and Styles of Usage." *Social Problems* 17 (1990), pp. 487–501.

David Dunkelman. "Is Aging for Us? Toward a Dialogue on Jewish Long-Term Care." *Journal of Jewish Communal Service* 77, no. 2 (2000), pp. 109–123.

Dayle A. Friedman, ed. *Jewish Pastoral Care: A Practical Handbook from Traditional and Contemporary Sources.* 2nd ed. Woodstock, VT: Jewish Lights Publishing, 2005.

Dayle A. Friedman and M. Muncie. "Freeing the Captives of the Clock: Time and Ritual in Long-Term Care." Presented at American Society on Aging Conference, San Francisco, 1990.

Erving Goffman. *Asylums.* Garden City, NY: Doubleday, 1961.

Jaber F. Gubrium. *Living and Dying at Murray Manor.* New York: St. Martin's Press, 1975.

Charlene A. Harrington, Helen Carrillo, and Courtney LaCava. *Nursing Facilities: Staffing, Residents, and Facility Deficiencies, 1998 through 2005.* San Francisco: University of California, 2001.

Richard Hastings. "Learned Helplessness." *Geriatric Care* 17, no. 10 (1985), pp. 1–2.

Stephan O. Kline. *The Continuum of Care in the 21st Century, An Action Guide: Helping Federations Meet the Needs of Our Jewish Elderly.* Washington, DC: United Jewish Communities, 2001.

Harold Koenig. *Aging and God: Spiritual Pathways to Mental Health in Midlife and Later Years.* Binghamton, NY: Haworth Press, 1994.

Cary Kozberg. "Let Your Heart Take Courage: A Ceremony for Entering a Nursing Home," from *A Heart of Wisdom: Making the Jewish Journey from Midlife through the Elder Years,* Susan Berrin, ed. Woodstock, VT: Jewish Lights, 2000.

Maggie Kuhn, Christina Long, and Laura Quinn. *No Stone Unturned.* New York: Ballantine Books, 1991.

Jeff Levin and Larry Dossey. *God, Faith, and Health: Exploring the Spirituality-Healing Connection.* Hoboken, NJ: John Wiley & Sons, 2002.

Morton A. Lieberman. "Institutionalization of the Aged: Effects on Behavior." *Journal of Gerontology* 24 (1969), pp. 330–340.

Wendy Lustbader. *Counting on Kindness: An Exploration of Dependency.* New York: Free Press, 1993.

Marian L. MacDonald. "The Forgotten Americans: A Sociopsychological View of Aging and Nursing Homes." *American Journal of Community Psychology* 3 (1973), pp. 272–294.

E. Mason. "Some Correlates of Self-Judgment of the Aged." *Journal of Gerontology* 9 (1954), pp. 324–337.

Florida Scott-Maxwell. *The Measure of My Days.* New York: Penguin Books, 1979.

Athena McClean. *The Person in Dementia: A Study of Nursing Home Care in the U.S.* Peterborough, Ontario: Broadview Press, 2007.

David O. Moberg. "Gerontology in Seminary Training." *Theological Education* 3 (Special issue, 1980), pp. 283–293.

Miriam Rieger. *The American Jewish Elderly.* New York: United Jewish Communities Report Series on the 2000–2001 National Jewish Population Survey, 2004.

Michael Salamon. Jewish Patients in Nursing Homes under Non-Jewish Auspices: Some Personal Observations, *Journal of Aging and Judaism,* Spring 1998, pp. 196–200.

Renee Rose Shield. *Uneasy Endings.* Ithaca, NY: Cornell University Press, 1988.

David J. Zucker. "Para-chaplaincy: A Communal Response to the Ill and Suffering." In *Jewish Pastoral Care,* Dayle A. Friedman, ed. Woodstock, VT: Jewish Lights, pp. 453–467.

Resources

Hiddur: The Center for Aging and Judaism of the Reconstructionist Rabbinical College, 1299 Church Rd., Wyncote, PA 19095. (215) 576-0800, www.hiddur.org. Trains professionals and distributes spiritual resources, such as Sacred Seasons celebration kits, available at www.sacredseasons.org.

Sacred Aging Project, Union for Reform Judaism, 633 Third Ave., New York, NY 10017. (212) 650-4000, www.urj.org/jfc/olderadults. Develops and distributes resources for congregations and individuals, including *10 Guiding Principles of Long-Term Healthcare Planning* and *A Time to Prepare*, a handbook for facing illness and death.

12

An Anchor amidst Anomie
Ritual and Aging

She was seated in the place of honor. It might well have been a throne, but it was actually the sofa of her daughter's home. One by one, her nine grandchildren came before her, each bearing one of the precious trinkets accumulated over her eighty-five years. It was the "Great Grammy Giveaway," necessitated by my Grammy Anne's impending move to an assisted-living complex, where her quarters would be dramatically smaller than those in the apartment she had inhabited for years. As each grandchild took a turn choosing an object from the stunning array arranged on the Ping-Pong table in the basement, Grammy Anne told the story of that tchotchke, *describing the trip on which it was acquired or the adventure she'd had bargaining for it. I got the "Grammy swans," swan-shaped crystal bowls, bought when a local hotel went under in the Depression. Floating on circular mirrors, their necks adorned with ribbons matching the color scheme of the affair, these swans had graced countless luncheon tables. They were a perfect embodiment of Grammy Anne's elegance and graciousness.*

Grammy Anne is long gone, sadly, but the swans and the memories of that sweet moment remain with me. That impromptu ritual passed along a treasured legacy to each of Grammy's dear ones. It also eased a difficult and sad transition for her and her family. Instead of merely discarding those belongings that would not fit in the new home, treating her treasures as flotsam and jetsam, Grammy was given an opportunity to savor them, and to bestow a priceless gift on her family members. This ritual transformed Grammy's experience; it created meaning in a moment of great loss.

Aging presents enormous challenges to a person's sense of significant being. We have a responsibility to address these threats to meaning, for, as the English writer Ronald Blythe teaches, we mustn't allow the old to fall into purposelessness: "To appreciate the transience of all things is one matter, to narrow the last years—and they can be numerous—down to a dreary thread is another."[1]

As the Great Grammy Giveaway narrative suggests, ritual has the potential to infuse painful passages and periods with meaning and sustenance. This is true of traditional religious ritual, as well as of idiosyncratic rituals specific to the individual or family, such as this one. This chapter examines the promise of meaning offered in ritual, and specifically examines rites of passage. Although human beings are inexorably drawn to ritual, we moderns may feel intimidated by the prospect of doing so. In order to facilitate the creation of new rituals to reflect the contemporary experience of aging, the chapter closes by offering guidance for shaping and conducting a ritual.

*R**itual can serve as an orienting anchor.***

Ritual as an Orienting Anchor

In the midst of confusing, alienating losses, changes, and stresses, ritual can serve as an orienting anchor. Ritual has been defined as an act or actions intentionally conducted by an individual or group employing one or more symbols in a repetitive, formal, precise, and highly stylized fashion.[2] As anthropologist Barbara Myerhoff taught, ritual suggests predictability and continuity: "Even when dealing with change, new events are connected to preceding ones, incorporated into a stream of precedents so that they are recognized as growing out of tradition and experience."[3] Ritual connects the individual to ancestors and those not yet born. Myerhoff noted that this sense of connection is heightened in religious rituals, in which the participant is linked also to "the forces of nature and purposes of the deities, reading the forms of macrocosm in the microcosm."[4] With the use of sacred symbols, the present moment is no longer a strange wilderness but connected to the whole of the person's life, so that he or she experiences his or her history as "a single phenomenological reality."[5]

Ritual also serves to reaffirm meaning. According to the pastoral theoretician Elaine Ramshaw, rituals "carry core meanings of the social group performing them."[6] In moments when the sense of the coherence of a person's life or the universe is threatened, ritual can reinforce the symbolic worldview, thus reaffirming order. Funerals provide a powerful example of this kind of bolstering, as they bring order amid chaos, and affirm theological and social meanings and beliefs. The widow facing a bleak and terrifying world without her husband of sixty years is symbolically reminded at the funeral of God's care, and of the goodness of life that exists alongside loss and finitude.

Ritual pierces isolation and creates community. While individuals can construct private rituals, rituals are most often shared in a social context. Ritual has the capacity to heighten a sense of shared values or history, while also creating common memories. Even an ordinary birthday party for a man who has reached the ripe age of seventy-five may bond participants in profound ways: informal reminiscence reminds them of precious shared experiences in the past; those who have already passed that milestone reflect on their lives before and since; and those not yet there are given an indelible model of how a person can age (gracefully or grumpily!). Ritual can intensify our bonds and deepen our awareness that we are all in the same human boat, sailing amid fragility and mortality, seeking dignity and joy, courage and love.

In moments when the sense of the coherence of a person's life or the universe is threatened, ritual can reinforce the symbolic worldview, thus reaffirming order.

Ritual can provide a safe container for ambivalence. In the context of ritual, we can have a "contained expression of unwanted, conflicting emotion."[7] For example, a worker retiring from a job of many years might jokingly express both his criticisms of his employers and his ambivalence about leaving in formal or informal remarks ("You nearly pushed me out with your confusing new computer system. Now I'm *really* leaving ... but watch out, I might decide to come back and haunt you!"). Rituals also bolster social norms, as they ultimately reinforce the "preferred emotion," so the worker is made to feel that this parting is a cause for celebration, and that something better awaits him in retirement.[8]

The Dearth of Ritual for Later Life

Sadly, elders in our society have little ritual to mark or frame their experiences. The great transitions of older adulthood go largely unmarked. Between retirement, which might be acknowledged in a social way, and death, there is no normative or even common ceremony. "That 'old age' may last for three decades, lacking even demarcations provided by clearly named phases, goals or features, is astonishing."[9] The result of this lack of clearly defined rituals and expectations is "cultural vagueness, anomie and isolation." Infusing old age with ritual can teach old and young "the meaning of their existence and the justifications for their continued being."[10]

Ritual can provide meaning in aging in the context of ongoing religious life, as well as in marking the transitions, losses, and gains of late life. We turn first to the role of religious ritual in bringing meaning to time.

Rites of Passage: Continuity and Change

Even in the absence of religious or communal ritual, older people often spontaneously create their own ways to mark the unique experiences of aging. As Myerhoff notes:

> Just as children fastidiously work to bring some cosmos into the chaos of their emerging world of boundless complexity, so older people are often noted to fuss obsessively with trivial

items, ordering a life that is ending, using the predictability and certainty that ritual provides during times of anxiety and helplessness.[11]

For example, Myerhoff compares sorting through mementos and personal belongings to nesting in late pregnancy, an effort toward "a final imposition of one's human purpose on the last random, untidy event of all."[12] Aside from these individual rituals and a few paltry social markings, the passages of old age have largely been bereft of ritual acknowledgment. As Myerhoff notes, "Retirements and funerals are crude markers for the stark beginning and end of old age; in between there is a universe of differentiation that remains a cultural wasteland for each to calculate and navigate alone, without the aid of ritual, ceremony, or symbol."[13]

Rites of passage are enormously helpful to all of us in getting through life passages, so their absence in aging is costly. Rites of passage are rituals that mark a change in place, state, social position, or age.[14] These rituals serve as a frame and call us to awareness of what we are experiencing.[15] In other words, they force us to pay attention. In the words of religion scholar Ronald Grimes, rites of passage "ensure that we attend to such events fully, which is to say, spiritually, psychologically and socially."[16]

Rites of passage help us place the current moment in context, both in terms of our own life span and in terms of cultural values that orient us. Grimes writes, "Even a single rite of passage can divide a person's life into 'before' and 'after.' An entire system of such rites organizes a life into stages.... These ceremonial occasions inscribe images into the memories of participants, and they etch values into the cornerstones of social institutions."[17]

> *Rites of passage help us place the current moment in context, both in terms of our own lifespan and in terms of cultural values that orient us.*

The rites of passage that our society offers older people are largely moments of celebration for gains or attainments. Myerhoff suggests that we need a corresponding set of rituals to mark losses.[18] There is no end to the transitions that call out for ritual acknowledgment. Here are some examples:

Positive Experiences/Gains

- Becoming a great-grandparent
- Taking on a new volunteer role
- Undertaking a new religious study or practice
- Entering a new community
- Making a new friend
- Recovering from acute illness or surgery
- Entering a new romantic relationship
- The anniversary of belonging to a congregation or organization
- Going on a journey

Negative Experiences/Losses

- Adapting to a disability (hearing loss, sight loss, immobility, incontinence) and/or accepting an assistive device (hearing aid, walker, wheelchair)
- Hearing bad news about your health or prognosis
- Losing a friend
- Leaving a home
- Leaving a congregation or community
- Giving up driving
- Becoming a caregiver to an incapacitated spouse or partner
- The end of menopause
- Becoming a "last twig" when the last surviving member of your generation in the family dies
- Entering a nursing home[19]

The very experience of entering old age can be transformed by ritual acknowledgment. For example, the scholar Savina Teubal decided she would not approach old age with dread. Instead,

Teubal created a ritual to *celebrate* becoming an older woman on the occasion of her sixtieth birthday. This ritual, *Simchat Hochmah* (the celebration of wisdom), drew upon biblical narratives and included a blessing, a change of name, a covenant, a reconciliation with death, and an affirmation of life.[20] *Simchat Hochmah* has been emulated and adapted by many other women, and is depicted in a documentary film called *Timbrels and Torahs*.[21]

Some of the transitions of aging could be meaningfully marked through ritual acknowledgment in the context of a religious community. The *mi-sheberakh* blessing in Jewish liturgy provides an example of a means of doing this. These blessings are traditionally offered to members of the congregation who are called up to say a blessing over the Torah when it is read in the synagogue. The individual receives a blessing in honor of his or her performing this treasured ritual, and in acknowledgment of any significant event in his/her life, such as a birthday, anniversary, departure on a trip for Israel, or a yahrzeit, the anniversary of the death of a close relative. This ritual makes the community aware of the important experiences of the individual. It also enables the person to share joys and sorrows, and invokes God's blessing at powerful moments.

Some of the transitions of aging could be meaningfully marked through ritual acknowledgment in the context of a religious community.

The *mi-sheberakh* blessing could easily be a context for marking the passages of late life. Elder members of a community could receive a *mi-sheberakh* in honor of moving out of their family home, or of surrendering a driver's license, or of becoming a great-grandparent. If utilized in this way, private, isolated experiences would become visible and honored. Both painful and joyous transitions would be intimately connected to community and to the Divine. Even in a more private context, the *mi-sheberakh* ritual points to the power of giving blessings. Family members, friends, and professionals can also help elders in our midst in their high and low moments by offering them our personal blessings, whether stated in religious language or framed in a secular context as an articulation of our own hopes for them.

Personal, family, and communal rituals can thus enrich aging and provide a container to hold our hopes, fears, dreams, and dreads in moving through the passages of later life. Many people would like to create or participate in rituals, but may wonder how to do it. The next section explores some simple guidelines for designing and conducting rituals for transitions of aging.

Constructing a Ritual of Transition[22]

In order to have an impact, a ritual needs to reflect the transition it is marking. To begin, you need to carefully examine the transition you are addressing. What are its significant features? Is there a "before" (status quo), "during" (liminality), and "after" (new state)? What are the salient characteristics of each? What are the emotional components and meanings of this transition for the person experiencing it, for family members/friends, and for members of the community, if they will be included?

A ritual is a kind of drama, so it is helpful to focus on physical action and behavior. Doing something will make the experience visceral.

Next, the ritual needs to have credibility. Essential in this regard is focusing on a guiding metaphor that has emotional resonance for those involved. The metaphor will help anchor and orient all involved, reaching from the unfamiliar in this situation toward a known and familiar realm.[23] In addition, a ritual is a kind of drama, so it is helpful to focus on physical action and behavior. *Doing something* will make the experience visceral; excessive explanation and didactic content are best avoided.

Finally, the ritual should tie in to personal and communal continuity through symbols, words, or actions.

Brainstorming is a helpful tool for the next stage of creating a ritual. Once you have analyzed the transition to be addressed, let your mind free associate. Search traditional literature, or whatever body of knowledge is most meaningful to you. Look for material associated with this transition, including heroes, texts, stories, symbols, blessings, prayers, and songs. Hone in on the image or metaphor that seems most apt and let that guide you as you create a ritual. Use this metaphor to frame and define the moment for the person undergoing the transition and those present.

Now you are ready to create a structure that includes ritual action or affect-based components for each stage of the rite. Here are some things to consider:

Timing/rhythm. Make sure the ritual is not too long. A relatively brief ritual is often more powerful than a long, drawn-out ceremony. In addition, make sure your ritual has a beginning, middle, and end, and that there are good transitions between them.

Involve key people. Be aware of people in the subject's life who need to be honored or acknowledged, or who can contribute to the meaning of the event.

Be sensitive to the community's role. Even though the ritual is primarily focused on the individual who is making a change, those who are in attendance will both affect and be affected by this experience.

Drama. Be alert to opportunities to make the moment magical. Think about aesthetic aspects, including setting, lighting, clothing/costume, food, and adornments, such as flowers and decorations.

Music. Music is an essential part of the power of many rituals. Music opens participants to the experience, touches their emotions, and provides a sense of continuity. You can include music through recorded music, performed music, and/or community singing.

Facilitator/leader. Think carefully about who will be conducting this ritual. Individuals who are the focus of rituals of transition need to be present to the magnitude of the moment. For this reason, it may be best if someone else takes responsibility for facilitating the ritual. The extent of this role ranges from creating the ritual to carrying out what the subject and/or others have designed.

Safety. Make sure that this ritual will be safe for the person on whom it is focused and all present. Do not make unexpected demands on anyone or violate boundaries by putting anyone on the spot. Make sure the person experiencing the transition knows about and is comfortable with what will happen in the ritual.

Evaluate. Once the ritual is completed, think about what went well and what did not go as you or others had hoped. Look at what contributed to a sense of connection and what fell flat. This reflection will prove invaluable to you for the next time you set out to shape a ritual of transition.

The anecdote that follows illustrates the incredible healing power of incorporating ritual into what could otherwise be a sad, isolating occurrence.

Carol and Bob decided to "downsize" from the home they had lived in for forty-three years. Grateful that they could make the decision for the sake of liberation from burden, rather than in crisis, they intentionally set about marking this transition for themselves, their children, and their grandchildren. On their last week in the house, the entire family came together for a special Shabbat dinner. With affection and good humor, they shared memories of the times they had shared in the house— funny moments of childhood, civil rights and anti-war organizing, and sad moments as well. Carol, Bob, and one of their adult children later went through the entire house, sharing memories specific to each room. Finally, they offered a spontaneous prayer, expressing their gratitude for the goodness they had experienced in this home, and affirming hopefulness for future blessings. When they had settled into the new house, close friends joined them to hang the new mezuzah. Carol said of this series of rituals, "It felt really important.... I don't miss the house, and I think that creating this closure contributed to that."

Final Words

As Carol and Bob's transition demonstrates, ritual is a powerful tool for finding and creating meaning in late life. We are all blessed with an innate human proclivity toward ritual, and we can draw upon this to enrich our own and others' experiences through the highs, lows, and in-betweens of aging. Ritual can be accessible to all older adults, religious and non-religious, frail and well. It can help us to "number our days," imbuing transitions and everyday experiences with holiness.[24]

We are all blessed with an innate human proclivity toward ritual, and we can draw upon this to enrich our own and others' experiences through the highs, lows, and in-betweens of aging.

For Further Investigation

Penina V. Adelman. *Miriam's Well: Rituals for Jewish Women around the Year.* New York: Biblio Press, 1990.

Susan Berrin, ed. *Celebrating the New Moon.* Northvale, NJ: Jason Aronson, 1996.

———, ed. *A Heart of Wisdom: Making the Jewish Journey from Midlife through the Elder Years.* Woodstock, VT: Jewish Lights Publishing, 1997.

Ronald Blythe. *The View in Winter: Reflections on Old Age.* New York: Harcourt Brace Jovanovich, 1979.

Arno van Gennep. *The Rites of Passage.* Chicago: University of Chicago Press, 1960.

Ronald L. Grimes. *Deeply into the Bone: Re-inventing Rites of Passage.* Berkeley: University of California Press, 2000.

Abraham Joshua Heschel. "To Grow in Wisdom." In *The Insecurity of Freedom*. Philadelphia: Jewish Publication Society, 1966, pp. 70–84.

———. *The Sabbath: Its Meaning for Modern Man*. (Repr.) New York: Farrar Straus & Giroux, 2005.

Barbara Myerhoff. "We Don't Wrap Herring in a Printed Page." In *Secular Ritual*, Sally Falk Moore and Barbara Myerhoff, eds. Assen, The Netherlands: Van Gorcum, 1977, pp. 199–224.

———. *Remembered Lives: The Work of Ritual, Storytelling, and Growing Older*. Marc Kaminsky, ed. Ann Arbor: University of Michigan Press, 1992.

———. "A Death in Due Time: Conviction, Order, and Continuity in Ritual Drama." In *Remembered Lives*, pp. 159–190.

———. "Experience at the Threshold: The Interplay of Aging and Ritual." In *Remembered Lives*, pp. 219–227.

Elaine Ramshaw. *Ritual and Pastoral Care*. Philadelphia: Fortress Press, 1987.

Florida Scott-Maxwell. *The Measure of My Days*. New York: Penguin Books, 1979.

Savina J. Teubal. *"Simchat Hochmah."* In *Four Centuries of Jewish Women's Spirituality*, Elaine Umansky and Diane Ashton, eds., pp. 257–264.

Elaine Umansky and Diane Ashton, eds. *Four Centuries of Jewish Women's Spirituality*. Boston: Beacon Press. 1992.

Resources

Ritualwell.org, ceremonies for Jewish living, is a source for innovative contemporary Jewish ritual where you can browse thousands of rituals for holidays and life-cycle occasions, listen to music, download a ritual, or cut and paste your own.

Transitional Keys offers a toolkit and *A Guidebook: Rituals to Improve Quality of Life for Older Adults* as well as trainings on using ritual to bring meaning to elders (www.transitionalkeys.org).

PART V

AGING AND COMMUNITY

13

L'Dor Va-Dor
Living the Chain of Tradition through Intergenerational Programs

> *"From generation to generation we shall tell of Your greatness."*
>
> SIDDUR

L'dor va-dor, from generation to generation. We invoke these words each time we open a siddur to pray. We fervently hope that the enterprise of Jewish life is a means for assuring the continuity of the chain of the tradition. Intergenerational programs, encounters between young people and older adults, transform *l'dor va-dor* from words on a prayer book page into reality by enabling Jews to personally experience the chain of tradition.

With the increasing graying of the Jewish community, and the separation of many families from older relatives due to geographical mobility, the profound benefits of intergenerational programming become evident.

Intergenerational programs, encounters between young people and older adults, transform l'dor va–dor from words on a prayer book page into reality.

For the young, contact with elders can break down stereotypes of the elderly; forge a connection to the Jewish past and Jewish values; and supply a very special kind of warmth, acceptance, and nurturance. For elders, experiences shared with young people reduce isolation in age-segregated ghettos; provide a connection to the Jewish future through relationships with those who will shape it;

177

*F*or the young, contact with elders can break down stereotypes of the elderly…. For elders, experiences shared with young people reduce isolation in age-segregated ghettos.

and enable them to feel affirmed through sharing of their time, their memories, and their caring.

Intergenerational programs have the potential for deep meaning and satisfaction for participants. However, these do not come merely by placing older and younger people in the same place at the same time. Rather, an intergenerational encounter requires considerable sensitivity to succeed. Two examples of intergenerational programs, the worst and the best, will illustrate this necessity for sensitivity.

> The religious school principal called the Jewish nursing home the week before Hanukkah saying that she would like to send over some children "to perform Hanukkah songs for the old people." When the day of the performance arrived, fifteen rather frightened-looking third graders came to the nursing home floor. They sang songs for a group that included a woman who walked about aimlessly, a man crying "nurse, nurse," and several older people sleeping in their wheelchairs, in addition to those men and women who were listening intently to the Hanukkah songs.
>
> When the ten-minute performance was over, a few older people applauded, several reached out to kiss the children (some of whom recoiled uncomfortably), and the teacher gathered up the children to meet their bus. The visit was never mentioned again, either in the nursing home or in the children's classroom, but the principal was discomfited the following year when these same children grumbled and complained at the prospect of returning to the nursing home.

This unfortunate scene provides a dramatic contrast to a very different, and very successful, event held in the same location.

The third-grade day-school students had each been assigned a "special friend," a resident of the Jewish nursing home. The friends had exchanged letters, telling a bit about themselves. The day-school class and the group of nursing home residents had also exchanged videos, in which each participant in the program was introduced and spoke briefly.

On the day of their first meeting, the children ran excitedly into the room in the nursing home where the older people awaited them, immediately picked out their "special friends," and began talking. The room was instantly abuzz with conversation. One student asked his older friend, who had mentioned on the videotape that she spent her childhood in Russia, "So how do you like this country?" That day, the week before Purim, the older and younger participants baked hamentaschen together, sang Purim songs, and shared Purim memories over lunch. The group continued to meet monthly for six months, and many of the friends stayed in touch afterward through letters, phone calls, and visits.

These two scenes illustrate that creating a meaningful intergenerational encounter requires thoughtful planning and careful preparation. We want older and younger people to have a rewarding experience, not to frighten or patronize one another. We hope to develop sensitivity and connection, not to engage in "show-and-tell." Successful intergenerational programs therefore require several essential components: clarifying goals, selecting program structure, attending to logistics for special needs, preparing older and younger participants, debriefing, and follow-up.

Goals and Program Structure

In creating an intergenerational program, as with any educational endeavor, it is important to clarify the goals for the experience. Is this experience primarily intended to build personal relationships, to teach about the aging process, to convey a specific body of material (e.g., reminiscences about the immigrant experience), to provide services, or to strengthen interorganizational ties? Based on the goals, a program planner might choose from among a variety of structures, including a one-time workshop or event, an ongoing learning experience, a worship service or holiday celebration, or an intensive encounter on a retreat.

Older participants could be either well or frail elders, chosen from synagogue members, participants in a senior adult club at a Jewish community center, or residents of a retirement residence or home for the aged. An intergenerational program can employ a variety of learning modalities, including sharing an experience, such as viewing a performance or a film; contributive moments, such as performing for or with one another; and interactive sharing, as in discussing personal reactions to a particular issue or experience. Ideally, the program will allow both older and younger participants to be involved in a mutual, interactive fashion.

Logistics

Planners of intergenerational programs need to be particularly sensitive to special needs of participants so that both young and old can participate with maximal comfort. The program site should be assessed to assure that it is accessible to older people using canes, walkers and/or wheelchairs. If the young participants are very small children, they may require child-sized chairs. Hearing and visual impairments should be anticipated and provided for through microphones, screening out of outside noise, and the provision of larger-type versions of any written materials. If food is served, participants' special dietary needs (e.g., kosher, low-salt, dietetic) must be ascertained beforehand.

Orienting Participants before the Encounter

By far the most important component in shaping a successful intergenerational program is preparing both younger and older participants for the encounter. Younger participants need to have a context in which to place the experience. Toward that end, they should first explore both their stereotypes and the realities of aging. They will need help to identify with some of the feelings and experiences of older people.

Young people will feel most comfortable in meeting frail elders if they have been told what to expect (wheelchairs, walkers, deafness, dementia), and if they meet impaired elders with the knowledge that the overwhelming majority of people over sixty-five are basically healthy and living independently. Finally, orientation of younger participants can include very concrete pointers on how to reach out to older participants, such as compensating for hearing loss, using touch to connect, and making conversation.

By far the most important component in shaping a successful intergenerational program is preparing both younger and older participants for the encounter.

Older participants will find it helpful to learn about the group who will be joining them, as well as the purpose and structure of the program. In addition, they may want to express concerns they have about the encounter, such as fear of rejection, embarrassment over physical impairment, or reluctance to enter a relationship that will be time-limited. Their sensitivity will be heightened through an exploration of their sense of the younger participants' feelings about the encounter. Contact before the program through letters, e-mail, or video may build interest and enthusiasm and ease any awkwardness in the initial meeting.

Debriefing and Follow-Up

An intergenerational experience provokes many emotional responses in participants, so it is vitally important to spend at least a few minutes with each group in sharing reactions to the experience. Often, children will not easily verbalize their feelings, but discussion time will at least give them a sense that their feelings are appropriate and valid. Celebrate triumphs and talk through what was challenging. In ongoing projects, it will be valuable to brainstorm and perhaps role-play alternative approaches to difficult situations. If the encounter has been a positive experience, participants may want to retain their connection in some way. They may do so through exchange of gifts or photographs (individually or as groups), telephone contact, letters, or subsequent visits.

Since loss is a pervasive part of many older people's experience, it is important to commit only to what the individual or group can actually follow through on. Also, the longer the relationship, the greater the chance that one or more of the older participants may become ill or die. Even fairly young children are able to cope with this loss, provided they are given support and an opportunity to express their feelings.

Josh, a ninth-grader, had been visiting the nursing home monthly with his synagogue youth group, and had become quite friendly with Ben, a crusty eighty-three-year-old resident. One week, when Josh went to bring Ben to the activity, he found another man in Ben's room. When he asked at the nurses' station, he learned that Ben had died the day before. Josh was crying when he reached the room where the program was taking place. The recreation therapist saw him and, on learning about Ben's death, stopped the program to allow participants to reminisce about Ben and to offer a moment of silence. The youth group leader invited Josh and the other children to share their feelings. They talked about grandparents who had died, and about how hard it was to make friends in the nursing home who might die. Josh came back the next month and donated a painting he had made in Ben's memory.

Practical Tips for Intergenerational Programs

- Allow time to orient both older and younger participants in advance of the encounter.
- Design an experience to give both old and young participants opportunities to give and receive.
- Create a memento of the experience so that participants can remember and savor the encounter.

- In debriefing after the encounter, invite participants to note something that was challenging, and also something they were proud of.

A Model Intergenerational Shabbat Program

This model is based on a sustained collaboration between Beth Sholom Congregation, of Elkins Park, Pennsylvania, and the Abramson Center for Jewish Life of Horsham, Pennsylvania (formerly Philadelphia Geriatric Center). Middle and high school students join elders from the nursing home monthly for Shabbat dinner and services.

Orientation. At the start of the year, orientation sessions are held for elders at the nursing home and for teens at the synagogue. Teens are introduced to the nursing home context and given practical tips on moving wheelchairs and talking to hard-of-hearing elders. They are invited to share anxieties ("what-ifs"), and to brainstorm together about how to handle potentially difficult situations ("What if someone wants me to take her to the bathroom?" "What if someone thinks I'm her daughter?").

Preparation. Invitations are distributed to elders the week before the event (teens receive a reminder), and elders are reminded the day of the event. When they arrive, teens are given nametags and the name of their partner (two teens are partnered with one elder). Teens go to the elders' rooms to bring them to dinner.

Ice breaker. Once teens and elders are seated, a short program invites them to get to know each other. They might be asked to discuss a particular topic (e.g., earliest Jewish memory, favorite hobby, family constellation) or invited to participate in a shared experience, such as [seated] Israeli dancing or group singing.

Shabbat rituals. Pairs of elders and teens make blessings over candles, Kiddush, and ha-Motzi, and teens serve the meal. Teens transport elders to services at which some of the teens and elders are given parts to lead.

Closure. Teens transport elders to their rooms. On the bus back to the synagogue, teens participate in a debriefing of the experience, noting particularly surprising, challenging, and funny aspects of the evening. Elders are informally enabled to talk about the program in the days following it. Nursing home staff (chaplain or recreation therapist) and youth group leaders touch base to review the program, note areas that could be improved, and make plans for next time.

Final Words

Taking into account the very sensitive nature of the intergenerational encounter and including the above components in program design can produce memorable meetings, moments that will allow both older and younger participants to feel they have had, in the words of one older intergenerational program participant, "A *mechayeh*!"—a life-giving and life-affirming experience.

For Further Investigation

Melissa Hawkins, Francis McGuire, and Kenneth Backman. *Preparing Participants for Intergenerational Interaction: Training for Success.* Binghamton, NY: Haworth Press, 1997.

Journal of Intergenerational Relationships: Programs, Policies and Research. Haworth Press. 10 Alice St., Binghamton, NY 13904. (800) 429-6784, www.haworthpress.com.

Resources

Dorot, a New York City-based initiative, mobilizes youth to serve elders and provides resources to volunteer-based efforts to enhance lives of elders. Dorot offers training and consultation, as well as a manual, *Friendly Visiting Plus: A*

Proven Method for Enhancing Connections between Older Adults and the Community. 171 W. 85th St., New York, NY 10024. (212) 769-2850, www.dorotusa.org.

Generations Together, an intergenerational studies program at the University of Pittsburgh, offers a wide variety of practical publications on intergenerational programming. 121 University Place, Pittsburgh, PA 15260. (412) 648-7155, www.gt.pitt.edu.

Generations United is a national membership organization focused on improving the lives of children, youths, and elders through intergenerational strategies, programs, and public policies. Their website includes a database of articles and programs. 1331 H St. NW, Ste. 900, Washington, DC 20005. (202) 289-3979, www.gu.org.

Temple University Center for Intergenerational Learning, *Connecting Generations, Strengthening Communities—Toolkit for Intergenerational Program Planners.* 1601 N. Broad St., Rm. 206, Philadelphia, PA 19122. (215) 204-6970, www.temple.edu/cil.

Weaving the Generations

Congregations as Communities for All Ages

Ideal and Reality

*P*eople who meet Milt are seldom able to guess his age. He is a fixture at the synagogue every Shabbat morning, at weekly Torah study, and often for daily minyan. He is a treasured volunteer in several congregational programs, and his craftsmanship is evident in sculptures he has forged for sites throughout the building. He offers active encouragement to teens and has created a prize to encourage them to participate in synagogue programs. No wonder everyone is surprised to learn he is ninety-one years old![1]

Milt's experience in synagogue life represents the best that we might hope for. He is growing and contributing to his community and is integrally involved with people of all ages. If Milt's synagogue life represents the ideal vision of engagement across the life span and intergenerational connection, Marilyn's experience embodies the gap between the ideal and the reality.

At seventy-six, Marilyn works as an academic researcher as she has for forty-five years. She is passionately involved with her garden, cooking, country home, husband, children, and grandchildren. She is also grieving the loss of dear, old friends, the

> *ones who remember her parents and childhood. Though gener-*
> *ally upbeat, Marilyn is bitter about the synagogue she has been*
> *involved with for twenty years. She has volunteered extensively*
> *in past years, but now, she says, "There is no place there for me*
> *… no one ever asks anything of me, and the new rabbi doesn't*
> *know I exist."*

Marilyn's experience is not unique. Though many elders like Milt find the synagogue to be a haven of nourishing ties and involvement, many others feel alienated, excluded, or invisible.

In this chapter I will explore the place of elders within a vital synagogue community. I will map the territory, investigating both the numbers of elders within synagogues currently and in coming years, and the nature of these groups. I will examine the current state of participation of elders within synagogues, as well as obstacles to their involvement. Finally, I will propose a shift in the way we conceive of elders' place within congregational life, and I will make suggestions for implementing this vision.

Our Congregations Are Graying

North American synagogues are profoundly affected by the age wave. The numbers of members in midlife and aging are surging. According to a 2006 report by Synagogue 3000,[2] the proportion of members over fifty-five ranges from 27 percent in the Orthodox movement to 47 percent in the Conservative; and the proportion over sixty-five ranges from 16 percent of Reconstructionist congregants to 34 percent of Conservative congregants. Proportions of congregants over seventy-five range from 8 percent in Orthodox congregations to 18 percent in Conservative synagogues. (See Figure 4.) These numbers can only be expected to grow as baby boomers move into older adulthood.

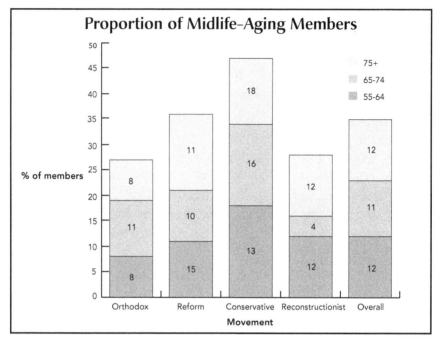

Figure 4

Interestingly, despite the impressive proportions of synagogue members in these age groups, a minority of American Jews in mid- and late-life actually belong to congregations. The rates, in Figure 5, of their synagogue affiliation are:

Synagogue Affiliation of Mid- and Late-Life Jews

Age	Percent affiliated
55–64	34
65–74	34
75+	36

Figure 5

This relatively low rate of affiliation mirrors the rest of the Jewish population. It suggests both challenge and opportunity as congregations contemplate affirmatively reaching out to unaffiliated Jews in midlife and beyond. Currently, these groups are seldom targeted in efforts to reach unaffiliated Jews. Tailored efforts to attract individuals in the second half of life might well bring new life and energy to congregations.

Who Are the Elders in Congregations?

These congregational members represent diverse age groups, including baby boomers, their parents, and even some of their grandparents. They range from individuals who are at the height of their work lives to active retirees and frail elders dependent on help at home or in assisted-living or other congregate settings.

Gerontological seminary educator Henry Simmons suggests that individuals in these groups experience a number of life stages and transitions. At first they encounter what he calls *extended middle age*, a period of continuity in which life retains the basic contours it had before. This stage might continue beyond retirement for a year, or even twenty. The basic questions faced are about goals and commitments—"Who am I? What will I do? With whom?"[3]

Extended middle age ends when something significant changes, such as a health crisis, bereavement, or relocation. This change requires a transition to a revised lifestyle, *the new me.*[4] The contours of life have changed, and after a period of transition, most people stabilize and find a *new normal*. Life might continue this way until death. For many, though, this period is followed by a stage of frailty and dependency that Simmons calls *like it or not* or *reluctant journey.*[5] In addition to physical challenges, individuals in this stage are facing mortality and striving to make meaning.

Given the wide range of life experiences faced by elders, no single approach to synagogue programming can possibly work for all. A successful strategy will involve addressing individuals across this continuum of stages of aging.

Obstacles to Elders' Participation

As we saw from Marilyn's experience, not all elders feel welcomed or engaged within their congregations. What follows are some factors that militate against full engagement of elders.

Focus on the Young

An urban congregation has been engaged for several years in a synagogue transformation initiative through which it has added diverse and innovative Shabbat programming. At a congregant focus group convened to offer feedback on the project, Sandy, a long-time member in her sixties reflected, "I haven't really taken part in any of the activities offered, but then again, I assumed that you were not trying to reach people at our stage of life. My husband and I figured you were going after the young people."

Synagogues are understandably focused on promoting Jewish continuity. In many communities, this concern with ensuring the future of Judaism is implemented through near-exclusive focus on the young. As in Sandy's congregation, the emphasis of outreach and programming is primarily on reaching and involving young children and their parents. In the context of the many dynamic initiatives to transform and revitalize congregational life, aging may be seen as a problem. James Ellor, a religious gerontologist, reflects on this tension within contemporary Christian congregations:

Traditional approaches to the revitalization of congregational systems treat "old" as the enemy. Old buildings, old worship styles, old clergy, and at times the old members are treated as if they are the source of the problem.[6]

In an environment in which "young" is valorized and "old" seen as problematic, it is natural that elders may feel peripheral or devalued. On the other hand, generation gaps between older and younger congregants may indeed make it challenging to satisfy and involve elders. Today's elders lived through the Holocaust and the establishment of Israel; their politics and identity were formed by these events, whatever direction they have taken. They grew up in an era when rabbis were seen as towering figures, and may not be patient or comfortable with the consensus models of leadership and decision making many congregations and rabbis have embraced. Elders may have decades of attachment to "the way things have been" liturgically and organizationally. Engaging elders will require addressing and bridging these (generation) gaps.

Present but Invisible

Well elders often comprise a significant proportion of "regulars" at daily and Shabbat worship. They may be valued long-time volunteers in the community. And, like Milt, they may not be perceived as "old." This can be a blessing but also a burden if important aspects of their life experiences are not addressed or acknowledged in congregational life. A retirement community chaplain reports that many of his residents who still worship in their churches say that they are bored by the experience. Nothing in the congregation's worship or program addresses topics important to their lives such as death, chronic illness, and suffering.[7]

Engaging elders will require addressing and bridging these (generation) gaps.

Absent and Invisible

When elders cross the line from well to frail, a transition that can happen over time with the onset of chronic illness, or in a flash with a stroke or hip fracture, they all too often lose connection with the congregational community. Participation may become impossible if they lack mobility, money, or transportation. While members of the congregation may reach out in an acute crisis, that connection too often falls away when the need is chronic. Then these elders may well become absent and invisible.

Segregation

Many congregations offer elders opportunities to be involved through senior adult clubs or groups. Their programs tend to be recreational in nature, featuring trips, secular lectures, and entertainment. They often do not reflect the richness of the spiritual offerings of the congregation's "general" programming.[8] In addition, programming by age group may miss the opportunities and richness of multigenerational community. Perhaps understandably, groups specifically for elders can become stigmatized. Elders who do not find segregated programming appealing, especially those who are relatively young and healthy, vote with their feet and stay away.

A New Paradigm: Transforming the Synagogue into a Community for All Ages

When Moses asks Pharaoh to let his people go, Pharaoh asks him, *Mi va'mi ha-holchim*—just who exactly will be going?[9] Moses responds, *Bizkeneinu uvineareinu nelech*—we will go with our elders and our youth. In other words, Moses asserts that the very essence of our community is inclusion of members across the life cycle. If this was true at the moment of our people's formation, how much more so should this vision be reflected in synagogues, perhaps the central institution of Jewish life today? As Rabbi Morris Allen passionately urges, "We must work to create synagogues where people across the age spectrum actually interact with one another, where young people are cherished and older people are nurtured."[10]

In a tradition that envisions connections *l'dor va-dor*, from generation to generation, active participation of elders alongside younger members can be an indicator of congregational vitality. It is time to abandon involvement of youth as the measure of success. We can now embrace a vision of the synagogue as a truly multigenerational community. The synagogue can and should be a "community for all ages," where young, old, and in-between will benefit from interdependence, reciprocity, inclusion, individual worth, and connectedness.[11]

Congregations as Communities for All Ages

The concept of communities for all ages has been developed at Temple University's Center for Intergenerational Learning. According to Nancy Z. Henkin, "Communities for all ages are those that promote the well-being of children, youth, and older adults, strengthen families, and provide opportunities for ongoing, mutually beneficial interaction among age groups."[12] A community for all ages thus embodies the vision promoted by Moses. It is a context in which care, engagement, and connection are available to members from birth to death. In a congregation for all ages, we will value participation at all ages and stages, as well as connections *across* life stages. We will validate everyone who crosses the threshold, and provide all with opportunities to contribute.

Rabbi Hayim Herring powerfully articulates the synagogue's multigenerational mandate:

> *Synagogues should consciously think of themselves as multi-generational institutions.* People undergo spiritual, emotional, cognitive and physical developmental changes throughout their lives. What suits them at one stage of life will not necessarily appeal to them at another stage, as is apparent in a multigenerational institution like a synagogue. This awareness should be reflected in all aspects of the congregation, including programs, dues structures and the ability of staff to relate to members regardless of age or stage of life.[13]

What Elders Can Contribute to the Multigenerational Congregation

Rabbi Richard Address suggests that elders offer tremendous potential "spiritual capital" to congregations.[14] Elders bring many assets to synagogue life, including accumulated skills, perspective, and available time and energy. Mid- and late-life members can bring many precious resources, highlighted below.

Avid Engagement in Congregational Life

Research by Bethamie Horowitz has revealed that "Jewish identity is not a fixed factor in one's life but rather a matter that parallels personal growth and development.

*E*lders bring many assets to synagogue life, including accumulated skills, perspective, and available time and energy.

There are critical periods and moments in people's lives that offer potential opportunities for Jewish institutions to play a role, if only these institutions can be open and available to individuals in a way that meets their changing needs and concerns."[15]

The vicissitudes and opportunities of later life can prompt a new or renewed openness to spiritual life, as Rabbi Sid Schwarz points out: "The aging process itself brings to consciousness one's own mortality and questions of one's legacy. Suddenly religion has a greater appeal."[16] Many baby boomers or elders who have not been involved earlier in life may find that prayer, study, and communal connection speak profoundly to them now.

Energy and Skills for Volunteering, Both Within and on Behalf of the Congregation

The experience and talents of elders infuse leadership and enthusiasm into service and community building. In a recent survey, 65 percent of Americans fifty to seventy-five surveyed viewed retirement as a time to begin a new chapter by starting new activities and being involved in their communities, rather than as a time to take it easy and take a much deserved rest from work.[17] In other words, elders and boomers are eager to reframe retirement as a time of service and growth.[18]

Sharing Wisdom

Elders can shine light on the path ahead for individuals and the community with insights gleaned from the road behind. Their accumulated perspective can be a boon for the work of organizing the congregation. New challenges can be confronted with guidance from past experience. Younger members can be inspired by the perspective and wisdom elders can offer in shaping a Jewish life, raising a family, building a community, and being a mensch.

Younger members can be inspired by the perspective and wisdom elders can offer in shaping a Jewish life, raising a family, building a community, and being a mensch.

Financial Support

While not all elders have the wherewithal to be philanthropic, many have accumulated wealth that could enrich congregational life, both in the present and, through planned giving, in the future. Too often, this key opportunity is missed, either because no one asked or because the elders have become marginalized or disconnected from the congregation.

Weaving Elders into the Multigenerational Congregation

How can a congregation tap the vast potential assets elders can offer? The vision of the congregation as a community for all ages impels us to focus on *inclusion* and *engagement* across the life cycle. Our ideal is a congregation in which everyone has opportunities for full participation in Jewish life, and in which the gifts and needs of each life stage are addressed.

Evaluating Inclusiveness of the Congregation

Elders want most of all to participate in the life of the congregation. Though some might like opportunities to gather with age peers, *inclusion* and *integration* in congregational programs and services are the priority for most. Ideally, people in every life stage will have opportunities to take part in the dimensions of wholeness outlined in Pirke Avot 1:2—lifelong learning and teaching, worship and ritual, and giving and receiving caring connection. Toward the aim of community for all ages, a congregation might want to conduct an inclusivity audit of its current programming (see Figure 6). This audit would include analysis of opportunities for engagement in Torah, *avodah*, and *g'milut chasadim* for members at every life stage.

The vision of the congregation as a community for all ages impels us to focus on inclusion and engagement across the life cycle.

Where gaps are evident, the audit should examine obstacles to participation (for example, physical inaccessibility or irrelevance of content). Surveying congregants or interviews with samples of various age groups may be helpful in understanding participation and non-participation. These gaps may produce priorities for new initiatives in the congregational program. When new programs are considered, it will be helpful to explicitly consider which age groups are being targeted and what steps will be necessary in order to foster inclusion.

Accessibility

In order to foster inclusion of elders, the congregation must ensure *accessibility*.[19] Among the factors to consider in examining accessibility are:

- Is the facility physically accessible?[20] Are the restrooms and seating accessible to individuals with wheelchairs or walkers?
- Is there a ramp to the *bimah*?
- Is amplification available for those with hearing loss?
- Is the lighting in the sanctuary and on the *bimah* adequate?
- Are large-type *siddurim* and *chumashim* available?

Additional aspects of accessibility include:

- **Welcome.** Is the congregation a "welcoming congregation" for elders?[21] Are older participants in worship or

Congregations for All Ages—Inclusivity Audit

Cohort	Torah: lifelong learning and teaching	*Avodah*: worship and ritual	*G'milut chasadim*: caring connection
Children and teens	Program/s	Program/s	Program/s
	Obstacle/s to participation	Obstacle/s to participation	Obstacle/s to participation
Young adults	Program/s	Program/s	Program/s
	Obstacle/s to participation	Obstacle/s to participation	Obstacle/s to participation
Midlife adults	Program/s	Program/s	Program/s
	Obstacle/s to participation	Obstacle/s to participation	Obstacle/s to participation
Independent elders	Program/s	Program/s	Program/s
	Obstacle/s to participation	Obstacle/s to participation	Obstacle/s to participation
Frail elders	Program/s	Program/s	Program/s
	Obstacle/s to participation	Obstacle/s to participation	Obstacle/s to participation

Figure 6

programs greeted and assisted in getting seated? Are they made to feel their participation in events and celebrations, as well as their ideas, are appreciated?[22]

- **Transportation.** How can members who do not drive get to services and programs? Can the congregation arrange carpools and/or taxi service?
- **Timing.** Are programs held at a time that works for working elders and/or for those who do not go out at night?
- **Money.** Are dues and fees structured so that older members on fixed incomes can be charged discounted dues without embarrassment?

Engagement in Key Dimensions of Wholeness

Here are some guidelines for fostering engagement of elders in Torah, *avodah*, and *g'milut chasadim*. While these suggestions address elders, they aim for a model of inclusion within the context of a multigenerational community.

Torah: Lifelong Learning and Teaching

Many elders have a profound desire to deepen their connection to Jewish learning. Increased free time, as well as the challenges of redefining a person's self in light of new roles and circumstances, may prompt a thirst for Jewish study that is more intense than at other points in life. The new challenges and opportunities of later life may be what Diane Tickton Schuster, an expert on adult Jewish learning, describes as *hineini* ("here I am") moments, "times in their lives, when, like Moses encountering the Burning Bush, they have felt prepared—even compelled—to open themselves to some kind of dialogue with Judaism, God, or their identities as Jews."[23] Even individuals who have not had prior Jewish education may seek opportunities to learn and grow Jewishly in later life.

We need to employ a respectful and effective educational approach in engaging older adult learners.

We need to employ a respectful and effective educational approach in engaging older adult learners. While research suggests that older learners are indeed able to extend their knowledge and continue to grow intellectually, they do it best when teaching touches and exploits what they already know. Successful adult learning programs in the congregation will include key aspects of the approach called andragogy:[24]

- Build from the known to the unknown—welcome (while channeling appropriately) students' sharing of life experience relevant to the topic at hand.
- Allow the learner to be self-directed in the educational process—invite students to articulate and evaluate their own learning objectives.

Tickton Schuster adds to this educational theory the important insight that adults in moments of change and transition may be most open to "study opportunities that are responsive to immediate concerns," such as programs on Jewish mourning practices for midlife individuals facing loss of parents.[25] For elders, opportunities to examine texts and models for encountering suffering, conducting life review, and bestowing your legacy may be particularly apt.

Bringing Torah to elders in the context of the multigenerational synagogue does not necessitate *segregated* educational programming. Older learners can be easily integrated into adult study opportunities within the congregation. The hallmarks of accessibility addressed above can make those learning experiences available to elders. In addition, creating a warm learning environment will enhance comfort and connection among older and other learners. Older learners sharing the class with younger learners are invariably also teachers; their experience and insight enliven the learning for all. Explicitly encouraging intergenerational learning can be a key to fostering a congregation for all ages. One model to consider is intergenerational *hevruta* (study partner) pairings for Torah study,[26] which can organically unite young and old congregants in pursuit of meaning and wisdom. This pairing can be dynamic and inspiring for both.

For frail elders who are not able to attend adult education programs, consider bringing learning to them. For example, a *hevruta* partner could come to an elder's home, or an adult education class could be held by telephone conference call, as is done in the diverse array of courses in Dorot's University Without Walls program.[27] The Internet offers exciting possibilities for study from remote locations; online courses and *hevruta* pairings can bring study and communal connection to those who have computer skills and access.

Avodah: Worship and Liturgy, Continuity and Change

One of the adult learners profiled by Tickton Shuster observed:

"At the [family bar mitzvah] service it hit me full force that what Judaism does is to really *embrace the generations*. There were old people and young people—and what hit me was the comprehensive way in which everyone was *held* by the community."[28]

Elders may find great comfort in the liturgical life of the congregation. The rhythm of daily, Shabbat, and festival observance can infuse their lives with meaning and holiness. The sense of continuity offered by praying with community can be precious amid change and loss; it can also be challenging for a congregation to balance some elders' desire for familiarity with other congregants' wish to innovate. However, it should not be assumed that elders uniformly want things the way they have always been. As James Ellor points out, "Many older adults are actually experts at handling change. Historically, persons who reach an advanced age have successfully survived many changes."[29]

*E*lders want to be warmly welcomed into congregational prayer. They also want to be seen and to have their significant life experiences noted.

Many elders will thus enthusiastically embrace novel spiritual experiences, while others may mourn or reject changes. Finding balance may involve creating moments in the congregation's wor-

ship life that honor continuity and others that foster experimenta-
tion. James Ellor suggests a strategy for engaging elders in the
process of liturgical change. He proposes employing reminiscence
in working to create change.[30] For example, in the synagogue's
undertaking a change of prayer book, congregants might be invited
to gather to share memories of the old prayer book and its meaning
to them. They could be engaged in capturing the memories they
have shared in some symbolic way, such as a document, a photo, or
a display. Memorial dedications might be preserved or transferred
to new books. This involvement of elders and sensitivity to their
concerns can facilitate congregational change:

> By honoring the memories rather than shunning them, the con-
> gregation then can move to the new books without conveying
> the message that the old is no longer wanted or useful.[31]

A spirit of inclusiveness in all worship services will help elders feel
comfortable and valued. Elders want to be warmly welcomed into
congregational prayer. They also want to be seen and to have their
significant life experiences noted. Including elders among lay participants in leading services is inspiring for congregants of all ages. In
addition, the spiritual life of elders and the congregation as a whole
may be enhanced by ritually acknowledging experiences and transitions of later life, such as:

- Retirement
- Re-partnering after widowhood
- Moving from a longtime residence
- Entering assisted living or nursing home
- Becoming a great-/grandparent
- Taking on a new volunteer role or study project
- Celebrating a significant interval of affiliation with the
  congregation

Ritual acknowledgment can take the form of inserting prayers or
blessings into regular services for Shabbat or holidays, or in some
cases, crafting rituals dedicated to the occasion in the individual's

home or the synagogue.[32] See chapter 12 for guidance on constructing a ritual for a moment or passage of later life.

G'milut Chasadim: Giving and Receiving Caring Connection

> "We older people who come regularly to synagogue struggle
> with both issues of *living* and issues of *leaving*. We want the
> synagogue to respond to both."[33]

GETTING SUPPORT

As this statement eloquently expresses, aging brings with it profound challenges, including:

- Redefining yourself outside of previous professional or
  family roles
- Coming to terms with your past—life review, completing
  unfinished business, forgiveness
- Coping with change and limits
- Caring for frail spouses and other relatives
- Losing dear ones
- Encountering illness and mortality
- Contemplating your legacy

The congregation's caring can be a vital source of support in the face
of these vicissitudes. Connection to community can bolster and
strengthen elders. Congregants' and clergy's responsiveness in
moments of need and crisis are invaluable. Elders may not be able to
ask for help, but they will appreciate any effort made toward them.
They may need friendly contact, assistance in participating in congregational activities, help in accessing social service support, or com-
panioning in facing spiritual dilemmas and challenges. Providing
support may be particularly challenging, since many of these needs
can continue chronically over extended periods of time. The congregation may therefore want to explore formal connections, such as
outplacement of a social worker or nurse at their facility.[34]

In accompanying elders spiritually, training and sensitivity are
essential for both clergy and lay volunteers (see chapter 9). Elders
need to know that their rabbi, cantor, or lay companion under-

stands something about what they are facing, and that this companion is open to their questions, doubts, and dilemmas. This is particularly important in "issues of leaving," the fears, hopes, and concerns connected to a person facing his or her own death.

CONTRIBUTING TALENTS

Today's and tomorrow's elders are a precious reservoir of skill and wisdom that can be tapped in service to and on behalf of the congregational community. The congregation's elders are likely well-educated and faced with multiple opportunities for engagement, including work, travel, leisure, family, and volunteering. In order to motivate and mobilize elders as volunteers within, or on behalf of, the congregation, it is essential to understand what elders seek in volunteer opportunities. Volunteer opportunities that appeal to older people feature:

- **Flexibility:** recognizing that older volunteers may travel or live in the community only part of the year
- **Choice:** enabling an individual to engage in a variety of roles and modes of involvement
- **Respect:** utilizing volunteers' experience and involving them in decision making
- **Making a difference:** doing meaningful work that addresses compelling needs
- **Opportunities:** for learning and building skills and relationships

A congregation that hopes to engage older members as volunteers will want to create opportunities that include these aspects. It should work to avoid obstacles to elder volunteerism, such as:

- Lack of transportation
- Disrespect among staff or volunteers
- Ageism-prejudice that minimizes older people's contributions

Ideally, a congregation will inventory older members' skills, talents, and interests in volunteering and use that information to create a

continuum of meaningful volunteer opportunities to serve synagogue and community. One model is Rev. Richard Gentzler's
Talent, Education and Expertise survey for elders within a congregation.[35] To utilize volunteers most effectively, the congregation
should consistently support them through appropriate lay and staff
organizational structures. With effective supervision and com-
pelling roles, older volunteers can not only find meaning, but also bring an infusion of energy and creativity into congregational life.

With attention to inclusion and integration in the full dimensions of Jewish living, congregations can bring meaning, inspiration, and solace to later life.

Final Words

Engaging elders in congregations for all ages requires rethinking our approach to elders and to members of all generations.[36] With attention to inclusion and integration in the full dimensions of Jewish living, congregations can bring meaning, inspiration, and solace to later life. But a
paradigm shift can do more than this, for it will also enrich the fabric
of life for *all* who participate in synagogue life. This multigenerational community will affirm the contribution and value of all, and
will empower and inspire members across the life cycle. The congregation for all ages can realize the vision of Psalm 148:12: "Boys
with girls, youths with elders will [together] praise God's name."

For Further Investigation

Richard F. Address and Andrew L. Rosenkranz. *To Honor and Respect: A
   Program and Resource Guide for Congregations on Sacred Aging.* New York:
   Union for Reform Judaism, 2005.

Terry Bookman and William Kahn. *This House We Build: Lessons for Healthy
   Synagogues and the People Who Dwell There.* Herndon, VA: The Alban
   Institute, 2007.

Steven M. Cohen. *Members and Motives: Who Joins American Synagogues and
   Why.* Los Angeles: S3K Synagogue Studies Institute, Fall 2006.

James W. Ellor. "Elements of Parish Revitalization." In *Aging, Spirituality, and Religion: A Handbook,* vol. 1, Melvin A. Kimble et al., eds., pp. 270–280.

Marc Freedman. *Prime Time: How Baby Boomers Will Revolutionize Retirement and Transform America.* New York: Public Affairs, 1999.

Jill Friedman Fixler, Sandee Eichberg, and Gail Lorenz. *Boomer Volunteer Engagement: Collaborate Today, Thrive Tomorrow,* 2008.

David P. Gallagher. *Senior Adult Ministry in the 21st Century: Step-by-Step Strategies for Reaching People over 50.* Eugene, OR: Wipf & Stock Publishers, 2006.

Richard Gentzler and Donald Clingan. *Aging: God's Challenge to Church and Synagogue.* Nashville: Discipleship Resources, 1996.

Zachary I. Heller, ed., *Re-envisioning the Synagogue.* Hollis, NH: Hollis Publishing, 2005.

Nancy Z. Henkin, April Holmes, Benjamin Walter, Barbara R. Greenberg, and Jan Schwarz. *Communities for All Ages: Planning across Generations.* Baltimore: Annie E. Casey Foundation, 2005.

Hayim Herring. "The Commanding Community and the Sovereign Self: Increasing Understanding between Synagogue Dwellers and Spiritual Seekers" in *Re-envisioning the Synagogue,* Zachary I. Heller, ed., pp. 55–108.

Lawrence A. Hoffman. *Rethinking Synagogues: A New Vocabulary for Congregational Life.* Woodstock, VT: Jewish Lights Publishing, 2006.

Bethamie Horowitz. "Connections and Journeys: Assessing Critical Opportunities for Enhancing Jewish Identity." Report. New York: UJA-Federation, 2000.

Melvin A. Kimble, Susan H. McFadden, James W. Ellor, and James J. Seeber, eds., *Aging, Spirituality, and Religion: A Handbook,* vol. I. Minneapolis: Augsbury Fortress Press, 1999.

Melvin A. Kimble and Susan H. McFadden, eds. *Aging, Spirituality, and Religion: A Handbook,* vol. II. Minneapolis: Augsbury Fortress Press, 2003.

Donald R. Koepke, ed. *Ministering to Older Adults: The Building Blocks.* Binghamton, NY: Haworth Press, 2005.

Nancy Morrow-Howell and Marc Freedman. "Civic Engagement in Later Life." *Generations, the Journal of the American Society on Aging* 30, no. 4 (Winter 2006–2007), pp. 6–10.

Thomas B. Robb. *Growing Up: Pastoral Nurture for the Later Years.* Binghamton, NY: Haworth Press, 1991.

Diane Tickton Schuster. *Jewish Lives, Jewish Learning: Adult Jewish Learning in Theory and Practice.* New York: UAHC Press, 2003.

Sidney Schwarz. *Finding a Spiritual Home: How a New Generation of Jews Can Transform the American Synagogue.* Woodstock, VT: Jewish Lights Publishing, 2003.

Henry Simmons. "A Framework for Ministry for the Last Third of Life." In *Aging, Spirituality, and Religion: A Handbook*, vol. II, Melvin A. Kimble and Susan H. McFadden, eds., pp. 81–98.

———. "Religious Education." In *Aging, Spirituality, and Religion*, vol. II, Marvin A. Kimble and Susan H. McFadden, eds., pp. 218–232.

David A. Teutsch. *Spiritual Community: The Power to Restore Hope, Commitment and Joy.* Woodstock, VT: Jewish Lights Publishing, 2005.

Ron Wolfson. *The Spirituality of Welcoming: How to Transform Your Congregation into a Sacred Community.* Woodstock, VT: Jewish Lights Publishing, 2006.

Resources

Hiddur: The Center for Aging and Judaism of the Reconstructionist Rabbinical College, 1299 Church Rd., Wyncote PA 19095. (215) 576-0800, www.hiddur.org.

Sacred Aging Project, Union for Reform Judaism, 633 Third Ave., New York, NY 10017-6778. (212) 650-4294, www.urj.org/jfc/olderadults.

Center for Spirituality and Aging, 891 S. Walnut St., Anaheim, CA 92802. (714) 239-6267, www.spiritualityandaging.org/.

AFTERWORD

In the Year 2108

In writing this book, I have tried to offer creative conceptions and responses to the experience of growing older as it exists here in the twenty-first-century North American community. I hope that the culture of aging will be transformed in the years to come; that aging will be welcomed, not dreaded; that elders will be included, not isolated; and that elders' lives will be infused with meaning and dignity.

What might the world of Jewish aging look like in one hundred years? Surely life expectancy, so dramatically increased in the previous century, will have surpassed ninety years of age. Four-generation families will be the norm. Fully one-third of the Jewish community will be sixty or older. There will not simply be more years of life, but more goodness in those years. In the year 2108, I imagine that:

- Envisioning and preparing for later life is part of every Jewish child's education, every couple's premarital counseling, and every life-cycle event.
- Ceremonies for transitions of later life are common, including passages such as:
  - Transitioning from previous careers to new volunteering or new careers
  - Moving from a home of longstanding
  - Giving up a driver's license
  - Commencing a new intimate relationship

- Synagogues pride themselves on vibrant engagement of members across the lifespan; old and young study, pray, and volunteer together, and support each other in formal and informal ways.
- Elders with physical or cognitive challenges are accompanied by rabbis and chaplains who support, challenge, and engage them; they participate in Jewish life from their homes, and in programs and buildings that are accessible and hospitable.
- Family members caring for frail elders are acknowledged, assisted, and bolstered by congregations and communal agencies.
- Dynamic service projects employ elders' talents to educate children, help the needy, and enhance the community's success in reaching Jews who are disconnected from Jewish life.
- Old age is eagerly anticipated as a time of creating, growing, and contributing.

How will we realize this vision? In part, the sheer demographic revolution will drive this transformation. The baby boomers will recast and reshape aging, just as we have redefined youth, parenting, and midlife. Beyond the presence of a generation that has felt empowered to change the world and entitled to experience bounty, though, this change will be propelled by fundamental changes in the institutions of Jewish life.

Seminaries will need to incorporate aging training as a core competency in rabbinic education. Jewish educators will be equipped with skill in fostering lifelong learning. Synagogues will have to rethink their priorities and structures away from near exclusive focus on the young and toward maximizing engagement and connection for members of all generations. Jewish institutions and aging-services providers will need to facilitate learning and growing for those they serve, and not just provide for their concrete needs. Initiatives and programs designed to enhance Jewish engagement through study and community service will need to expand their target populations to include Jews in later life.

My Prayer

May we all work to realize these old and new visions of aging. May we both fulfill and experience the promise of the psalmist: "I will satisfy [you] with length of days; and enable [you] to experience My salvation."[1]

NOTES

Introduction: Seasons of Splendor—
New Visions for Jewish Aging

1. The term "age wave" was coined by Ken Dychtwald. See *Age Wave: How the Most Important Trend of Our Time Will Change Your Future*, New York: Bantam Books, 1990.

2. Miriam Rieger, *The American Jewish Elderly*. Report from the 2000–2001 National Jewish Population Study (NJPS). New York: United Jewish Communities, 2004 (www.ujc.org). A study by the Myers-JDC-Brookdale Institute reported by the Jewish Telegraphic Agency on May 17, 2005, found that the proportion of Jews who are elderly is more than twice the average proportion of elderly worldwide.

3. According to 2004 U.S. Census Bureau data, the average life expectancy for sixty-year-old white females is twenty-four years, for white males twenty years. Department of Health and Human Services, National Center for Health Statistics, *National Vital Statistics Reports* 54, no. 19, June 28, 2006 (www.dhhs.gov).

4. According to the 2000–2001 NJPS, fully 33 percent of Jewish elders had household incomes below $25,000.

5. See Marc Freedman, *Encore: Finding Work That Matters in the Second Half of Life*, New York: Public Affairs, 2007.

6. Rieger, *The American Jewish Elderly*.

7. See Chaim Waxman, *Jewish Baby Boomers: A Communal Perspective*, New York: SUNY Press, 2000.

8. N. E. Cutler, N. A. Whitelaw, and B. L. Beattie, *American Perceptions of Aging in the 21st Century*, Washington, DC: National Council on the Aging, 2002.

9. Exodus 20:12 and Leviticus 19:3 are foundational sources for these concepts. See chapter 8 of this volume for further explication.

10. H. R. Moody, paraphrasing M. Scott Peck in a presentation at Association of Jewish Aging Services symposium, May 2007.

11. Translations in this book, except if noted otherwise, are from *Tanakh: The Jewish Bible*, Philadelphia: Jewish Publication Society, 2007, Babylonian Talmud, Soncino edition.

12. Danny Siegel, "The Mitzvah of Bringing Out the Beauty in Our Elders' Faces," in *A Heart of Wisdom: Making the Jewish Journey from Midlife through the Elder Years*, Susan Berrin, ed., Woodstock, VT: Jewish Lights Publishing, 1997, p. 51.

Chapter 1   Crown Me with Wrinkles and Gray Hair: Traditional Views and Visions of Aging

1. Midrash Rabbah—Genesis LXV:9.
2. BT Shabbat 152a.
3. Tanhuma Miketz 10.
4. BT Shabbat 152a.
5. BT Shabbat 152a.
6. Leviticus Rabbah 8:1.
7. BT Shabbat 89b.
8. Midrash Petirat Moshe, Adolph Jellineck, ed., *Bet ha-Midrash*, Jerusalem: Wahrmann Books, 1967, p. 127.
9. BT Ta'anit 23a.
10. Yalkut Shimoni, Parashat Ekev.
11. BT Berakhot 8a.
12. BT Megillah 27b.
13. BT Ta'anit 20b.
14. See chapter 9.
15. Hayye Adam 69:2.
16. Tosefta Megillah 3 [4].
17. BT Kiddushin 33a.
18. BT Berakhot 8b.
19. Hayye Adam 69:3.
20. Exodus Rabbah 3:8.
21. Megillah 31b.
22. BT Berakhot 39a.
23. BT Yevamot 62b.
24. BT Kiddushin 30a.
25. Ecclesiastes Rabbah 2:20, 1–21.
26. BT Ta'anit 23a.

Chapter 2   The Mitzvah Model: Meaning and Mission in Late Life

1. Ronald Blythe, *The View in Winter: Reflections on Old Age*, New York: Harcourt Brace Jovanovich, 1979, p. 122.
2. The concept of mitzvah may be interpreted differently in liberal and traditional communities. Traditional Jews hold that a person learns of his or her

precise obligation through halachah; post-halachic Jews maintain that a person "hears" the commandment in community, or through his or her own autonomous relationship with God. Regardless of which view someone holds, participating in the mitzvot—what Mordecai Kaplan called "sancta"—grants a person a connection to holiness and meaning.

3. Abraham J. Heschel, "To Grow in Wisdom," in *The Insecurity of Freedom*, Philadelphia: Jewish Publication Society, 1966, p. 78.
4. Orah Hayyim 94:6; Mishnah Berurah 100:20.
5. *Shulchan Arukh* Orah Hayyim 94:6 and gloss.
6. Ibid., 100a; and Tur, Orah Hayyim 110a.
7. Mishnah Berurah Orah Hayyim 100:21.
8. Heschel, "To Grow in Wisdom," p. 78.

Chapter 3   Everything I Needed to Know I Learned in the Nursing Home: Torah for Confronting Fragility and Mortality

1. Maimonides, *Mishneh Torah*, Hilchot Talmud Torah 1:8 and 1:10.
2. Rachel Naomi Remen, *Kitchen Table Wisdom*, New York: Riverhead Trade, 2006.
3. BT Menachot 43b.
4. David Spangler, *Blessing: The Art and the Practice*, Riverhead Books, 2001, p. 7.

Chapter 4   Seeking the *Tzelem*: Making Sense of Dementia

1. An earlier version of this material was presented as a plenary address at the 2005 National Association of Jewish Chaplains conference in Philadelphia.
2. As in other chapters, details have been changed to protect the confidentiality of these individuals.
3. Miriam Rieger, *The American Jewish Elderly*, United Jewish Communities Report Series on the National Jewish Population Survey 2000–2001, New York: United Jewish Communities, September 2004. Note that this number is likely an underestimate because the study did not include elders in nursing homes or other institutional settings, which are likely populated with disproportionate numbers.
4. Larry VandeCreek, ed., *Spiritual Care for Persons with Dementia: Fundamentals for Pastoral Practice*, Binghamton, NY: Haworth Press, 1999, p. 79.
5. Diana Friel McGowin, *Living in the Labyrinth: A Personal Journey through the Maze of Alzheimer's*, New York: Delacorte Press, 1993, p. 114.
6. Rita Bresnahan, *Walking One Another Home: Moments of Grace and*

Possibility in the Midst of Alzheimer's, Linguori, MO: Linguori/Triumph, 2008, p. 82.

7. Daily morning service, Shacharit; my translation. See, for example, *Daily Prayer Book*, Philip Birnbaum, trans., New York: Hebrew Publishing Company, 1977, p. 71.

8. Tom Kitwood, *Dementia Reconsidered: The Person Comes First*, Buckingham, England; Philadelphia: Open University Press, 1997. Kitwood developed a list of seventeen depersonalizing tendencies of what he calls "malignant social psychology" in relating to individuals with dementia.

9. I learned this term from the late Maggie Kuhn, founder of the Gray Panthers.

10. David Keck, *Forgetting Whose We Are: Alzheimer's Disease and the Love of God*, Nashville: Abingdon Press, 1996.

11. Kenneth J. Doka, ed., *Disenfranchised Grief: Recognizing Hidden Sorrow*, Lexington, MA: Lexington Books, 1989.

12. These are the two basic aspects of obligations toward parents, according to BT Kiddushin 31b.

13. Bresnahan, *Walking One Another Home*, p. 110.

14. See Deuteronomy 10:19 for one of the many examples in the Torah of this commandment.

15. Exodus 23:9.

16. Betsy Sholl, in *Mother to Daughter, Daughter to Mother, Mothers on Mothering: A Daybook and Reader*, Tillie Olsen, ed., Old Westbury, NY: Feminist Press, 1984, p. 245, cited in Bresnahan, *Walking One Another Back Home*.

17. Kitwood, p. 14.

18. Susan McFadden, Mandy Ingraum, and Carla Baldauf, "Actions, Feelings, and Values: Foundations of Meaning and Personhood in Dementia," in *Viktor Frankl's Contribution to Spirituality and Aging*, Melvin A. Kimble, ed., Binghamton, NY: Haworth Press, 2000, p. 83.

19. Christine Bryden and Elizabeth MacKinlay, "Dementia—A Spiritual Journey Towards the Divine: A Personal View of Dementia," *Journal of Religious Gerontology* 13, no. 3/4 (2002), pp. 69–75.

20. Ibid.

21. Stephen Sapp, "To See Things as God Sees Them: Theological Reflections on Pastoral Care to Persons with Dementia," in *Spiritual Care for Persons with Dementia: Fundamentals for Pastoral Practice*, Larry VandeCreek, ed., Binghamton, NY: Haworth Press, 1999, p. 37.

22. Hershel Matt, "Fading Image of God? Theological Reflections of a Nursing Home Chaplain," *Judaism* 36, no. 1 (Winter, 1987), pp. 75–83.

23. Cited in *Itturei Torah*, Aaron Jacob Greenberg, ed., Tel Aviv: Yavneh, 1985, on Parashat Bereishit.

24. See the prayer *Elohai Neshamah* from the daily Shacharit service (my translation) "The soul that you have implanted within me is pure. You created it, you formed it, and you are destined to take it from me and to return it to me in the time to come [after death]." For the context, see, for example, *Daily Prayer Book*, Philip Birnbaum, trans., New York: Hebrew Publishing Company, 1977, pp. 15–16.

25. Translation mine. For the context, see, for example, *The Metsudah Machzor*, Avrohom Davis, trans., Brooklyn, NY: Metsudah Publications, 1985, p. 317f.

26. Zichronot, translation mine. For the context, see, for example, *The Metsudah Machzor*, p. 320.

27. Interestingly, BT Berachot 10a indicates that the soul "sees and is not seen."

28. Bryden, "Dementia: A Spiritual Journey," p. 69–75.

29. BT Berachot 64a.

30. BT Eruvin 10a.

31. BT Menachot 99a, my translation. I'm grateful to Rabbi Beth Naditch for pointing me to the connections between these texts.

32. Sapp, "To See Things as God Sees Them," p. 37.

33. Bresnahan, *Walking One Another Home*, p. 50.

34. McGowin, *Living in the Labyrinth*, p. 14.

35. Melvin A. Kimble, cited in Susan McFadden, et al., "Actions, Feelings, and Values," p. 83.

36. Bresnahan, *Walking One Another Home*, p. 38.

37. Debbie Everett, "Forget Me Not: The Spiritual Care of People with Alzheimer's Disease" in Larry VandeCreek, ed., *Spiritual Care for Persons with Dementia*, p. 87.

Chapter 5   *Lilmod U'lilamed:* Elders as Learners and Teachers of Torah

1. Translation is mine.

2. See, for example, Lisa Grant, Meredith Woocher, Diane T. Schuster, and Steven M. Cohen, *A Change of Heart: Jewish Text Study at the Florence Melton Adult Mini-School*, a self-study that reports that 30 percent of students in this community-based adult-education program are fifty to fifty-nine years old, and fully 28 percent are over sixty (www.fmams.org.il).

3. For a rich discourse on older adult learning theory and practice, contact the Lifetime Education and Renewal Network (LEARN), a constituent group of the American Society on Aging, 833 Market St., Ste. 511, San Francisco, CA 94103; (800) 537-9728, www.asaging.org.

4. See, for example, Malcolm Knowles, Elwood F. Holton III, and Richard A. Swanson, *The Adult Learner: The Definitive Classic in Adult Education and Human Resource Development*, 6th ed., Amsterdam; Boston: Elsevier, 2005.

5. For a fuller examination of the role of religious education in later life, see Henry Simmons, "Religious Education," in *Aging, Spirituality, and Religion: A Handbook*, vol. I, Melvin A. Kimble, Susan H. McFadden, James J. Seeber, and James W. Ellor, eds., Minneapolis: Augsbury Fortress Press, 1995, pp. 218–232.

6. This idea was suggested to me in conversation more than twenty years ago by Rabbi Kerry Olitzky.

7. Exodus Rabbah 3:8.

Chapter 6   Help with the Hardest Mitzvah: Spiritually Supporting Family Caregivers

1. Tanhuma 'Ekev, 2.

2. The 2000-2001 National Jewish Population Survey reported the lower rates of fertility of Jewish women than their non-Jewish peers over the past generation, as well as significant geographic mobility—35 percent of Jewish adults lived in a different location than five years before, 10 percent in different cities, 10 percent in different states, and 2 percent in a different country.

3. See Elaine M. Brody, "Parent Care as a Normative Family Stress," *The Gerontologist* 25, no. 1 (1985), pp. 19–29.

4. Ibid.

5. This material was developed by me as part of "Training Professionals to Engage Jewish Elders," a project of Hiddur: The Center for Aging and Judaism of the Reconstructionist Rabbinical College. Training team members include Carol P. Hausman, PhD; Rabbi Gary Lavit; Chaplain Sheila Segal; Lynne P. Iser; and myself.

6. See chapter 7 for an explication of some of these sources.

7. See, for example, P. V. Rabins, M. D. Fitting, J. Eastham, and J. Zabora, "Emotional Adaptation over Time in Caregivers for Chronically Ill Elderly People," *Age and Aging* 19 (1990), pp. 185–190.

8. This collection of tools was developed by Chaplain Sheila Segal and Carol P. Hausman, PhD, as part of "Training Professionals to Engage Jewish Elders."

Chapter 7   Beyond Guilt: Perspectives from Tradition on Obligations to Aging Parents

1. Collected in *Yiddish Folktales*, Beatrice Silverman Weinreich, ed., New York: YIVO Institute for Jewish Research, 1988, p. 24.

2. The literal translation of the verse, "A man shall revere his mother and his father," has been rendered here in a more inclusive manner.

3. BT Kiddushin 31b.

4. This term emerged out of the Normalization movement, which sought to transform care for disabled people to give them the benefits of normal living.

Key thinkers included: Wolf Wolfensberger, *The Principle of Normalisation in Human Services*, Toronto: National Institute of Mental Retardation, 1972; B. Nirje, "The Right to Self-determination"; and Robert Perske, "The Dignity of Risk," in W. Wolfensberger, ed., *Normalization*, Toronto: National Institute on Mental Retardation, 1972.

5. See, for example, BT Kiddushin 32a, and compare JT Kiddushin 1:7 and Maimonides' Mishneh Torah Mamrim 6:3.

6. BT Kiddushin 31a–b.

7. Applying such an exemption of women would be greatly at odds with contemporary gender roles, wherein, most commonly, women assume caregiving roles not only for their partners and children but also for their own and their spouses' parents. Nonetheless, this exemption hints at the challenges of juggling multiple caregiving responsibilities for intimate others.

8. Mishneh Torah Ishut 13:14.

9. Ishut 13:15.

10. Maggid Mishnah (citing a responsum of Alfasi) suggests she must prove in a Bet Din that they are causing her suffering and/or damaging her marital bond. She is required to do this, since the husband is presumed to own the house and thus has complete authority to determine who visits. In this reading, the wife's right is only to be free from suffering in the home she shares with her husband.

11. See, for example, BT Kiddushin 31a–32a.

12. Maimonides Mishneh Torah Mamrim 6:10. Ravad disagrees, suggesting that if the child will not care for the parent, no one else will either; Radbaz, however, affirms the Rambam's position, suggesting that there are times when nonrelatives may have an easier time dealing with the elder's behaviors than an adult child, who is emotionally involved.

13. *Sefer Hasidim*, section 343, p. 257.

14. Pirke Avot 1:14.

15. The reference is to Leviticus 19:14, "Do not place a stumbling block before the blind." This term is used to refer to causing another to sin (stumbling in the most consequential sense).

16. Maimonides Mishneh Torah Mamrim 6:8–9. Translation mine.

17. *Shulhan Aruch* 240:18.

18. Pirke Avot 2:21.

Chapter 8   Balancing Parents' and Children's Quality of Life: Ethical Dilemmas in Family Caregiving

1. Kiddushin 31a–b.

2. See the paper by Deena Zimmerman in *Quality of Life in Jewish Bioethics*, Lannum, MD: Lexington Books, 2006, pp. 89–98.

3. See, for example, Carol Gilligan, *In a Different Voice: Psychological Theory and Women's Development*, Cambridge: Harvard University Press, 1982, pp. 28–32.

4. See Nel Noddings, *Caring: A Feminine Approach to Ethics and Moral Education*, Berkeley: University of California Press, 1984.

5. Joan C. Tronto, "Beyond Gender Difference to a Theory of Care," in *Feminism*, vol. II, Susan Moller Okin and Jane Mansbridge, eds., Brookfield, VT: Edward Elgar Publishing Company, 1994, p. 648.

6. Carol Gilligan, "Moral Orientation and Moral Development," in *Women and Moral Theory*, Eva F. Kittay and Diana T. Meyers, eds., Rowman & Littlefield 1987, p. 24, suggests the importance of interdependence and reciprocity in the ethics of care.

7. For a lucid summary of the various positions in the debate between the ethics of care and the ethics of justice, see Suzanne Poirier and Lioness Ayres, *Stories of Family Caregiving*, Indianapolis: Center Nursing Publishing, 2002.

8. A fascinating model for infusing the theological dialogue with the gleanings of care theory is offered by Ruth E. Groenhout, *Theological Echoes in an Ethic of Care*, Notre Dame, IN: Erasmus Institute, 2003. Groenhout investigates elements of the worldview of the ethic of care that are congruent with Jewish and Christian ethics and those that might offer correctives to significant "blind spots." Importantly, Groenhout suggests that the ethics of care's focus on human finitude and interdependence can enrich theological approaches to ethics.

9. See Daniel Gordis. "Wanted—The Ethical in Jewish Bioethics," *Judaism* 38 (1989), p. 29.

10. See David A. Teutsch, "Values-Based Decision Making," *The Reconstructionist* 65, no. 2, pp. 22–28.

11. Although it is beyond the scope of this chapter, it would be worthwhile to investigate filial caregiving in Jewish sources outside of the rabbinic realm, such as folktales and folk songs and modern Yiddish and Hebrew literature.

12. Genesis Rabbah 39:7.

13. The text offers another justification for this abandonment: Terah is wicked and thus was in the category of those who are "called dead even while they are alive."

14. This case was the basis for the panel's discussion when this paper was presented at the 2004 Academic Coalition for Jewish Bioethics conference.

15. BT Kiddushin 31a.

16. Interestingly, once in Eretz Yisrael, when Rav Assi learned that his mother was on her way to him, he asked for advice from his teachers about whether he could leave the holy land of Israel to go to meet her. He did eventually set out toward her, but learned that she had died before he got to her. I have wondered in reading this text if he was actually seeking to meet his mother or escape her. The ambiguity of his situation is tantalizing, and also very believable.

Chapter 9   Enabling Their Faces to Shine: Spiritual Accompaniment with Aging Individuals

1. See chapter 6.
2. See Wendy Lustbader, *Counting on Kindness: An Exploration of Dependency*, New York: Free Press, 1991, for a fascinating examination of the meaning of dependency in a society that prizes independence above almost all else.
3. Robert N. Butler, "The Life Review: An Interpretation of Reminiscence in the Aged," *Psychiatry* 26 (1963), pp. 65–76.
4. Florida Scott-Maxwell, *The Measure of My Days*, New York: Penguin, 1979.
5. For example, homebound elders can participate in a synagogue service via a tele-phone hook-up to the public address system. See Amy L. Sales and Shira Kandel, *Synagogue Hope: Help, Opportunities and Programs for Jewish Elders*, Waltham, MA: Brandeis University, 1998. In addition, some congregations broadcast Shabbat, High Holy Day services, or both over the radio to those who are too ill or frail to attend services. Finally, ill or homebound people can join in study with each other and a teacher using conference-call technology, as has been demon-strated with great success by Dorot in New York City (www.dorotusa.org).
6. For information about appropriate print size and format for individuals with low vision, contact JBI International, 110 E. 30th St., New York, NY 10016; (212) 889-2525, www.jewishbraille.org.
7. A sound system that includes infrared amplification with headsets for individ-uals who are hearing impaired is an option to consider.
8. Maimonides, *Hilchot Talmud Torah* 1:6; translated by Danny Siegel.
9. For an explication of the theory of andragogy, see Malcolm Knowles, *The Modern Practice of Adult Education: From Pedagogy to Andragogy*, Cambridge, MA: Cambridge Book Company, 1988.
10. Polly Young-Eisendrath, *The Resilient Spirit: Transforming Suffering into Insight and Renewal*, Reading, MA: Addison-Wesley, 1997.
11. Maggie Kuhn et al., *No Stone Unturned: The Life and Times of Maggie Kuhn*, New York: Ballantine Books, 1991, pp. 212–213.
12. Abraham Joshua Heschel, *The Sabbath: Its Meaning for Modern Man*, New York: Farrar, Straus & Giroux, 1951.
13. Cited in Kathy Calkins, "Time Perspective, Marking and Styles of Usage," in *Social Problems* 17 (1990), pp. 487–501.
14. Heschel, *The Sabbath*, p. 82.
15. Barbara Myerhoff, "Ritual and Signs of Ripening" in *Age and Anthropological Theory*, D. I. Kertzer and J. Keith, eds., Ithaca, NY: Cornell University Press, 1984. pp. 325, 322.
16. Ibid., p. 306.
17. See chapter 11 for a fuller discussion on this point. Staff, or volunteers with-out extensive Jewish backgrounds, can lead an observance of Shabbat or a

holiday using Sacred Seasons celebration kits, a resource created and distributed by Hiddur: The Center for Aging and Judaism. Kits are available online at www.sacredseasons.org.

18. See chapter 12 for a more detailed examination of the impact of ritual, as well as guidance on constructing rituals for aging. Also see www.ritualwell.org for both examples of creative rites of passage and guidance on creating them.

19. Rabbi Margaret Holub, personal communication.

20. For an explanation of this new Hebrew term for pastoral care, see my introduction to *Jewish Pastoral Care: A Practical Handbook from Traditional and Contemporary Sources*, Dayle A. Friedman, ed., Woodstock, VT: Jewish Lights Publishing, 2005.

21. BT Baba Kama 92b.

22. Viktor Frankl, *Man's Search for Meaning: An Introduction to Logotherapy*, New York: Touchstone Books, 1984, p. 151.

23. See, for example, the exercises in "Healing a Painful Memory," "Giving Yourself the Gift of Forgiveness," and "A Testimonial Dinner for the Severe Teachers," Zalman Schachter-Shalomi and Ronald S. Miller, *From Age-ing to Sage-ing*, New York: Warner Books, 1995, pp. 276–280.

24. See chapter 19 in Friedman, *Jewish Pastoral Care*, "Grief and Bereavement," p. 407.

25. *So That Your Values Live On: Ethical Wills and How to Prepare Them*, Jack Riemer and Nathaniel Stampfer, eds., Woodstock, VT: Jewish Lights Publishing, 1991.

26. Rabbi Richard Address has compiled an excellent manual for older adults to use in preparing for death and dying. *A Time to Prepare: A Practical Guide for Individuals and Families in Determining One's Wishes for Extraordinary Medical Treatment and Financial Arrangements*, New York: Union of American Hebrew Congregations, 2002, contains advance directive forms, background on Jewish values, a format for a person to indicate wishes about his or her funeral, and an ethical will format.

Chapter 10   PaRDeS: Compassionate Spiritual Presence with Elders

1. Charles V. Gerkin, *The Living Human Document: Re-Visioning Pastoral Counseling in a Hermeneutical Mode*, Nashville: Abingdon Press, 1984, p. 40.

2. Rachel Mikva, "Text and the Human Document: Toward a Model for Rabbinical Counseling," *Journal of Reform Judaism*, Summer 1990, pp. 23–33.

3. Charles Taylor, *The Skilled Pastor: Counseling as the Practice of Theology*, Minneapolis: Fortress Press, 1991, pp. 19–20.

4. Gerkin, *The Living Human Document*, pp. 122–124.

5. Viktor Frankl, address to American Society on Aging Conference, Washington, DC, 1988; based on my notes.

6. See Genesis 21:17, where God is described as hearing the voice of Ishmael *ba'asher hu sham*, in all that he faces, exactly where he is. Interestingly, the text actually does not mention that Ishmael has either spoken or cried. This offers us a model of listening and presence that meets the other where he or she is, and which can hear and understand more than he or she is able to say about his or her troubles.

7. Martin Buber, *I and Thou*, New York: Charles Scribner's Sons, 1958, p. 133.

8. Gabriel Fackre, "Ministry of Presence," in Rodney J. Hunter, ed., *Dictionary of Pastoral Care and Counseling*, Nashville: Abingdon Press, 1990, p. 951.

9. BT Hagigah 14b.

10. Ibid.

11. Translation mine.

12. Personal communication.

Chapter 11 Spiritual Challenges and Possibilities for Jews in Long-Term Care Facilities

1. While this chapter specifically addresses the nursing home context, much of it is applicable to assisted-living facilities as well.

2. Charlene A. Harrington, Helen Carrillo, and Courtney LaCava, *Nursing Facilities: Staffing, Residents, and Facility Deficiencies, 1998 through 2005*, San Francisco: University of California, 2006.

3. Erving Goffman, *Asylums*, Garden City, NY: Doubleday, 1966.

4. Athena McClean, *The Person in Dementia: A Study of Nursing Home Care in the U.S.* Peterborough, Ontario: Broadview Press, 2007, p. 33.

5. Gubrium's study of a nursing home, *Living and Dying at Murray Manor*, New York: St. Martin's Press, 1975.

6. Ibid., p. 171.

7. Florida Scott-Maxwell, *The Measure of My Days*, New York: Penguin Books, 1971, p. 41.

8. Kathy Calkins, "Time Perspective, Marking and Styles of Usage," *Social Problems* 17 (1990), pp. 487–501.

9. Gubrium, *Murray Manor*, p. 162.

10. Ibid., p. 164

11. Renee Rose Shield, *Uneasy Endings*, Ithaca, NY: Cornell University Press, 1988, p. 185.

12. Dayle A. Friedman and M. Muncie, "Freeing the Captives of the Clock: Time and Ritual in Long-Term Care." Presented at American Society on Aging Conference, San Francisco, 1990.

13. Marian L. MacDonald, "The Forgotten Americans: A Sociological View of

Aging and Nursing Homes," *American Journal of Community Psychology* 3 (1973), pp. 272–294.

14. Wendy Lustbader, *Counting on Kindness: An Exploration of Dependency*, New York: Free Press, 1993.

15. Morton A. Lieberman, "Institutionalization of the Aged: Effects on Behavior," *Journal of Gerontology* 24 (1969), pp. 330–340.

16. Shield, *Uneasy Endings*, p. 197.

17. Heschel, 1966, 81.

18. Richard Hastings, "Learned Helplessness," *Geriatric Care* 17, no. 17 (1985), pp. 1–2.

19. E. Mason, "Some Correlates of Self-Judgment of the Aged" *Journal of Gerontology* 9 (1954), pp. 324–337.

20. MacDonald, "The Forgotten Americans," p. 281.

21. Shield, *Uneasy Endings*, p. 207.

22. I have not located statistics quantifying the precise numbers of Jewish elders in Jewish and non-Jewish long-term care facilities. My estimate of tens of thousands in non-Jewish settings is based on data from 2000-2001 National Jewish Population Survey. The NJPS counted 956,000 Jews over sixty-five (see Miriam Rieger, *The American Jewish Elderly*, 2004; www.ujc.org). This was by definition an undercount, since the telephone survey included only community-dwelling elders. Using that number, however, if 5 percent of Jewish elders, or an additional 48,000, are in nursing homes, then there are at least 1,013,250 million Jewish elders. If we include elders in continuing care and other retirement communities, the numbers of Jewish elders would certainly be even higher.

    Some communities, such as Providence, Rhode Island, have closed Jewish long-term care facilities. Other smaller communities have never had them. Even communities with exceptional facilities do not have adequate space for all Jewish elders needing long-term care at any given moment.

23. Many American Jews affiliate while they have young children, and fall away from synagogue life when their children grow up. Others drift away when they experience obstacles, such as fixed income or disability, and are reluctant to ask for accommodations. The NJPS data report that 44 percent of Jews over sixty-five belong to a congregation; this statistic is taken from a subset of respondents. The report gives no estimate of affiliation for the "old-old," those over seventy-five or eighty-five, who represent the overwhelming majority of long-term care residents.

24. Harold Koenig, *Aging and God: Spiritual Pathways to Mental Health in Midlife and Later Years*, Binghamton, NY: Haworth Press, 1994; Jeff Levin and Larry Dossey, *God, Faith, and Health: Exploring the Spirituality-Healing Connection*, Hoboken, NJ: John Wiley & Sons, 2002.

25. I am indebted to Susan Rosenthal of the National Center for Jewish Healing for connecting me to her healing center colleagues from across North America, who generously shared their work with me as I researched this chapter. I am grateful to all of the professionals who responded to my queries with descriptions of their community's efforts.
26. David Zucker, "Para-chaplaincy: A Communal Response to the Ill and Suffering," in *Jewish Pastoral Care*, Dayle A. Friedman, ed., Woodstock, VT: Jewish Lights Publishing, 2005, pp. 453–467.
27. In Philadelphia, a grant from the Federation Endowments Corporation supported Hiddur and the Joan Grossman Center for Chaplaincy and Healing of the Jewish Family and Children's Service in mailing hard copies of the kits to 400 local recreation therapists, Jewish chaplains, and parachaplains. Workshops were also offered to recreation therapists and non-Jewish chaplains on how to use the kits to celebrate Passover and Hanukkah in their facilities. Jewish chaplains were trained to train staff in facilities they serve to use the kits.
28. (Moberg, 1980). Hiddur: The Center for Aging and Judaism of the Reconstructionist Rabbinical College offers a specialization in aging for rabbinical students. Its initiative, Embracing Aging, has been funded by the Retirement Research Foundation to develop models for infusing aging throughout seminary training. In addition, Hiddur is developing training for rabbis, chaplains, and other professionals in the field.

Chapter 12   An Anchor amidst Anomie: Ritual and Aging

1. R. Blythe, *The View in Winter: Reflections on Old Age*, New York: Harcourt Brace Jovanovich, 1979, p. 23.
2. Barbara Myerhoff, "We Don't Wrap Herring in a Printed Page," in *Secular Ritual*, Sally Falk Moore and Barbara Myerhoff, eds., Assen, The Netherlands: Van Goraum, 1977, pp. 199–224.
3. Barbara Myerhoff (1992), p. 163.
4. Ibid.
5. Ibid.
6. E. Ramshaw, *Ritual and Pastoral Care*, Philadelphia: Fortress Press, 1987, p. 25.
7. Ibid., p. 31.
8. Ibid.
9. Myerhoff, p. 221.
10. Ibid.
11. Ibid., p. 225.
12. Ibid.
13. Ibid.
14. Arnovan Gennep, *The Rites of Passage*, Chicago: University of Chicago Press, 1960.

15. Myerhoff, "We Don't Wrap Herring."

16. Ronald Grimes, *Deeply into the Bone: Re-inventing Rites of Passage*, Berkeley: University of California Press, 2000, p. 5.

17. Ibid.

18. Myerhoff, p. 225.

19. See, for example, Cary Kozberg, "Let Your Heart Take Courage: A Ceremony for Entering a Nursing Home," in Susan Berrin, ed., *A Heart of Wisdom. Making the Jewish Journey from Midlife through the Elder Years*, Woodstock, VT: Jewish Lights Publishing, 1997, pp. 289–297.

20. Savina J. Teubal, "*Simchat Hochmah*," in Elaine Umansky and Diane Ashton, *Four Centuries of Jewish Women's Spirituality*, Boston: Beacon Press, 1992, pp. 257–264.

21. For more information, see www.timbrelsandtorahs.com. Other examples of rituals for entering old age are: Marcia Cohn Spiegel, "Havdalah: A Time to Acknowledge Growing Old," in Berrin, *A Heart of Wisdom*, pp. 275–278; and Anne Tolbert, "A Personal 'Seder' to Celebrate Aging," in Berrin, pp. 279–88.

22. The following draws heavily on Debra Orenstein, "Afterword: How to Create a Ritual," *Lifecycles: Jewish Women on Life Passages and Personal Milestones*, vol. 1, Woodstock, VT: Jewish Lights Publishing, 1994, pp. 359–376.

23. Myerhoff, "We Don't Wrap Herring."

24. Psalm 90:12.

Chapter 14   Weaving the Generations: Congregations as Communities for All Ages

1. This chapter draws upon *Gearing Up for the Age Wave: A Guide for Synagogues*, by Rabbi Dayle A. Friedman. This is a report from *Aging and the 21st Century Synagogue: A Think Tank on Creating Positive Futures*, jointly sponsored by Sacred Aging Project of the Union for Reform Judaism and Hiddur: The Center for Aging and Judaism of the Reconstructionist Rabbinical College. The report is available at www.hiddur.org and www.urj.org/jfc/olderadults.

2. Synagogue 3000 Cohen, 2006.

3. Henry Simmons, "A Framework for Ministry for the Last Third of Life," in *Aging, Spirituality, and Religion*, vol. I, Melvin A. Kimble, Susan H. McFadden, James W. Ellor, and James J. Seeber, Minneapolis: Augsbury Fortress Press, 2003, p. 85.

4. Ibid., pp. 86–87.

5. Ibid., p. 87.

6. James W. Ellor, "Elements of Parish Revitalization," In *Aging, Spirituality, and Religion: A Handbook*, 1995, p. 271.

7. Donald R. Koepke, *Ministering to Older Adults: The Building Blocks*, Binghamton, NY: Haworth Press, 2005, p. 5.

8. The United Synagogue of Conservative Judaism (USCJ) has created a special network of congregationally based membership groups for Jews fifty-five and above called Hazak, an acronym for *hochmah* (wisdom), *ziknah* (maturity), and *kadimah* (looking ahead).

9. Exodus 10:8.

10. Morris Allen, "The Synagogue of Tomorrow: A Non-prophetic Vision" in *Re-envisioning the Synagogue*, Zachary Heller ed., Hollis, NH: Hollis Publishing, 2005, p. 145.

11. This term was coined by Temple University's Center for Intergenerational Learning, www.temple.edu/cil.

12. Nancy Z., Henkin, April Holmes, Benjamin Walter, Barbara Greenberg, and Jan Schwarz, *Communities for All Ages: Planning across Generations*, Baltimore: Annie E. Casey Foundation, 2005.

13. Hayim Herring, "The Commanding Community and the Sovereign Self: Increasing Understanding between Synagogue Dwellers and Spiritual Seekers" in Zachary I. Heller, *Re-envisioning the Synagogues*, 2005, p. 89. Emphasis mine.

14. Richard F. Address and Andrew L. Rosenkranz, *To Honor and Respect: A Program and Resource Guide for Congregations on Sacred Aging*, New York: URT, 2005, p. ix.

15. Bethamie Horowitz, "Connections and Journeys: Assessing Critical Opportunities for Enhancing Jewish Identity," Raport, New York: USA-Federation, 2000.

16. Sidney Schwarz, *Finding a Spiritual Home: How a New Generation of Jews Can Transform the American Synagogue*, San Francisco: Jossey-Bass, 2000, p. 19.

17. Peter Hart Associates, *The New Face of Retirement: Older Americans, Civic Engagement, and the Longevity Revolution*, Civic Ventures, 1999. www.civicventures.org.

18. See Freedman, *Prime Time: How Baby Boomers Will Revolutionize Retirement and Transform America*, New York: Public Affairs, 2002.

19. Two excellent accessibility inventories are Richard Gentzler and Donald Clingan's Church-Synagogue Accessibility Survey (1996) and Lillian Maltzer's checklist for user-friendly synagogues (Address and Rosenkranz, *To Honor and Respect*, 2005).

20. For an excellent guide to making your congregation accessible, see Elizabeth Patterson and Neal Vogel, *Accessible Faith: A Technical Guide for Accessibility in Houses of Worship*, Retirement Research Foundation, 2003, available at www.rrf.org.

21. Wolfson (2006) offers an excellent introduction to the importance of a wel-

coming culture for all within the synagogue (*The Spirituality of Welcoming: How to Transform Your Congregation into a Sacred Community*, Woodstock, VT: Jewish Lights Publishing, 2006).

22. Terry Bookman and William Kahn, *This House We Build: Lessons for Healthy Synagogues and the People Who Dwell There*, Herndon, VA: The Alban Institute, 2007, pp. 41–43.

23. Diane Tickton Schuster, *Jewish Lives, Jewish Learning: Adult Jewish Learning in Theory and Practice*, New York: UAHC Press, 2003, p. 15.

24. See, for example, Malcolm Knowles and Elwood F. Holton III, *The Adult Learner: The Definitive Classic in Adult Education and Human Resource Development*, 6th ed. Amsterdam; Boston: Elsevier, 2005.

25. Tickton Schuster, *Jewish Lives, Jewish Learning*, p. 37.

26. Beth El Synagogue in Durham, NC, creates intergenerational pairings for congregation-wide Torah study during the Omer period. For information, contact (919) 682-1238, info@betheldurham.org.

27. Contact Dorot for more information: (212) 769-2850, www.dorotusa.org.

28. Tickton Schuster (2003), p. 111.

29. Ellor, "Elements of Parish Revitalization," p. 277.

30. Ibid., p. 278.

31. Ibid.

32. For a rich assortment of creative rituals for life passages, see Ritual Well, an online resource of Kolot: The Center for Women's and Gender Studies, www.ritualwell.org.

33. Dr. Ernest Kahn, private communication.

34. UJA-Federation of New York has pioneered the outplacement of social workers in synagogue settings through its Partners in Caring initiative. For more information, contact UJA-Federation 130 East 59th St., New York, NY 10022; (212) 980-1000, www.ujafedny.org.

35. Richard Gentzler and Donald Clingan, *Aging: God's Challenge to Church and Synagogue*, Nashville: Discipleship Resources, 1996, p. 137.

36. The directions for change outlined in this chapter will no doubt require investment. Capable lay and rabbinic leadership, careful attention to community process, and challenging debates about allocation of congregational resources will all be required to realize this vision. Many of the works cited in "For Further Investigation" can be helpful in guiding congregations in the process of effective transformation.

Afterword

1. Psalm 91:16, translation mine.

GLOSSARY

Amidah. Hebrew for "standing." This prayer is at the center of most Jewish religious services. Also known as the *Shemoneh Esrei* or the *Tefilah*.

bikur cholim. The mitzvah of visiting the sick. Its earliest reference is in a rabbinic commentary on Genesis 18:1, when Abraham circumcised himself at age ninety-nine and God sent three angels to his side to comfort and heal him. It is said that each visit to a sick person takes away one-sixtieth of his or her illness.

bracha. A blessing.

brit milah. Hebrew for "covenant of circumcision," also referred to as a *bris.* The ritual circumcision of a male Jewish child is conducted on the eighth day of his life, or, if previously uncircumcised, on a male convert to Judaism. The ritual traces back to the covenant established with the biblical patriarch Abraham.

Eretz Yisrael. The Land of Israel.

g'milut chasadim. Hebrew for "bestowal of lovingkindness" or "acts of compassion." A major aspect of *g'milut chasadim* was traditionally charity and almsgiving for the poor, but today it refers to a wide range of compassionate activities undertaken for another person.

halachah. Hebrew for "the path that one walks." Halachah is the term used to describe all of Jewish law. It is the complete body of rules and practices that have evolved in Jewish tradition, including 613 biblical commandments, laws later instituted by the Rabbis, as well as folk customs that evolved and eventually became "binding" by the Rabbis.

hevruta. A traditional style of Jewish learning that involves studying in pairs.

High Holy Days. Together, the holidays of Rosh Hashanah and Yom Kippur are commonly referred to as the High Holy Days, or the Days of

Awe. During this ten-day period of reflection, Jews contemplate the beginning of the new year (in the Hebrew calendar), and make atonement for the wrongs they committed in the previous year. Rosh Hashanah means "Head of the Year" in Hebrew, and Yom Kippur means "Day of Atonement."

hineini. Hebrew for "here I am!" The word is often used in Torah as a response to God's call, as in the story of the Binding of Isaac.

Malach haMavet. Hebrew for "Angel of Death."

mensch. Literally, human being; this Yiddish term is used to refer to a good person.

midrash (midrashim). From a Hebrew root meaning "to study," "to seek out," or "to investigate." Midrashim are stories elaborating on incidents in the Bible, which often provide a principle of Jewish law or provide a moral lesson.

Mishnah. The collection of oral laws compiled circa 200 CE by Rabbi Judah Hanasi. It later became the foundational text of the Talmud.

mitzvah (mitzvot). "Commandment" in Hebrew. All of the 613 biblically based commandments are called mitzvot. The term can also refer to any Jewish religious obligation in general, or any good deed a person intentionally does.

neshomeh, neshamah. Soul, or spirit.

Omer. A biblical measure of grain. The Counting of the Omer (*Sefirat Ha'omer*) is a verbal counting of each of the forty-nine days between Passover and Shavuot.

parasha (parashat, parashot). The five books of the Torah have been divided into weekly Torah portions, according to an established calendar adhered to by Jews around the world. Each week beginning on Shabbat, the new weekly parasha (*parashat hashavua*) is read during religious services.

Pesach. Known as Passover in English, Pesach is one of the three biblical pilgrimage festivals, a holiday commemorating the Exodus from Egypt. The holiday also marks the beginning of the harvest season.

pidyon shevuyim. The mitzvah of redeeming the captive.

Pirke Avot. Hebrew for "Ethics/Teachings of the Fathers." This tractate of the Mishnah is devoted to ethical advice from many of the greatest rabbis of the early Talmudic period.

Purim. A Jewish holiday that involves a raucous public recitation of the Book of Esther (known as the Megillah reading) with participants dressed in costumes, wearing masks, and drinking wine. The Book of Esther tells the story of the evil leader Haman's plot to annihilate the Jews of the Persian empire. Other customs of the holiday include giving food and small gifts to friends, giving charity to the poor, and enjoying a celebratory meal.

pushke. A Yiddish word derived from the Polish word *puszka.* A *pushke* is a small can or container kept in the home, often in the kitchen, in which money to be donated to a charity is accumulated. They are sometimes called *tzedakah boxes, tzedakah* being the Hebrew word for justice or righteous behavior.

Rosh Hashanah. See High Holy Days.

Seder (sedarim). Hebrew for "order." Usually refers to the celebratory meal held at Passover, when the Jews recount the story of their enslavement and subsequent Exodus to the land of Israel.

Shabbat. Hebrew for "rest;" also known as the Sabbath or Shabbes. Shabbat is the weekly day of rest, symbolizing the seventh day in the Book of Genesis after six days of creation. It is observed from sundown on Friday until the appearance of three stars in the sky on Saturday night. Traditionally Shabbat is ushered in by the lighting of two candles; the candlelighting times vary by region, depending on when the sun sets.

Shema. A central section of all Jewish prayer services, the Shema is a declaration of the Jewish people's belief in one God.

Siddur. The traditional Jewish prayer book, used for Shabbat and daily services.

Sitz im Leben. In biblical criticism, *Sitz im Leben* is a German phrase roughly translating to "setting in life," and it describes the situations for which biblical passages were written. Examples include classifying material as a letter, poem of lament, parable, psalm, or song. The term also refers to the identity of a passage's speaker, his occupation or audience.

Talmud. Written over several generations, and compiled around 500 CE, the Talmud is a most significant collection of the Jewish oral tradition interpreting the Torah. Similar to an encyclopedia, it consists of sixty-three volumes and is made up of two parts: an earlier text, the Mishnah, and commentary on the Mishnah, known as Gemara.

tchochke. Knickknack. Originally a Yiddish word.

Torah. In its narrowest sense, Torah refers to the first five books of the Bible: Genesis, Exodus, Leviticus, Numbers, and Deuteronomy, also known as the Pentateuch. In its broadest sense, Torah is the entire body of Jewish teachings.

tzedakah. Hebrew for "righteousness." In English, *tzedakah* is usually translated as "charity," although in the Jewish context, it carries a connotation of responsibility and obligation. The giving of *tzedakah* is considered an obligation, something all Jews are required to do, as well as a mitzvah, a good deed.

yahrzeit. Yiddish for "anniversary." A yahrzeit is the anniversary of the death of a close relative or loved one.

Yom Kippur. See High Holy Days.

CREDITS

Chapter 1 is adapted from "Crown Me with Wrinkles and Gray Hair: Traditional Views and Contemporary Implications," in *A Heart of Wisdom: Making the Jewish Journey from Midlife through the Elder Years*, Susan Berrin, ed., Woodstock, VT: Jewish Lights Publishing, 1997, pp. 5–18. Used with permission.

Chapter 2 is adapted with permission from "The Mitzvah Model: Meaning and Mission in Late Life," *Aging Today* 24, no. 1 (Winter 2003), p. 17. American Society on Aging, San Francisco, CA (www.asaging.org).

Chapter 3 originally appeared as "Everything I Need to Know I Learned in the Nursing Home: Torah for Confronting Fragility and Mortality," *The Reconstructionist*, Spring 2004, pp. 70–81. Reprinted with permission.

Chapter 4 is adapted from Dayle A. Friedman, ed., "Seeking the *Tzelem*: Making Sense of Dementia" in *Jewish Pastoral Care: A Practical Handbook from Traditional and Contemporary Sources*, 2nd ed., Woodstock, VT: Jewish Lights Publishing, 2005, pp. 75–92. Used with permission.

Chapter 5 originally appeared as "*Lilmod U'lilamed*: Elders as Learners and Teachers of Torah," *Jewish Education News* 26, no. 3 (Summer 2005), pp. 13-15, published by the Coalition for the Advancement of Jewish Education (www.caje.org). Reprinted with permission.

Chapter 6 includes material adapted with permission from "Eldercare: An Unacknowledged Challenge for the Jewish Family," *Sh'ma: A Journal of Jewish Responsibility*, June 2003, pp. 9–10. (www.sh'ma.com).

Chapter 7 is adapted with permission from "Beyond Guilt: What We Owe Our Aging Parents," in *That You May Live Long: Caring for Our Aging Parents, Caring for Ourselves*, Richard F. Address and Hara E. Person, eds., New York: UAHC Press, 2003, pp. 78–89.

Chapter 8 is adapted with permission from "Balancing Parents' and Children's Quality of Life: Dilemmas in Care Giving," in *Quality of Life in Jewish Bioethics*, Noam J. Zohar, ed., Lannum, MD: Lexington Books, 2006, pp. 78–87.

Chapter 9 is adapted from "Letting Their Faces Shine: Spiritual Accompaniment in Aging," in *Jewish Pastoral Care*, 2nd ed., Dayle A. Friedman, ed., Woodstock, VT: Jewish Lights Publishing, 2005, pp. 344–373. Used with permission.

Chapter 10 is adapted with permission from "PaRDeS: A Model from Jewish Tradition for Compassionate Spiritual Presence with Elders," *Aging & Spirituality* 14, no. 3 (Fall 2002), pp. 4–5. American Society on Aging, San Francisco, CA (www.asaging.org); and from "PaRDeS: A Model for Pastoral Presence," in *Jewish Pastoral Care*, 2nd ed., Dayle A. Friedman, ed., Woodstock, VT: Jewish Lights Publishing, 2005, pp. 42–55.

Chapter 11 is adapted with permission from "Spiritual Challenges of Nursing Home Life," in *Aging, Spirituality, and Religion: A Handbook*, vol. I, Melvin A. Kimble, Susan H. McFadden, James W. Ellor, and James J. Seeber, eds., Minneapolis: Augsbury Fortress Press, 1995, pp. 362–373. Also includes material adapted from "Forsake Them Not: The Jewish Community and Elders in Non-Jewish Long-Term Care Facilities," *Journal of Jewish Communal Service*, Winter 2006, pp. 149–155. Used with the permission of the Jewish Communal Service Association, publishers of the *Journal of Jewish Communal Service* (www2.jesana.org).

Chapter 12 is adapted with permission from "An Anchor amidst Anomie: Ritual and Aging," in *Aging, Spirituality, and Religion: A Handbook*, vol. II, Melvin A. Kimble and Susan H. McFadden, eds., Minneapolis: Augsbury Fortress Press, 2003, pp. 134–144.

Chapter 13 includes material used with permission from "*L'Dor Va-Dor*: Living the Chain of Tradition through Intergenerational Programs," *Compass* 12, no. 12 (Winter 1990), pp. 6–7.

INDEX

233

Bar/Bat Mitzvah

The JGirl's Guide: The Young Jewish Woman's Handbook for Coming of Age
By Penina Adelman, Ali Feldman, and Shulamit Reinharz
This inspirational, interactive guidebook helps pre-teen Jewish girls address the many
issues surrounding coming of age. 6 x 9, 240 pp, Quality PB, 978-1-58023-215-9 **$14.99**
  Also Available: **The JGirl's Teacher's and Parent's Guide**
  8½ x 11, 56 pp, PB, 978-1-58023-225-8 **$8.99**

Bar/Bat Mitzvah Basics: A Practical Family Guide to Coming of Age Together
  Edited by Cantor Helen Leneman 6 x 9, 240 pp, Quality PB, 978-1-58023-151-0 **$18.95**
The Bar/Bat Mitzvah Memory Book, 2nd Edition: An Album for Treasuring the
  Spiritual Celebration *By Rabbi Jeffrey K. Salkin and Nina Salkin*
  8 x 10, 48 pp, Deluxe HC, 2-color text, ribbon marker, 978-1-58023-263-0 **$19.99**
For Kids—Putting God on Your Guest List, 2nd Edition: How to Claim the
  Spiritual Meaning of Your Bar or Bat Mitzvah *By Rabbi Jeffrey K. Salkin*
  6 x 9, 144 pp, Quality PB, 978-1-58023-308-8 **$15.99** *For ages 11–13*

Putting God on the Guest List, 3rd Edition: How to Reclaim the Spiritual
  Meaning of Your Child's Bar or Bat Mitzvah *By Rabbi Jeffrey K. Salkin*
  6 x 9, 224 pp, Quality PB, 978-1-58023-222-7 **$16.99**; HC, 978-1-58023-260-9 **$24.99**
  Also Available: **Putting God on the Guest List Teacher's Guide**
  8½ x 11, 48 pp, PB, 978-1-58023-226-5 **$8.99**
Tough Questions Jews Ask: A Young Adult's Guide to Building a Jewish Life
  By Rabbi Edward Feinstein 6 x 9, 160 pp, Quality PB, 978-1-58023-139-8 **$14.99** *For ages 12 & up*
  Also Available: **Tough Questions Jews Ask Teacher's Guide**
  8½ x 11, 72 pp, PB, 978-1-58023-187-9 **$8.95**

Bible Study/Midrash

**Abraham's Bind & Other Bible Tales of Trickery, Folly, Mercy
and Love** *By Michael J. Caduto*
Re-imagines many biblical characters, retelling their stories.
6 x 9, 224 pp, HC, 978-1-59473-186-0 **$19.99** *(A SkyLight Paths book)*
Ancient Secrets: Using the Stories of the Bible to Improve Our Everyday Lives
By Rabbi Levi Meier, PhD 5½ x 8½, 288 pp, Quality PB, 978-1-58023-064-3 **$16.95**
The Genesis of Leadership: What the Bible Teaches Us about Vision,
Values and Leading Change *By Rabbi Nathan Laufer; Foreword by Senator Joseph I. Lieberman*
Unlike other books on leadership, this one is rooted in the stories of the Bible.
6 x 9, 288 pp, Quality PB, 978-1-58023-352-1 **$18.99**; HC, 978-1-58023-241-8 **$24.99**

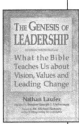

Hineini in Our Lives: Learning How to Respond to Others through 14 Biblical Texts and
  Personal Stories *By Norman J. Cohen* 6 x 9, 240 pp, Quality PB, 978-1-58023-274-6 **$16.99**
Moses and the Journey to Leadership: Timeless Lessons of Effective Management from
  the Bible and Today's Leaders *By Dr. Norman J. Cohen*
  6 x 9, 240 pp, Quality PB, 978-1-58023-351-4 **$18.99**; HC, 978-1-58023-227-2 **$21.99**
Self, Struggle & Change: Family Conflict Stories in Genesis and Their Healing Insights for
  Our Lives *By Norman J. Cohen* 6 x 9, 224 pp, Quality PB, 978-1-879045-66-8 **$18.99**
The Triumph of Eve & Other Subversive Bible Tales *By Matt Biers-Ariel*
  5½ x 8½, 192 pp, Quality PB, 978-1-59473-176-1 **$14.99**; HC, 978-1-59473-040-5 **$19.99**
  (A SkyLight Paths book)
The Wisdom of Judaism: An Introduction to the Values of the Talmud
By Rabbi Dov Peretz Elkins
Explores the essence of Judaism. 6 x 9, 192 pp, Quality PB, 978-1-58023-327-9 **$16.99**
  Also Available: **The Wisdom of Judaism Teacher's Guide**
  8½ x 11, 18 pp, PB, 978-1-58023-350-7 **$8.99**

Or phone, mail or e-mail to: **JEWISH LIGHTS Publishing**
An imprint of Turner Publishing Company
4507 Charlotte Avenue • Suite 100 • Nashville, Tennessee 37209
Tel: (615) 255-2665 • www.jewishlights.com
Prices subject to change.

Congregation Resources

The Art of Public Prayer, 2nd Edition: Not for Clergy Only *By Lawrence A. Hoffman*
6 x 9, 272 pp, Quality PB, 978-1-893361-06-5 **$19.99** *(A SkyLight Paths book)*

Becoming a Congregation of Learners: Learning as a Key to Revitalizing
Congregational Life *By Isa Aron, PhD; Foreword by Rabbi Lawrence A. Hoffman*
6 x 9, 304 pp, Quality PB, 978-1-58023-089-6 **$19.95**

Finding a Spiritual Home: How a New Generation of Jews Can Transform the
American Synagogue *By Rabbi Sidney Schwarz*
6 x 9, 352 pp, Quality PB, 978-1-58023-185-5 **$19.95**

Jewish Pastoral Care, 2nd Edition: A Practical Handbook from Traditional &
Contemporary Sources *Edited by Rabbi Dayle A. Friedman*
6 x 9, 528 pp, HC, 978-1-58023-221-0 **$40.00**

Jewish Spiritual Direction: An Innovative Guide from Traditional and Contemporary
Sources *Edited by Rabbi Howard A. Addison and Barbara Eve Breitman*
6 x 9, 368 pp, HC, 978-1-58023-230-2 **$30.00**

The Self-Renewing Congregation: Organizational Strategies for Revitalizing
Congregational Life *By Isa Aron, PhD; Foreword by Dr. Ron Wolfson*
6 x 9, 304 pp, Quality PB, 978-1-58023-166-4 **$19.95**

Spiritual Community: The Power to Restore Hope, Commitment and Joy
By Rabbi David A. Teutsch, PhD 5½ x 8½, 144 pp, HC, 978-1-58023-270-8 **$19.99**

The Spirituality of Welcoming: How to Transform Your Congregation into a
Sacred Community *By Dr. Ron Wolfson* 6 x 9, 224 pp, Quality PB, 978-1-58023-244-9 **$19.99**

Rethinking Synagogues: A New Vocabulary for Congregational Life
By Rabbi Lawrence A. Hoffman 6 x 9, 240 pp, Quality PB, 978-1-58023-248-7 **$19.99**

Children's Books

What You Will See Inside a Synagogue
By Rabbi Lawrence A. Hoffman and Dr. Ron Wolfson; Full-color photos by Bill Aron
A colorful, fun-to-read introduction that explains the ways and whys of Jewish
worship and religious life. 8½ x 10½, 32 pp, Full-color photos, Quality PB, 978-1-59473-256-0 **$8.99**
For ages 6 & up (A SkyLight Paths book)

The Kids' Fun Book of Jewish Time
By Emily Sper 9 x 7½, 24 pp, Full-color illus., HC, 978-1-58023-311-8 **$16.99**

In God's Hands
By Lawrence Kushner and Gary Schmidt 9 x 12, 32 pp, HC, 978-1-58023-224-1 **$16.99**

Because Nothing Looks Like God
By Lawrence and Karen Kushner
Introduces children to the possibilities of spiritual life.
11 x 8½, 32 pp, Full-color illus., HC, 978-1-58023-092-6 **$17.99** *For ages 4 & up*

Also Available: **Because Nothing Looks Like God Teacher's Guide**
8½ x 11, 22 pp, PB, 978-1-58023-140-4 **$6.95** *For ages 5–8*
     Board Book Companions to *Because Nothing Looks Like God*
5 x 5, 24 pp, Full-color illus., SkyLight Paths Board Books *For ages 0–4*

What Does God Look Like? 978-1-893361-23-2 **$7.99**

How Does God Make Things Happen? 978-1-893361-24-9 **$7.95**

Where Is God? 978-1-893361-17-1 **$7.99**

The Book of Miracles: A Young Person's Guide to Jewish Spiritual Awareness
By Lawrence Kushner. All-new illustrations by the author
6 x 9, 96 pp, 2-color illus., HC, 978-1-879045-78-1 **$16.95** *For ages 9 and up*

In Our Image: God's First Creatures
By Nancy Sohn Swartz 9 x 12, 32 pp, Full-color illus., HC, 978-1-879045-99-6 **$16.95** *For ages 4 & up*

Also Available as a Board Book: **How Did the Animals Help God?**
5 x 5, 24 pp, Board, Full-color illus., 978-1-59473-044-3 **$7.99** *For ages 0–4 (A SkyLight Paths book)*

What Makes Someone a Jew?
By Lauren Seidman
Reflects the changing face of American Judaism.
10 x 8½, 32 pp, Full-color photos, Quality PB Original, 978-1-58023-321-7 **$8.99** *For ages 3–6*

Current Events/History

A Dream of Zion: American Jews Reflect on Why Israel Matters to Them
Edited by Rabbi Jeffrey K. Salkin Explores what Jewish people in America have to say about Israel. 6 x 9, 304 pp, HC, 978-1-58023-340-8 **$24.99**
  Also Available: **A Dream of Zion Teacher's Guide** 8½ x 11, 18 pp, PB, 978-1-58023-356-9 **$8.99**

The Jewish Connection to Israel, the Promised Land: A Brief Introduction for Christians *By Rabbi Eugene Korn, PhD* 5½ x 8½, 192 pp, Quality PB, 978-1-58023-318-7 **$14.99**

The Story of the Jews: A 4,000-Year Adventure—A Graphic History Book
  Written & illustrated by Stan Mack 6 x 9, 288 pp, illus., Quality PB, 978-1-58023-155-8 **$16.99**

Hannah Senesh: Her Life and Diary, the First Complete Edition
  By Hannah Senesh; Foreword by Marge Piercy; Preface by Eitan Senesh
  6 x 9, 368 pp, Quality PB, 978-1-58023-342-2 **$19.99**; 352 pp, HC, 978-1-58023-212-8 **$24.99**

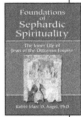

The Ethiopian Jews of Israel: Personal Stories of Life in the Promised Land *By Len Lyons, PhD; Foreword by Alan Dershowitz; Photographs by Ilan Ossendryver*
Recounts, through photographs and words, stories of Ethiopian Jews.
10½ x 10, 240 pp, 100 full-color photos, HC, 978-1-58023-323-1 **$34.99**

Foundations of Sephardic Spirituality: The Inner Life of Jews of the Ottoman Empire
  By Rabbi Marc D. Angel, PhD 6 x 9, 224 pp, HC, 978-1-58023-243-2 **$24.99**

Judaism and Justice: The Jewish Passion to Repair the World
  By Rabbi Sidney Schwarz 6 x 9, 352 pp, Quality PB, 978-1-58023-353-8 **$19.99**

Ecology/Environment

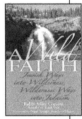

A Wild Faith: Jewish Ways into Wilderness, Wilderness Ways into Judaism
By Rabbi Mike Comins; Foreword by Nigel Savage
Offers ways to enliven and deepen your spiritual life through wilderness experience.
6 x 9, 240 pp, Quality PB, 978-1-58023-316-3 **$16.99**

Ecology & the Jewish Spirit: Where Nature & the Sacred Meet
  Edited by Ellen Bernstein 6 x 9, 288 pp, Quality PB, 978-1-58023-082-7 **$18.99**

Torah of the Earth: Exploring 4,000 Years of Ecology in Jewish Thought
  Vol. 1: Biblical Israel: One Land, One People; Rabbinic Judaism: One People, Many Lands
  Vol. 2: Zionism: One Land, Two Peoples; Eco-Judaism: One Earth, Many Peoples
  Edited by Arthur Waskow Vol. 1: 6 x 9, 272 pp, Quality PB, 978-1-58023-086-5 **$19.95**
  Vol. 2: 6 x 9, 336 pp, Quality PB, 978-1-58023-087-2 **$19.95**

The Way Into Judaism and the Environment
  By Jeremy Benstein 6 x 9, 224 pp, HC, 978-1-58023-268-5 **$24.99**

Grief/Healing

Healing and the Jewish Imagination: Spiritual and Practical Perspectives on Judaism and Health *Edited by Rabbi William Cutter, PhD*
Explores Judaism for comfort in times of illness and perspectives on suffering.
6 x 9, 240 pp, HC, 978-1-58023-314-9 **$24.99**

Grief in Our Seasons: A Mourner's Kaddish Companion *By Rabbi Kerry M. Olitzky*
4½ x 6½, 448 pp, Quality PB, 978-1-879045-55-2 **$15.95**

Healing of Soul, Healing of Body: Spiritual Leaders Unfold the Strength & Solace in Psalms *Edited by Rabbi Simkha Y. Weintraub, CSW*
6 x 9, 128 pp, 2-color illus. text, Quality PB, 978-1-879045-31-6 **$14.99**

Mourning & Mitzvah, 2nd Edition: A Guided Journal for Walking the Mourner's Path through Grief to Healing *By Anne Brener, LCSW*
7½ x 9, 304 pp, Quality PB, 978-1-58023-113-8 **$19.99**

Tears of Sorrow, Seeds of Hope, 2nd Edition: A Jewish Spiritual Companion for Infertility and Pregnancy Loss *By Rabbi Nina Beth Cardin*
6 x 9, 208 pp, Quality PB, 978-1-58023-233-3 **$18.99**

A Time to Mourn, a Time to Comfort, 2nd Edition: A Guide to Jewish Bereavement *By Dr. Ron Wolfson*
7 x 9, 384 pp, Quality PB, 978-1-58023-253-1 **$19.99**

When a Grandparent Dies: A Kid's Own Remembering Workbook for Dealing with Shiva and the Year Beyond *By Nechama Liss-Levinson, PhD*
8 x 10, 48 pp, 2-color text, HC, 978-1-879045-44-6 **$15.95** *For ages 7–13*

Inspiration

Happiness and the Human Spirit: The Spirituality of Becoming the Best You Can Be *By Abraham J. Twerski, MD*
Shows you that true happiness is attainable once you stop looking outside yourself for the source.   6 x 9, 176 pp, HC, 978-1-58023-343-9 **$19.99**

The Bridge to Forgiveness: Stories and Prayers for Finding God and Restoring Wholeness *By Rabbi Karyn D. Kedar*
Examines how forgiveness can be the bridge that connects us to wholeness and peace.
6 x 9, 176 pp, HC, 978-1-58023-324-8 **$19.99**

God's To-Do List: 103 Ways to Be an Angel and Do God's Work on Earth
By Dr. Ron Wolfson 6 x 9, 150 pp, Quality PB, 978-1-58023-301-9 **$16.99**

God in All Moments: Mystical & Practical Spiritual Wisdom from Hasidic Masters
Edited and translated by Or N. Rose with Ebn D. Leader
5½ x 8½, 192 pp, Quality PB, 978-1-58023-186-2 **$16.95**

Our Dance with God: Finding Prayer, Perspective and Meaning in the Stories of Our Lives *By Karyn D. Kedar* 6 x 9, 176 pp, Quality PB, 978-1-58023-202-9 **$16.99**
Also Available: **The Dance of the Dolphin** (HC edition of *Our Dance with God*)
6 x 9, 176 pp, HC, 978-1-58023-154-1 **$19.95**

The Empty Chair: Finding Hope and Joy—Timeless Wisdom from a Hasidic Master, Rebbe Nachman of Breslov *Adapted by Moshe Mykoff and the Breslov Research Institute*
4 x 6, 128 pp, 2-color text, Deluxe PB w/flaps, 978-1-879045-67-5 **$9.99**

The Gentle Weapon: Prayers for Everyday and Not-So-Everyday Moments—Timeless Wisdom from the Teachings of the Hasidic Master, Rebbe Nachman of Breslov
Adapted by Moshe Mykoff and S. C. Mizrahi, together with the Breslov Research Institute
4 x 6, 144 pp, 2-color text, Deluxe PB w/flaps, 978-1-58023-022-3 **$9.99**

God Whispers: Stories of the Soul, Lessons of the Heart *By Karyn D. Kedar*
6 x 9, 176 pp, Quality PB, 978-1-58023-088-9 **$15.95**

Restful Reflections: Nighttime Inspiration to Calm the Soul, Based on Jewish Wisdom
By Rabbi Kerry M. Olitzky & Rabbi Lori Forman 4½ x 6½, 448 pp, Quality PB, 978-1-58023-091-9 **$15.95**

Sacred Intentions: Daily Inspiration to Strengthen the Spirit, Based on Jewish Wisdom
By Rabbi Kerry M. Olitzky and Rabbi Lori Forman 4½ x 6½, 448 pp, Quality PB, 978-1-58023-061-2 **$15.95**

Kabbalah/Mysticism/Enneagram

Awakening to Kabbalah: The Guiding Light of Spiritual Fulfillment
By Rav Michael Laitman, PhD 6 x 9, 192 pp, HC, 978-1-58023-264-7 **$21.99**

Seek My Face: A Jewish Mystical Theology *By Arthur Green*
6 x 9, 304 pp, Quality PB, 978-1-58023-130-5 **$19.95**

Zohar: Annotated & Explained
Translation and annotation by Daniel C. Matt; Foreword by Andrew Harvey
5½ x 8½, 176 pp, Quality PB, 978-1-893361-51-5 **$15.99** (*A SkyLight Paths book*)

Ehyeh: A Kabbalah for Tomorrow
By Arthur Green 6 x 9, 224 pp, Quality PB, 978-1-58023-213-5 **$16.99**

The Flame of the Heart: Prayers of a Chasidic Mystic *By Reb Noson of Breslov. Translated by David Sears with the Breslov Research Institute* 5 x 7¼, 160 pp, Quality PB, 978-1-58023-246-3 **$15.99**

The Gift of Kabbalah: Discovering the Secrets of Heaven, Renewing Your Life on Earth
By Tamar Frankiel, PhD 6 x 9, 256 pp, Quality PB, 978-1-58023-141-1 **$16.95;**
HC, 978-1-58023-108-4 **$21.95**

Kabbalah: A Brief Introduction for Christians
By Tamar Frankiel, PhD 5½ x 8½, 208 pp, Quality PB, 978-1-58023-303-3 **$16.99**

The Lost Princess and Other Kabbalistic Tales of Rebbe Nachman of Breslov
The Seven Beggars and Other Kabbalistic Tales of Rebbe Nachman of Breslov
Translated by Rabbi Aryeh Kaplan; Preface by Rabbi Chaim Kramer
Lost Princess: 6 x 9, 400 pp, Quality PB, 978-1-58023-217-3 **$18.99**
Seven Beggars: 6 x 9, 192 pp, Quality PB, 978-1-58023-250-0 **$16.99**

See also *The Way Into Jewish Mystical Tradition* in Spirituality / The Way Into... Series

Life Cycle
Marriage / Parenting / Family / Aging

The New Jewish Baby Album: Creating and Celebrating the Beginning of a Spiritual Life—A Jewish Lights Companion
By the Editors at Jewish Lights. Foreword by Anita Diamant. Preface by Rabbi Sandy Eisenberg Sasso.
A spiritual keepsake that will be treasured for generations. More than just a memory book, *shows you how—and why it's important*—to create a Jewish home and a Jewish life. 8 x 10, 64 pp, Deluxe Padded HC, Full-color illus., 978-1-58023-138-1 **$19.95**

The Jewish Pregnancy Book: A Resource for the Soul, Body & Mind during Pregnancy, Birth & the First Three Months
By Sandy Falk, MD, and Rabbi Daniel Judson, with Steven A. Rapp
Includes medical information, prayers and rituals for each stage of pregnancy, from a liberal Jewish perspective. 7 x 10, 208 pp, Quality PB, b/w photos, 978-1-58023-178-7 **$16.95**

Celebrating Your New Jewish Daughter: Creating Jewish Ways to Welcome Baby Girls into the Covenant—New and Traditional Ceremonies *By Debra Nussbaum Cohen; Foreword by Rabbi Sandy Eisenberg Sasso* 6 x 9, 272 pp, Quality PB, 978-1-58023-090-2 **$18.95**

The New Jewish Baby Book, 2nd Edition: Names, Ceremonies & Customs—A Guide for Today's Families *By Anita Diamant* 6 x 9, 336 pp, Quality PB, 978-1-58023-251-7 **$19.99**

Parenting as a Spiritual Journey: Deepening Ordinary and Extraordinary Events into Sacred Occasions *By Rabbi Nancy Fuchs-Kreimer*
6 x 9, 224 pp, Quality PB, 978-1-58023-016-2 **$16.95**

Parenting Jewish Teens: A Guide for the Perplexed
By Joanne Doades
Explores the questions and issues that shape the world in which today's Jewish teenagers live.
6 x 9, 200 pp, Quality PB, 978-1-58023-305-7 **$16.99**

Judaism for Two: A Spiritual Guide for Strengthening and Celebrating Your Loving Relationship *By Rabbi Nancy Fuchs-Kreimer and Rabbi Nancy H. Wiener; Foreword by Rabbi Elliot N. Dorff* Addresses the ways Jewish teachings can enhance and strengthen committed relationships. 6 x 9, 224 pp, Quality PB, 978-1-58023-254-8 **$16.99**

Embracing the Covenant: Converts to Judaism Talk About Why & How
By Rabbi Allan Berkowitz and Patti Moskovitz 6 x 9, 192 pp, Quality PB, 978-1-879045-50-7 **$16.95**

The Guide to Jewish Interfaith Family Life: An InterfaithFamily.com Handbook
Edited by Ronnie Friedland and Edmund Case 6 x 9, 384 pp, Quality PB, 978-1-58023-153-4 **$18.95**

Introducing My Faith and My Community
The Jewish Outreach Institute Guide for the Christian in a Jewish Interfaith Relationship
By Rabbi Kerry M. Olitzky 6 x 9, 176 pp, Quality PB, 978-1-58023-192-3 **$16.99**

Making a Successful Jewish Interfaith Marriage: The Jewish Outreach Institute Guide to Opportunities, Challenges and Resources *By Rabbi Kerry M. Olitzky with Joan Peterson Littman*
6 x 9, 176 pp, Quality PB, 978-1-58023-170-1 **$16.95**

The Creative Jewish Wedding Book: A Hands-On Guide to New & Old Traditions, Ceremonies & Celebrations *By Gabrielle Kaplan-Mayer*
9 x 9, 288 pp, b/w photos, Quality PB, 978-1-58023-194-7 **$19.99**

Divorce Is a Mitzvah: A Practical Guide to Finding Wholeness and Holiness When Your Marriage Dies *By Rabbi Perry Netter; Afterword by Rabbi Laura Geller.*
6 x 9, 224 pp, Quality PB, 978-1-58023-172-5 **$16.95**

A Heart of Wisdom: Making the Jewish Journey from Midlife through the Elder Years
Edited by Susan Berrin; Foreword by Harold Kushner
6 x 9, 384 pp, Quality PB, 978-1-58023-051-3 **$18.95**

So That Your Values Live On: Ethical Wills and How to Prepare Them
Edited by Jack Riemer and Nathaniel Stampfer
6 x 9, 272 pp, Quality PB, 978-1-879045-34-7 **$18.99**

Holidays/Holy Days

Rosh Hashanah Readings: Inspiration, Information and Contemplation
Yom Kippur Readings: Inspiration, Information and Contemplation
Edited by Rabbi Dov Peretz Elkins with Section Introductions from Arthur Green's These Are the Words

An extraordinary collection of readings, prayers and insights that enable the modern worshiper to enter into the spirit of the High Holy Days in a personal and powerful way, permitting the meaning of the Jewish New Year to enter the heart.
RHR: 6 x 9, 400 pp, HC, 978-1-58023-239-5 **$24.99**
YKR: 6 x 9, 368 pp, HC, 978-1-58023-271-5 **$24.99**

Jewish Holidays: A Brief Introduction for Christians
By Rabbi Kerry M. Olitzky and Rabbi Daniel Judson
5½ x 8½, 144 pp, Quality PB, 978-1-58023-302-6 **$16.99**

Reclaiming Judaism as a Spiritual Practice: Holy Days and Shabbat
By Rabbi Goldie Milgram
7 x 9, 272 pp, Quality PB, 978-1-58023-205-0 **$19.99**

7th Heaven: Celebrating Shabbat with Rebbe Nachman of Breslov
By Moshe Mykoff with the Breslov Research Institute
5⅛ x 8¼, 224 pp, Deluxe PB w/flaps, 978-1-58023-175-6 **$18.95**

Shabbat, 2nd Edition: The Family Guide to Preparing for and Celebrating the Sabbath
By Dr. Ron Wolfson 7 x 9, 320 pp, illus., Quality PB, 978-1-58023-164-0 **$19.99**

Hanukkah, 2nd Edition: The Family Guide to Spiritual Celebration
By Dr. Ron Wolfson. Edited by Joel Lurie Grishaver.
7 x 9, 240 pp, illus., Quality PB, 978-1-58023-122-0 **$18.95**

The Jewish Family Fun Book, 2nd Edition: Holiday Projects, Everyday Activities, and Travel Ideas with Jewish Themes *By Danielle Dardashti and Roni Sarig. Illus. by Avi Katz.*
6 x 9, 304 pp, 70+ b/w illus. & diagrams, Quality PB, 978-1-58023-333-0 **$18.99**

The Jewish Lights Book of Fun Classroom Activities: Simple and Seasonal Projects for Teachers and Students *By Danielle Dardashti and Roni Sarig*
6 x 9, 240 pp, Quality PB, 978-1-58023-206-7 **$19.99**

Passover

My People's Passover Haggadah
Traditional Texts, Modern Commentaries
Edited by Rabbi Lawrence A. Hoffman, PhD, and David Arnow, PhD
A diverse and exciting collection of commentaries on the traditional Passover Haggadah—in two volumes!
Vol. 1: 7 x 10, 304 pp, HC, 978-1-58023-354-5 **$24.99**
Vol. 2: 7 x 10, 320 pp, HC, 978-1-58023-346-0 **$24.99**

Leading the Passover Journey
The Seder's Meaning Revealed, the Haggadah's Story Retold
By Rabbi Nathan Laufer
Uncovers the hidden meaning of the Seder's rituals and customs.
6 x 9, 224 pp, HC, 978-1-58023-211-1 **$24.99**

The Women's Passover Companion: Women's Reflections on the Festival of Freedom
Edited by Rabbi Sharon Cohen Anisfeld, Tara Mohr, and Catherine Spector
6 x 9, 352 pp, Quality PB, 978-1-58023-231-9 **$19.99**

The Women's Seder Sourcebook: Rituals & Readings for Use at the Passover Seder
Edited by Rabbi Sharon Cohen Anisfeld, Tara Mohr, and Catherine Spector
6 x 9, 384 pp, Quality PB, 978-1-58023-232-6 **$19.99**

Creating Lively Passover Seders: A Sourcebook of Engaging Tales, Texts & Activities
By David Arnow, PhD 7 x 9, 416 pp, Quality PB, 978-1-58023-184-8 **$24.99**

Passover, 2nd Edition: The Family Guide to Spiritual Celebration
By Dr. Ron Wolfson with Joel Lurie Grishaver 7 x 9, 352 pp, Quality PB, 978-1-58023-174-9 **$19.95**

Theology/Philosophy

A Touch of the Sacred: A Theologian's Informal Guide to Jewish Belief
By Dr. Eugene B. Borowitz and Frances W. Schwartz Explores the musings from the
leading theologian of liberal Judaism. 6 x 9, 256 pp, HC, 978-1-58023-337-8 **$21.99**

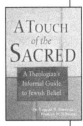

Talking about God: Exploring the Meaning of Religious Life with
Kierkegaard, Buber, Tillich and Heschel *By Daniel F. Polish, PhD*
Examines the meaning of the human religious experience with the greatest theolo-
gians of modern times. 6 x 9, 160 pp, HC, 978-1-59473-230-0 **$21.99** *(A SkyLight Paths book)*

Jews & Judaism in the 21st Century: Human Responsibility, the
Presence of God, and the Future of the Covenant
Edited by Rabbi Edward Feinstein; Foreword by Paula E. Hyman
Five celebrated leaders in Judaism examine contemporary Jewish life.
6 x 9, 192 pp, HC, 978-1-58023-315-6 **$24.99**

Christians and Jews in Dialogue: Learning in the Presence of the Other
By Mary C. Boys and Sara S. Lee; Foreword by Dr. Dorothy Bass
6 x 9, 240 pp, HC, 978-1-59473-144-0 **$21.99** *(A SkyLight Paths book)*

The Death of Death: Resurrection and Immortality in Jewish Thought
By Neil Gillman 6 x 9, 336 pp, Quality PB, 978-1-58023-081-0 **$18.95**

Ethics of the Sages: Pirke Avot—Annotated & Explained
Translation & Annotation by Rabbi Rami Shapiro
5½ x 8½, 208 pp, Quality PB, 978-1-59473-207-2 **$16.99** *(A SkyLight Paths book)*

Hasidic Tales: Annotated & Explained
By Rabbi Rami Shapiro; Foreword by Andrew Harvey
5½ x 8½, 240 pp, Quality PB, 978-1-893361-86-7 **$16.95** *(A SkyLight Paths Book)*

A Heart of Many Rooms: Celebrating the Many Voices within Judaism
By David Hartman 6 x 9, 352 pp, Quality PB, 978-1-58023-156-5 **$19.95**

The Hebrew Prophets: Selections Annotated & Explained
Translation & Annotation by Rabbi Rami Shapiro; Foreword by Zalman M. Schachter-Shalomi
5½ x 8½, 224 pp, Quality PB, 978-1-59473-037-5 **$16.99** *(A SkyLight Paths book)*

A Jewish Understanding of the New Testament
By Rabbi Samuel Sandmel; Preface by Rabbi David Sandmel
5½ x 8½, 368 pp, Quality PB, 978-1-59473-048-1 **$19.99** *(A SkyLight Paths book)*

Keeping Faith with the Psalms: Deepen Your Relationship with God Using the Book
of Psalms *By Daniel F. Polish* 6 x 9, 320 pp, Quality PB, 978-1-58023-300-2 **$18.99**

A Living Covenant: The Innovative Spirit in Traditional Judaism
By David Hartman 6 x 9, 368 pp, Quality PB, 978-1-58023-011-7 **$20.00**

Love and Terror in the God Encounter
The Theological Legacy of Rabbi Joseph B. Soloveitchik
By David Hartman 6 x 9, 240 pp, Quality PB, 978-1-58023-176-3 **$19.95**

The Personhood of God: Biblical Theology, Human Faith and the Divine Image
By Dr. Yochanan Muffs; Foreword by Dr. David Hartman 6 x 9, 240 pp, HC, 978-1-58023-265-4 **$24.99**

Traces of God: Seeing God in Torah, History and Everyday Life
By Neil Gillman 6 x 9, 240 pp, HC, 978-1-58023-249-4 **$21.99**

We Jews and Jesus: Exploring Theological Differences for Mutual Understanding
By Rabbi Samuel Sandmel; Preface by Rabbi David Sandmel
6 x 9, 176 pp, Quality PB, 978-1-59473-208-9 **$16.99** *(A SkyLight Paths book)*

Your Word Is Fire: The Hasidic Masters on Contemplative Prayer
Edited and translated by Arthur Green and Barry W. Holtz
6 x 9, 160 pp, Quality PB, 978-1-879045-25-5 **$15.95**

I Am Jewish
Personal Reflections Inspired by the Last Words of Daniel Pearl
Almost 150 Jews—both famous and not—from all walks of life, from all around
the world, write about many aspects of their Judaism.
Edited by Judea and Ruth Pearl
6 x 9, 304 pp, Deluxe PB w/flaps, 978-1-58023-259-3 **$18.99**
Download a free copy of the *I Am Jewish Teacher's Guide* at our website:
www.jewishlights.com

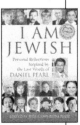

Pastoral Care Resources

LifeLights/™אורות החיים

LifeLights/™אורות החיים are inspirational, information-al booklets about challenges to our emotional and spiritual lives and how to deal with them. Offering help for wholeness and healing, each *LifeLight* is written from a uniquely Jewish spiritual perspective by a wise and caring soul—someone who knows the inner territory of grief, doubt, confusion and longing.

In addition to providing wise words to light a difficult path, each *LifeLight* booklet provides suggestions for additional resources for reading. Many list organizations, Jewish and secular, that can provide help, along with information on how to contact them.

> "Invaluable for those needing comfort and
> instruction in times of difficulty and loss."
> **Rabbi David Wolpe**, Sinai Temple, Los Angeles, CA

> "Particularly useful for hospital visits and shiva calls—and
> they enable me to help at those times when I feel helpless."
> **Rabbi Sally Priesand**, Monmouth Reform Temple,
> Tinton Falls, NJ

Categories/Topics:

Health & Healing

Abortion and Judaism: Rabbinic Opinion and Jewish Law
Caring for Your Aging Parents
Caring for Yourself/When Someone Is Ill
Facing and Recovering from Surgery
Facing Cancer as a Family
Finding Spiritual Strength in Pain or Illness
Jewish Response to Dementia: Honoring Broken Tablets
Living with Cancer, One Day at a Time
Recognizing a Loved One's Addiction, and Providing Help
When Madness Comes Home: Living in the Shadow of a Loved One's Mental Illness

Loss / Grief / Death & Dying

Coping with the Death of a Spouse
From Death through Shiva: A Guide to Jewish Grieving Practices
Jewish Hospice: To Live, to Hope, to Heal
Making Sacred Choices at the End of Life
Mourning a Miscarriage
Taking the Time You Need to Mourn Your Loss
Talking to Children about Death
When Someone You Love Is Dying
When Someone You Love Needs Long-Term Care

Categories/Topics continued:

Judaism / Living a Jewish Life

Bar and Bat Mitzvah's Meaning: Preparing Spiritually with Your Child

Choosing a Congregation That Is Right for You

Considering Judaism: Choosing a Faith, Joining a People

Do Jews Believe in the Soul's Survival?

Exploring Judaism as an Adult

Jewish Meditation: How to Begin Your Practice

There's a Place for Us: Gays and Lesbians in the Jewish Community

To Meet Your Soul Mate, You Must Meet Your Soul

Yearning for God

Family Issues

Jewish Adoption: Unique Issues, Practical Solutions

Are You Being Hurt by Someone You Love? Domestic Abuse in the Jewish Community

Grandparenting Interfaith Grandchildren

Healing Estrangement in Your Family Relationships

Interfaith Families Making Jewish Choices

Jewish Approaches to Parenting Teens

Looking Back on Divorce and Letting Go

Parenting through a Divorce

Raising a Child with Special Needs

Talking to Your Children about God

Spiritual Care / Personal Growth

Bringing Your Sadness to God

Doing Teshuvah: Undoing Mistakes, Repairing Relationships and Finding Inner Peace

Easing the Burden of Stress

Finding a Way to Forgive

Finding the Help You Need: Psychotherapy, Pastoral Counseling, and the Promise of Spiritual Direction

Praying in Hard Times: The Soul's Imaginings

Surviving a Crisis or a Tragedy

Now available in hundreds of congregations, health-care facilities, funeral homes, colleges and military installations, these helpful, comforting resources can be uniquely presented in *LifeLights* display racks, available from Jewish Lights. **Each *LifeLight* topic is sold in packs of twelve for $9.95.** General discounts are available for quantity purchases.

Visit us online at **www.jewishlights.com** for a complete list of titles, authors, prices and ordering information, or call us at (802) 457-4000 or toll free at (800) 962-4544.

About Jewish Lights

People of all faiths and backgrounds yearn for books that attract, engage, educate, and spiritually inspire.

Our principal goal is to stimulate thought and help all people learn about who the Jewish People are, where they come from, and what the future can be made to hold. While people of our diverse Jewish heritage are the primary audience, our books speak to people in the Christian world as well and will broaden their understanding of Judaism and the roots of their own faith.

We bring to you authors who are at the forefront of spiritual thought and experience. While each has something different to say, they all say it in a voice that you can hear.

Our books are designed to welcome you and then to engage, stimulate, and inspire. We judge our success not only by whether or not our books are beautiful and commercially successful, but by whether or not they make a difference in your life.

For your information and convenience, at the back of this book we have provided a list of other Jewish Lights books you might find interesting and useful. They cover all the categories of your life:

Bar/Bat Mitzvah	Life Cycle
Bible Study / Midrash	Meditation
Children's Books	Parenting
Congregation Resources	Prayer
Current Events / History	Ritual / Sacred Practice
Ecology/ Environment	Spirituality
Fiction: Mystery, Science Fiction	Theology / Philosophy
Grief / Healing	Travel
Holidays / Holy Days	12-Step
Inspiration	Women's Interest
Kabbalah / Mysticism / Enneagram	

Stuart M. Matlins, Publisher

Or phone, mail or e-mail to: **JEWISH LIGHTS Publishing**
An imprint of Turner Publishing Company
4507 Charlotte Avenue • Suite 100 • Nashville, Tennessee 37209
Tel: (615) 255-2665 • www.jewishlights.com
Prices subject to change.

For more information about each book, visit our website at www.jewishlights.com

Printed in the USA
CPSIA information can be obtained
at www.ICGtesting.com
JSHW022217140824
68134JS00018B/1100